87-00782

LIBRARY BOSS

Thoughts On
Library Personnel

ROBERT S. ALVAREZ, Ph.D.

ADMINISTRATOR'S DIGEST PRESS

Published by Administrator's Digest Press
P.O. Box 993, So. San Francisco, CA 94080

Printed in the United States of America
Library of Congress Catalog Card No. 87-70126

ISBN 0-9618247-0-0

I would like to dedicate this book to my father, Dr. Walter C. Alvarez, a much beloved and admired fellow writer and editor. I believe much of his love of books, new ideas, writing, and helping people, rubbed off on me, thus making my work and this book possible.

CONTENTS

INTRODUCTION

Twenty-two years ago I started the ADMINISTRA-TOR'S DIGEST, an 8-page monthly newsletter of new ideas for library administrators. It was designed to keep them abreast of new thinking and new developments in all fields that seemed to have applications and implications for their libraries.

For the first five years I wrote an editorial column that filled a quarter of the back page. It slowly grew to fill the entire page, then two pages, and finally—with the inclusion of letters from our readers—filled five of the eight pages of each issue.

By the 20th year I began to think of putting together a book or two made up of selections from these columns. Recalling the many readers who have been kind enough to remark over the years that my writings about my own ideas and experiences were the most interesting and challenging *to them,* as most first-person accounts are likely to be, I decided to use only those sections of the columns and see what they might produce.

I was surprised to find that I had enough such material to make four books. It then seemed sensible to change from a chronological arrangement of the material—certainly the easiest to prepare—to a topical arrangement. This quickly led to the decision to devote the first book to the people who work in the library, with the main emphasis given to the person "who runs the library." There would be nothing here about library buildings, collections, finances, equipment, services or programs.

The result is this volume to which I have given the title "LIBRARY BOSS: Thoughts on Library Personnel." I am delighted that this first book from "The Digest" is all about people, because they are the most important part of any operation. Get the right people—management and staff—and they will in time secure the buildings, the equipment, materials and income that they ought to have. And they will surpass comparable organizations that started with all the other needed elements but never had the same high quality of personnel. This is as true in the academic field as in professional sports, and as true in the library field as in the world of business.

People are everywhere the productive element. Look around you for a minute. Everything you see was conceived, designed and built by people. Everything you see in the library stems from the idea of some individual. He or she organized the library, secured the building, wrote each of the books on the shelves, produced the furniture, etc. Likewise, all the library policies, methods, routines, arrangements, services and programs have come from library board and staff members who either had ideas of their own or were good "idea borrowers."

This being the case, why aren't employers more careful in the selection of their personnel? People are so often hired as if there was thought to be no difference between any two of them, and as if nobody cared if there *was* a real difference between them.

If I could offer employers just one bit of advice, it would be this: Be more careful in your selection of new staff. Hire only people whom you feel you and your staff and the public will be happy to "live with." Be patient and wait until the right person can be found. Look especially for enthusiasm and imagination, together with a happy disposition and a real interest in the job and in helping people. Seek people whom you believe have a desire to excel and the capacity to do so.

Remember that your happiness is determined more by the people you work with and for than by anything else. Most unhappiness is caused by "people trouble." One may not be satisfied with one's building, equipment, library materials or budget, but I have rarely known anyone to become seriously troubled over such matters. Thus, since supportive, contented and capable people are one's best key to happiness and success, let your first priority be to get the right people and then help them grow, by providing the training, motivation, opportunity and leadership.

This is not intended to be a comprehensive book on library personnel. It is rather an accumulation of writings on a wide variety of topics as they came to my mind . . . many of them suggested by Letters to the Editor. Each separate writing is terminated by five small "boxes" (▪▪▪▪▪). If the item appeared originally in "The Digest," the date of the issue is indicated in parentheses.

The ideas I have expressed in these 17 chapters have come from what I have seen and heard and felt and thought in an unusually long and varied career. But I couldn't, and certainly wouldn't, have written this material, or this book, without the contributions and the encouragement from the hundreds of librarians who have written at one time or another to share their problems and their successes. Their letters presented an endless number and variety of situations and topics, and it was then a simple matter to express one's thoughts and feelings about each one.

I would like to take this opportunity to thank all those who have thus made these writings possible. This is their book, too; they are in a real sense co-authors.

Most of the material in this book is from the public library field, simply because that's where I've done my work and where almost all my correspondents are employed, but that doesn't mean that I've written for public librarians alone or that the ideas, opinions and attitudes discussed in LIBRARY BOSS don't apply equally to all types and sizes of libraries. The principles are the same everywhere and they never change.

If you're not a "library boss," and don't ever expect or

want to be one, don't be put off by the title of this book. The material is intended for all library supervisors—department or division heads, branch librarians, bookmobile librarians, section chiefs, high school librarians, special librarians, many levels of academic librarians, senior assistants, and many others. The *Library Administrator's Digest* is read by more people who *aren't* library directors, simply because there are more librarians in this group in the libraries that receive *LAD*. And their letters to me show that they read the publication with the same amount of interest as *their* bosses. I believe that they can profit equally as much from this book.

Robert S. Alvarez
Foster City, California

LIBRARY BOSS

Thoughts On Library Personnel

CHAPTER **I**

Staff—Selection and Training

PEOPLE—MOST IMPORTANT: "What's the most important element in running a successful business?" a reporter asked Allan Roy Thieme who was named Small Business Person of the Year in recognition of his accomplishments with the three-wheeled motorized wheelchair.

"The people, definitely," Thieme said. "You can't do anything alone. You have to find good people and help them grow."

That thought was reflected in his reaction when told he had won the award. "The people in the company will be so proud of themselves," said Thieme.

It is always a pleasure to quote someone else saying what one has tried to say so often in the past, and saying it so succinctly. Which reminds me of the expression we used so often in teaching a course on supervision to engineering supervisors in a large industrial plant: "A Supervisor Gets Results Through People."

One of these supervisors' greatest faults was trying to do too much of the work themselves, instead of spending enough time with their men, "helping them grow." Most engineers and draftsmen belong to the group of professionals who like to work alone, seeking their own solutions to difficult design problems. They are normally poor supervisors as they are more interested in their own work than in the problems and needs of the people working under them. It was always difficult trying to get them to see that a little time spent helping each of their men with his work would increase the productivity of the group more than they could accomplish by themselves working 80-hour weeks. Some of the top draftsmen, supervising 15 or 20 other draftsmen, were turning out eight or ten times as much work as some of the newer people, which was a good indication that they were largely ignoring their supervisory responsibilities and continuing to work as if they had only themselves to think about.

I thought about that some years later when I was given the job of cataloging government documents in a large library. I had never done any cataloging before in a library, and working with government documents is the toughest job I ever encountered in library work. Cataloging books for the average public library is a comparative breeze, as there is rarely any question as to the author, title or publisher. But the Federal documents I handled for four months posed nothing but problems. In almost every case it was a real question as to what the main entry should be. The Federal Government is a conglomeration of thousands of departments, offices, bureaus and other units, most of them issuing publications, and determining what heading to use in each case is certainly one of the most difficult assignments that an outsider can be given in a library. I had no instruction for this job and there was no one else I could call on for help. I quickly learned what it is like to be confronted by an unending series of little puzzles, with no assurance that the solutions one picks are the correct ones. The result was a tremendous waste of time spent trying to figure out how to head each catalog card. I was in the same boat as the junior draftsmen who had a supervisor only a dozen feet away to help them but could rarely get this person's attention.

IT MIGHT BE INTERESTING for all of us to stop and think whether we have ever given someone on our staff a special assignment and then become almost completely unavailable when this person needed some further direction or help from us. Or do we have some supervisors in the library who do precious little supervising—spending almost all their time on their own work. Do all our department heads act as if they truly believe that they get results through the work of all the people in their department, and are they helping these people grow? The L.A. Raiders had more rookies on the team a few years ago than ever before and weren't expected to be in the running for the Super Bowl. The reason they won it, in my humble opinion, is that the coaching staff did a superb job of building into these new young players, "helping them grow."

I often think that libraries—like most other educational and business institutions—are weakest in this area of training and staff development. We take young people out of library school and figure that with their professional training they can handle any early assignments in the library and, thereafter, take care of their own professional growth. We don't do very much to encourage or inspire them, or to prepare them for supervisory assignments, or to help them see and understand what an administrative job involves, or even counsel with them as to their individual goals and ambitions.

Perhaps we could learn something from the professional teams, in almost any sport. A football team, for instance, may have nine coaches, each one working closely and steadily with from two to six men in a particular area of activity. The one goal of each unit is to improve the proficiency and skills of its members, both individually and collectively. They study and plan and drill and then spend more hours viewing films of their (and their opponent's) performance. The emphasis is always on growth and perfection. There is nothing like it in business or education, or in any area of library work.

While our operation and objectives are quite unlike that of a sports team, who would say that we couldn't use a certain amount of the various elements mentioned above? Certainly there are departments in a library that could devote more time to study, planning, drilling, and reviewing their performance in action, just as there are complete staffs that might benefit from a new emphasis on improving the skills of each member. And any organization might profit from having more "coaches" on hand to work closely with individual employees in improving their job skills. I don't mean more of the usual kind of coordinators and supervisors who do everything else but help individual growth. I'd prefer the kind of dedicated coach whose job depends on his success in improving employee performance to such an extent that the overall operating efficiency and productivity of the organization is increased to a clearly discernible degree.

■   ■   ■   ■   ■

LET'S STOP LABELING PEOPLE: When I grew up in San Francisco there seemed to be just one population. Everyone we knew, and read about in the newspapers, was simply another person in the community. I never thought of any of my classmates at Madison School as belonging to any racial or religious or ethnic group, or as being different or separated from me in any way. We all had different names, different families and addresses, and different interests and activities. But that was all.

And life was a lot simpler and more pleasant in those days, before we started labeling people and putting them into a myriad of separate categories. Why we find it necessary to do this I don't know. I hope the media will some day solemnly agree never again to label any person on the basis of his racial, religious, ethnic, or any other affiliation.

How nice it would be to pick up the newspaper and no longer find people on every page identified as Jewish or Catholic, or as Hispanics (or Latinos) or Asians, or Filipinos or Samoans, or gays, or blacks. To me, it's divisive and objectionable, and I am sure that many of the people so publicly labeled find it demeaning.

The situation is perhaps worse right now with all the articles about the Jewish vote, the Hispanic vote, the Gay vote, the Labor vote, and the anticipated preferences of a hundred other groups in the population. I am surprised that nobody yet has talked about the Librarian vote, or the Ph.D. vote. As if people should vote alike according to their religious, ethnic, or economic grouping.

What started me off on this topic was a story in tonight's *Examiner* stating that women and Hispanics will take over more jobs of power if the San Mateo County Board of Supervisors is able to implement an ambitious affirmative action plan during the next two years.

The county's 155 administrative jobs are currently filled predominantly by white males, with blacks "adequately represented in this group," but "in order to find a balance in keeping with the rest of the county population, there is a need to hire 13 Hispanics, one Asian and five Filipinos." In addition, the county was also urged to hire 35 women to balance the male-female ratio in administrative jobs.

I believe most of us are opposed to any sort of quota system and believe that nothing could be more harmful to any organization. It would be hard to think of, or even imagine, any business firm or public institution that operates successfully under such a system. People are the most important part of any operation, and the one with the best people (those best qualified to perform their individual assignments) will generally come out on top.

We see evidence of this on all sides. The Los Angeles Raiders remain near the top in professional football because they are one of the most single-minded in seeking the best person possible for each position on their team, along with being perhaps the best in evaluating the potential of all would-be Raiders. The day they start thinking of the racial or religious or ethnic affiliations of these football players, or put anything ahead of finding and developing the best young men available, will mark the start of their decline as a football power.

The Mayo Clinic has long been our preeminent medical institution because none other has been more careful or selective in inviting top quality physicians to join their group in Rochester, Minn. I hope the day will never come when the Mayo Board of Governors will say, "We need now to hire 13 Hispanics, one Asian and five Filipinos," or anything similar to this which our County Board of Supervisors is quoted as saying.

Any such quotation seems to suggest that one is more interested in giving jobs to members of particular minorities than in finding well qualified individuals to fill administrative positions. For the fact of the matter is that one could hardly go out and find qualified minority members in such numbers to fill such positions anywhere, at any given time. Certainly not for the Mayo Clinic and probably not for your library either. Hence, when anyone makes such a statement as the one quoted above, he or she is admitting a willingness to accept some less qualified people.

That is something that no good administrator would consider doing. It would be the biggest mistake he could make. I can't imagine Dr. J. L. Wheeler, the great director of the Enoch Pratt Library in Baltimore some 40 years ago, doing anything like that. He was the closest thing to a successful football coach in the way he recruited personnel for his library. His primary interest in attending library conventions was to see and meet and gather information about all the likely looking newcomers to the profession. He always carried a notebook in which he would jot down the particulars about anyone who interested him. I'll never forget the time I bumped into him, literally, at an ALA convention. He immediately said to me, "Sit down here, young fella, and tell me about yourself."

Six weeks later, I received a long, handwritten letter from him, telling about his hopes for having someone come in and reorganize/simplify the book selection and book ordering process at the EPFL with its 24 branch libraries. He wanted to know if I would be interested in the assignment. I wrote back to say that it sounded wonderful but I had to admit that I had no experience in this field. He answered my letter by saying that that was precisely why he wanted me for this job. He wanted somebody with no preconceived ideas about book ordering, who would look at everything with a completely open mind.

ALWAYS GO FOR THE BEST: I hope all our readers will remember Dr. Wheeler and make a greater effort to seek out and appoint the best people that can be found . . . for every library position. And I mean *every* position, including all your library pages.

A pleasant and attractive high school student, one who is sharp and a joy to have around, costs not a penny more than one who is slow or glum and lacking in the kind of personality and animation that is so appreciated by both library patrons and the rest of the staff.

Don't take just anybody to fill your page positions, any more than you would hire anyone who asks for a job to fill your clerical positions. Like attracts like. When we opened our new main library in a city of 50,000 population I wanted to staff it with people who looked as bright and attractive as the colorful new building in which they would be working. I interviewed some 220 applicants for the clerical positions and concluded by hiring all 20 of those whom I'd graded "A" or "A −". I was equally selective in picking the starting group of 8 high school pages. Most of them were cheerleader types.

SOME READERS MAY NOT APPROVE of this. But I wanted warm, friendly personalities . . . both because I knew they would be coming into contact with the public, and because I wanted young people who the other pages would like. I knew that the more congenial the group was, the more pleasure they found working together, the longer they would stay on the job, and who wants a lot of turnover? And I knew also that if we could start off with a top group of young people, the job of library page would take on a positive image in the eyes of other teenagers and we would have no trouble in filling future page positions with quality workers.

And so it worked out for both the pages and the adult clericals. For a dozen years afterwards we had the greatest group of people in both categories that I ever encountered in a library. What does that mean for the administrator? Just about everything!

When a library director sees the things that need doing in and with the library, and really wants to do them, and yet nothing is accomplished, the answer is generally found to be not budget deficiencies but staff deficiencies. And I'm not thinking of the quantity of staff but, rather, the quality.

A staff of 20 happy-dispositioned, positive thinking, ready

to try anything, people will always out-perform a staff 30 percent larger, in the same size library and community, when the senior members of this group are humorless, status quo types who feel every new idea is a threat to them, as well as being "stupid."

I've had libraries where I felt we could accomplish anything we set our mind on, simply because I knew the staff was always prepared to give a new idea their best shot, and was confident that nobody would be fighting the change and causing staff problems over it. I've also experienced situations where I knew that even the thought of change would upset the department heads and lead to a lot of unhappiness.

Many of you reading this have experienced one or both of these types of situations. I make mention of them here simply to emphasize again that all people aren't the same by any means, and that the success and happiness of any manager is largely determined by the kind of people he or she has to work with.

ONE CAN'T DO MUCH ABOUT the employees one inherits. But one can certainly do a great deal to see that all the new people appointed to the library are the kind that you and your staff and the public will be happy to "live with."

It has always been my feeling that most library administrators don't give enough thought and attention to the selection of new staff members. I'm thinking mainly about the selection of non-professional personnel, since there are so many more of them on the staff and the area of recruitment is far greater for them than for the professional people. By this I mean that there are many more people of the type we have been talking about who can be found in your community for clerical positions. But one must often go looking for them, rather than wait to give the job to the first person who comes to the library wanting employment.

And, most important, one must be prepared to be patient

and wait until the right person can be found. It is far better to operate for a few months with an unfilled position on the staff than it is to hire just anyone to fill the opening, just because a department head says she must have another person right away. Your impatience may mean that you will have to get along with a substandard or problem employee for the next thirty years.

Don't misunderstand me. I am not saying that librarians are any different from any other vocational group in their hiring practices. As a former personnel officer for a large engineering firm I can assure you that engineers are no different when it comes to filling clerical positions. However, it must be noted that *their* clericals had no contact with the public, which is quite different from the situation in libraries.

My first piece of advice to any new administrator will always be: Hire only people you feel you would really like to have on your staff, who would be a definite asset and a source of real pleasure to your existing staff members. Select individuals, no matter how long it takes to find them, who are pleasant, animated and comfortable to be with, who seem to have imagination and enthusiasm, and who you believe would give a lift to your patrons and be a good representative of the library in any group.

On the other hand, don't hire anyone just because they could probably do the job at hand, or because someone else wants this person to have a job. If they clearly have no interest in the library, or have a lot of personal problems, or don't seem to be very happy with themselves or anybody else, or appear to be slow or gloomy or without any positive or joyful feelings, let some other organization have them. If you fill more than 10 percent of your positions with this kind of personnel your chances for real happiness and achievement in that library will be greatly reduced and you and your staff will long regret these hiring mistakes.

Needless to say, one should apply the same thinking and the same standards in the hiring of minority members. Seek and accept only the best, don't take someone simply because of his or her minority status, and resist anything resembling a quota system. If you are ever required to increase the number of people on your staff representing certain racial or ethnic groups, don't let other forces decide who these people will be. Immediately get out into the community and try to find the kind of representatives of these groups that you would be happy to have on the library staff, and then try to sell them on a library job. We have had a good number of such employees and have been completely satisfied with each one.

■　　　■　　　■　　　■　　　■

CHOOSE WHAT'S BEST FOR YOU, regardless of what's traditional or what all the other libraries are doing. I'm speaking now of staff selection, but these words could apply equally well to other aspects of your operation.

I was interested to learn that one of San Francisco's most luxurious hotels, The Stanford Court, is now hiring men as room cleaners. The men are Cambodian refugees, and they are being hired because the hotel was having a difficult time finding women for the same positions. The slight build of these men doesn't scare the women guests. The personnel director said he finds Asian refugees more willing and available to do less desirable jobs at the hotel than others applying for work.

Several years ago I was lunching with the owner of a local company who complained strongly about the unreliability of the young people that they had been employing. He was totally discouraged about the whole matter. I suggested that he try hiring older workers—people who really wanted to work, who had good working habits, and who could be depended upon to be loyal, industrious, appreciative employees. He was immediately interested, saying that he had never thought about such a possibility before; everyone else seemed to be looking only at the new high school crop for the clerical help they needed.

I ran into this gentleman last week and, recalling our earlier conversation, asked him if he had tried hiring some older people. He said he certainly had, and he couldn't be happier with the way they have all worked out. Their attitude and output is better, they are more interested in what they are doing, waste less time and have a better attendance record, and are much easier to get along with. For his situation, at least, they have proved to be the right choice.

■   ■   ■   ■   ■

FORTY-SIX APPLICANTS: We are happy to learn that the Search Committee appointed to find a new Director for Baltimore's Enoch Pratt Free Library, has received applications from forty-six candidates for the position. About twenty of this number will be interviewed, and the Board hopes to arrive at a decision by August 1.

It is good to know that there are still plenty of librarians with ambition and the desire to take on more demanding and challenging jobs. Ten years ago when we asked some 200 questions of as many top public library directors, one of the questions was, "Would you like a bigger job?" We were surprised when over two-thirds of them answered, "No." Whether they were perfectly content in their present post, or thought that a library that size was tough enough to handle, or just looking forward to retirement, we don't know. All we know is that the majority of these library directors had no interest in a new and larger position. But, fortunately, there have always been applicants for every administrative position, and seemingly there still are and doubtless always will be.

Even though a library director's job is increasingly more difficult. The whole field has expanded so greatly in the last fifteen years. I felt this so much last month on my brief visit to the exhibits hall of the ALA convention in San Francisco. So many computer terminals and exhibits of different types of library automation and networking and all the other new developments that library directors didn't have to contend with a dozen years ago.

And as a Massachusetts director remarked to me: "It's a harder job these days. Everyone seems to be watching what you are doing. Not only one's library board but various citizens' groups are attentive to what's going on at the library and concerned to a degree they never were before." I believe many of you would agree with this fine librarian . . . and agree too, that this makes the Librarian's job more difficult. (9/1981)

■   ■   ■   ■   ■

NEW CLASS GRADUATES: The latest issue of "Branching Out" carries a picture of the 1980 class of Library Associates graduated that week at the Baltimore County Library. The nine young people (8 women and 1 man) are a mighty nice looking group. "Attractive," "capable," "happy," "ready to go," are descriptive words that spring to the mind of the viewer. These are the kind of young people that a library needs and that the public wants to find there. I think I'll cut out the picture and show it to the manager of our branch bank. He has about 18 young women working behind the counter; none of them seem to stay more than three months and, whatever the reason for their departure, one doubts that either the employer or the customers care. Out of the last 100 tellers we've seen there, there haven't been more than three or four that I would seriously consider for a job at the library. The bank seems willing to hire just anybody, no matter how dull, unfriendly, or unattractive they may be. I'll never understand it. Better people can be found at any salary. (10/1980)

■   ■   ■   ■   ■

THOSE OFFENSIVE WORKERS: Some of you may have wondered why we ran the article about the "Bosses Hate List of Offensive Workers" since there is no information there that is new or that you can act upon.

I wanted to run it simply to emphasize the fact that there are many qualities that your job applicants have, or lack, that can mean more than their training or experience.

Most of us know librarians who, in hiring people for non-professional positions, would be primarily concerned with the grades these people made in high school. As if grades were more important than the personal qualities that were so clearly apparent if the administrator only took a good look at each applicant and tried to imagine him or her in the position to be filled.

Some of us can recall librarians who would contact a library school and say, "Please send me a cataloger or a reference librarian." As if all librarians are the same and there was no need to want to know something about the individual's personal qualities. In those days when there were more jobs than librarians, some employers seemed only to want another body with a professional degree attached. It's still hard for me to understand how anyone could employ someone sight unseen, without knowing anything about their personality and disposition, their interests and attitudes, and the likelihood of their turning out to have some of the deadly sins that make up the "Bosses Hate List." (4/1985)

■   ■   ■   ■   ■

LETTERS OF APPLICATION: One of our relatively new subscribers writes the following interesting letter and says she would be interested in knowing what our readers think about it.

"Why is it that some library directors refuse to acknowledge letters of application for positions that they receive in the mail? One excuse I have heard is, 'They get so many unsolicited applications.' Is that a valid excuse? I think not. Ignoring a letter of application is, to my mind, just plain rude. It takes only a few minutes to write a letter saying sorry, we have no openings on our staff at the present time; good luck in your professional career. An extra-busy administrator could have a standard letter in the file that could be sent to answer such inquiries—though an especially courteous administrator would individualize such a letter . . . I would think that library directors who don't acknowledge these inquiries are probably those who do not remember their spouses' birthdays or who do not answer an invitation that specifies R.S.V.P. . . . And doesn't our profession have enough image problems without adding rudeness?

"I speak from experience: when my husband and I were moving to this state from the midwest, I wrote to every public library in the two-county metropolitan area where we'd be living. Each letter stated up front that my husband's new position was as the director of the major academic library in the region (implied: as a professional courtesy, the public librarians would therefore give me their consideration). My letter also stated my qualifications as a public library director and my professional accomplishments. The result? *Three* responses out of thirty letters sent . . . As you can tell, I *was* able to find a position, and fortunately it was one that represented a career advancement. But the slight still rankles, especially now that I am in contact with a number of these library directors who are otherwise very nice people.

"Isn't it unfortunate that well-educated adults holding responsible positions need to be reminded of their manners? What a discouragement it must be to the newly-minted librarian to send applications out only to hear nothing at all. Perhaps a mention of this matter from you would help.''

UNFORTUNATE BUT NOT SURPRISING: Well, how do *you* feel about that? My own feeling is that it is indeed unfortunate, but certainly not surprising. Most people nowadays do not return phone calls, or reply to letters, or say thank you for favors, gifts, invitations or kind words. Such normal courtesies seem to have gone the way of most good manners, such as standing up when a woman enters the room, taking one's hat off in the elevator, opening doors for other people, etc. Most men used to do these things automatically; now, a great many of them don't.

The number of people who fail now to respond to phone calls, letters, and the receipt of favors and gifts, is also greater now than it used to be. Unfortunately, these people are not getting away with their discourtesies as they doubtless believe they are—if they ever think about the matter. Because the people they ignore so blithely have feelings and expectations. A good portion of them expect a response from the other party. They look for it and wait for it and feel hurt and puzzled and increasingly irritated when they don't hear anything.

The person who doesn't express thanks for a gift or a kind deed may feel it's no big deal. But he or she may have just lost a friend; at the very least, there will be no more gifts or favors coming to them from that address. The businessman who doesn't return phone calls is going to lose a lot of business. The library director who doesn't thank the media for their helpful efforts in behalf of the library will receive less support in the future. And so it goes.

Replying to letters of application is not quite in the same category, but if one gets in the habit of ignoring these letters and gives no thought to their writers, many of whom are most anxious and troubled and eager for any sign of encouragement to ease their feeling of fear and hopelessness, it is easy to become careless and lazy in other areas where the failure to make a courteous response can really hurt one.

And, actually, a library director does not receive that many letters from job applicants. In my fifteen years as a director of a public library in the Bay Area—one of the most popular work areas in the country—I don't believe I received more than one such letter every three weeks . . . and anybody has enough time to respond to that.

However, I confess that I didn't reply to all the letters I received. Many years ago I adopted my own policy regarding such letters. I decided that I would not bother to reply to anyone who didn't care enough to look up my library in the American Library Directory and learn the name of the library director. It was my opinion then, and it still is now, that such a person is either lazy or unimaginative, and I wouldn't want such a person on my staff. So all the letters that came addressed to "The Librarian," rather than to "Dr. Robert S. Alvarez, Director" went right into the waste basket. These were always form letters that I knew were going to a hundred other libraries at the same time. I figured that since the writer wasn't giving any thought to me, or my library, we really didn't owe him or her any special thought either.

BUT ALL APPLICANTS WHO CARED enough and were intelligent enough to personalize their letter, if only to the extent of addressing it to me personally, got a reply. And no form letter reply either. I tried to give them the best advice and the most encouragement that I could. Many times I warned them against giving up a job back East to come to California to look for a new position. This area was already full of unemployed librarians so nobody should come out here until he or she had a definite offer of a job in California. I would direct them to more likely areas and suggest persons and places to contact. I would try to end on a note of encouragement, saying that I had no doubt that they would get the kind of job they wanted; the only question was *When*. It might take three months, it might take five months, but it would be worth waiting for.

But to get back to the letter we just received and to its writer who finds it hard to forget that only 10 percent of the librarians she applied to, responded to her application letter, we can all understand her feelings and agree that library directors *should* be more considerate. At the same time, I feel sure that most of you reading this would want to urge her to forget this "slight" and put it completely out of her mind for all time. First, because it really isn't that important. There was nothing personal about it. The 90 percent of librarians who didn't answer her application letter doubtless treated every other such letter in the same way. In other words, the problem is with them, not her.

Just chalk it up to Human Nature, or to poor training, but don't again think of it in connection with particular individuals. Nobody's perfect, and if one can't forget the individuals just be glad that their particular imperfection is as mild and painless as this.

Another reason to forget it is that it is past and done with. It's old business. It doesn't rate consideration by anyone trying to live a day at a time, with no regrets about the past or worries about the future. Which is how a good administrator should live.

And finally, I'm so impressed with her wonderful good fortune in finding a new, career-advancement directorship so close to her husband's job that they can maintain their joint home and pursue their separate careers right there, I can't believe that she isn't in reality so happy and so appreciative of the great way everything turned out for her that this 10 percent response matter is pretty well forgotten by her. Nevertheless she brought up an interesting and important topic and we are indebted to her for it. We look forward to hearing from her again. (2/1984)

■   ■   ■   ■   ■

A "BIAS TOWARD LIBRARIES": "Once in a while I am tempted to read a good book, for better or for worse," writes Maria Patermann, Director of Libraries in Sunnyvale, California. "This one which I may want to provide with a caption, 'Library Research, Library Fiction,' may be of interest to our readers. In Jan Venolia's *Better Letters, a Handbook of Business and Personal Correspondence,* Periwinkle Press, 1981, appears the following paragraph under the Chapter, 'Job Applications and Resumes,' to wit: 'I have some mailroom experience, a California driver's license, and I'm six feet tall, so I can reach high places. I could perform errands, clerical duties, odd jobs, or library research, to name a few.'

"The author's intellectual vigor suggests to me that somewhere in the real world there still is a bias towards libraries and librarians which deserves reexamination."

Your editor doesn't quite know whether he should laugh or cry! That is one of the most amazing paragraphs that we have published as well as the strangest resume that we have seen. We can only assume that the young man felt he wasn't the proper height to be a surgeon, or at least a good engineer. (4/1982)

■   ■   ■   ■   ■

TRAINING NEW EMPLOYEES: The April issue of *Communication Briefings* offers the following do's and don'ts for anyone training new employers to keep in mind:

DON'T:

• Assume employees know how to do something well if they've had experience. It could be experience in doing it wrong.

• *Act* interested in the trainee's learning. *Be* interested.

• Feel that a task is easy because you found it easy to learn. Everyone learns at a different pace.

• Ridicule trainees for making mistakes. Let them learn from their errors.

DO:

• Ask employees what you can do to help them do a better job.

• Make sure you expect them to continue doing things correctly.

• Remember to keep them informed on how well they're doing or what they need to improve.

• Remember this axiom: Tell, show, watch, give feedback.

■   ■   ■   ■   ■

CHAPTER II

Personnel Matters

LIBRARIAN—No. 80: Anita Gates' new book, *90 Highest Paying Careers for the '80s* (Monarch Pres), ranges from (1) investment banker—$100,000 plus, to (90) TV industry technician—$15,340. Librarian rates the 80th position—$21,300.

All careers listed as most lucrative are based on the average, not the outstanding, earnings. But average salaries shouldn't mean much to ambitious young people trying to find the right career for themselves. In all the career counseling I've done I urged the young people to pay no attention to the average salary given for each vocation. If anyone thinks he probably won't do any better than average in the field of his choice he or she had better stop right there and pick another line of work where he can easily imagine himself doing a lot better than average. Then, the "average salary" no longer has any meaning for the beginner.

Actually, Gates says, you can get rich in any number of

fields if you are really good, work hard and are lucky. I've always believed that one could make a good living in any line of work provided he or she was one of the best in it. Hence it makes more sense to pick a job doing what you most like to do as you will work harder and be more successful at it. Pay no attention to anything you read or hear about the average pay in that field because you are not "average" and are never going to allow yourself to fall in that category. Top library administrators make more than many physicians, though the latter's average salary is $100,000. (12/1984)

.   .   .   .   .

SALARIES MUST REALLY BE LOW at the Ingham County Library in Michigan. One staff member is quoted in the Lansing State Journal (Nov. 15) as saying her daughter who works at McDonald's makes more per hour than she does. And another commented, "professional librarians should receive more than 50 cents an hour more than a beginning, inexperienced page who is paid minimum wage." (7/1980).

.   .   .   .   .

DISPARITY IN SALARIES: "One more thing that has concerned me more and more lately," writes Arthur Goertz, the director of the Wicomico County Library (Md.),

"is the growing disparity between salaries of public library employees and those of library personnel in other settings. Of particular note is the fact that school media personnel seem to be paid on the average several thousands of dollars more annually than do similar personnel in public libraries. Yes, Bob, I did say several thousands and have found it to be true. . . .

"I realize, of course that unionization of school personnel is the reason for higher salaries, but I don't see that as a solution for public librarians. As administrators, though, we can be aware of the dangers of such a problem to public libraries and do what we can to alleviate or correct the situation. I wonder if you've been aware of the growing salary gaps, Bob, and if your readers are also concerned? I also would like to hear of any suggestions to correct such a problem in a positive way. What say you or your readers?"

Well, I wouldn't be surprised if some of our readers are, or have been, concerned about this situation. However, I wouldn't say that this is anything new, or even that the salary gaps are growing. I was struck with this situation and wrote about it in the late 1960s, expressing some wonderment that the public libraries could continue to attract young people graduating from library schools when the school libraries were offering jobs with far better pay and much longer vacations. Librarians were in short supply in those days, and when I learned that the school librarians in our city started at almost a third more money than the public librarians, and worked only 9 months in comparison to the public librarians' 11½ months, I was afraid we would never be able to attract a new one. The competition seemed overwhelming, but somehow the public libraries throughout the land managed to continue to get their share of the new graduating classes. Apparently, most of the new professionals were more interested in the nature of the job than in the salary or fringe benefits. Which remains true today.

So I haven't been as concerned about this matter as perhaps I should have been. I can't say what the feelings of our readers are about this situation, but would be happy to hear from anyone who has thought about it. As to how to correct it, I wouldn't know of any way other than trying to get more money from your city or county, or trying to cut back on your other expenditures to make more money available for salaries. I know of a number of large libraries that greatly reduced the number of professional librarians on their staff but never learned whether this action was followed by an increase in the salaries of the remaining personnel. But I would certainly doubt it. (5/1982)

.   .   .   .   .

PRESIDENTS OF THE UNIVERSITY of California have an irritating habit of complaining about what to them are the shockingly low salaries of their faculty. They continually assert that the University is going to lose a lot of good people if the salaries aren't "made competitive" with those of some of the schools east of the mountains. To me, this is downright dishonest, and I wouldn't be surprised if some of the people in Sacramento felt the same way about it. No UC professor is going to leave the renowned university of sunny California to move back East to the City University of New York or any other institution that might offer a few thousand more dollars a year in gross pay. President Saxon, and his predecessors in Berkeley, certainly know this. They are well aware that UC never has experienced such a loss of personnel, and they know enough about what's important to faculty people to know that it's never likely to happen. They know full well what a recent study of university faculty confirmed: that salary ranks only fifth or sixth among the factors considered by faculty in the process of job selection. Location, the prestige of the institution, and the calibre and makeup of the particular department under consideration, are all more important to the average professor than the accompanying salary. The former have to do with one's self esteem, personal relationships, the enjoyment of life, the opportunity for productive and satisfying work—and getting a little more money can never mean as much to the individual. Why would a university president purport not to realize such basic truth? (9/1979)

■   ■   ■   ■   ■

SALARY ADVANCEMENT: We confess that the three articles in this issue on collective bargaining between public agencies and their employees leave us a bit depressed. There is nothing happy about demanding employee groups, agencies under pressure, administrators reduced in authority, or individuals considered en masse. We predict that the new era will make many people (administrators, agency representatives, city fathers, and taxpayers) more troubled and unhappy without really pleasing all those who will financially benefit from the efforts and pressures of the employee groups. There can be no real satisfaction to anyone in financial benefits that have nothing to do with merit or an individual's accomplishments. In the several years we served as salary administrator for an aircraft corporation we never heard an employee, at any level, express any particular pleasure over a general salary increase that affected everyone alike. A salary raise is important to the average employee only to the extent that it moves him ahead of his fellows and indicates that his work is appreciated and that he is really advancing in the organization. Most men would still rather receive a $15 raise when their co-workers are receiving $10, than get a $20 or $25 raise when everyone else is getting the same treatment.

In the old days we were able to use salary raises to motivate people and to help them become better workers. We could give the raise when the person had done something to earn it, and then tell him why he got it so he couldn't fail to see the relationship between the greater contribution and the greater paycheck. Nowadays, automatic increases make little more impression than would an announced drop in the cost-of-living, and employees rarely hear the one thing that would really please them: that they are doing a good job and that both they and their work are pleasing to, and appreciated by, their boss. Employees often demand more and more in salary in lieu of the praise that is withheld from them. The New York City teachers we read about on p. 1 could conceivably demand and get any number of additional salary increases without necessarily improving their morale or their teaching performance. (11/1969)

.   .   .   .   .

HIGHER SALARIES WON'T DO IT: We were reminded of last months tabulation of the Public Library Directors' Poll when we chanced this morning to read a newspaper statement that increasing teachers' salaries would provide our young people with a better group of teachers. It was good to recall that only a minority of our library administrators felt that a sizable increase in library salaries would attract a higher type of student to our library schools. We don't believe increasing salaries—or decreasing them either—is likely to have a noticeable effect on the quality of our teachers, or our librarians—and the same thing goes for our barbers, our architects, our policemen, dentists, astronauts, or garbage collectors. If teachers and physicians were obliged to permanently exchange salaries tomorrow, and the same thing happened between librarians and business executives, we wouldn't expect to see any change in the performance of the teachers and librarians, or any desire on the part of the now poorly paid medics and businessmen to switch to school teaching and library work. We read of laborers making as much as $22,000 a year working for the City of New York, and electricians there reaching $35,000 a year, but nowhere do we read of their being a different type, or doing a better job, than laborers or electricians serving other cities at less than half those wages. (3/1971)

■   ■   ■   ■   ■

MERIT PAY POLICY: According to the new Salt Lake County (Utah) plan for awarding merit pay, all employees will be evaluated twice each year, in January and July. Each employee has a copy of his or her performance standards, and all should know how they will be evaluated.

Both supervisors and employees should keep track of the employees' performance. Supervisors will be evaluated on the fairness and accuracy of their evaluations of employees.

Merit pay steps will be 2.5 percent each, rather than the current 5 percent. Each grade will have fifteen, seventeen or nineteen steps (Wow! I've never heard of such a system. When I was a Salary Administrator in a large engineering company we had only five steps per grade, which seemed about right. We conducted an evaluation/rating of all 1800 professional employees every three months and all those whose actual salary was below that called for by their individual rating could receive a raise even though they got one three months before. Roughly one-sixth of the employees were rated and reviewed every two weeks, on an even and continuous cycle. Ed.)

As Salt Lake County funds allow, merit pay will be awarded on the basis of the following performance evaluation average ratings: meets standards—2.5 percent (one step), exceeds standards—5 percent (two steps) and outstanding—7.5 percent (three steps.)

Those who consistently meet standards will be rewarded and those who are unusually productive will receive higher awards. If budget shortages occur, the Commission may authorize that the basic amounts be reduced as much as half, but the same proportions of awards will be retained and merit pay WILL be awarded. Eligible employees will receive increases once each year.

A County committee is now developing a proposal for a bonus plan for all employees who are at the top step of their pay range.

MERIT INCREASES—how nice to hear of them again! We've hardly heard a mention of them in the past 25 years. Merit pay plans are almost non-existent in city, state and federal government. One reason of course is that it's a lot easier to simply increase all salaries by the same percentage—in times when money for doing so is available. And it does avoid a lot of unpleasantness and having to try and explain to unhappy and resentful employees why they didn't get the increase that certain others did.

Treating everyone the same, as far as raises are concerned, may not create as much unhappiness and ill-will as paying people on the basis of their performance, but it will not make for any real happiness or employee-motivation either. And most employers would rather have a number of energetic, highly motivated real performers on their staff, even though that meant a few unhappy employees, too, than a group where everyone was content to work and to progress at the same rate.

We will hope to hear from other libraries that have an active merit pay plan. And perhaps some day we will hear from one that is on merit pay—straight merit, nothing but merit—from the top to the bottom.

We are thinking here of the school district in Barrington, Illinois, which back in 1968 reported having the only 100 percent merit system in the country . . . "We don't have any salary schedules at all, reported Supt. Robert M. Finley.

"I don't see degrees making better teachers—or years of service," he said. "Degrees, years of service—blah! We don't consider either in our evaluations. We are only interested in these things: How well does a teacher teach? Is he or she ethical and professional? Helpful to the rest of the staff? And something we call 'extra mile service'—that's the extra willingness some teachers display, the ones you have to kick out of the school at night."

HOW THE SYSTEM WORKS: At the start of the school year each principal assigns specific numbers to specific teachers. Only the principal and the teacher know a teacher's evaluation; subsequently the number alone appears on anything bearing on the teacher's evaluation. Principals, directors, and department heads must spend at least an hour or as much as all day with a teacher on at least three occasions—more with new teachers—and follow up each visit with a discussion with the teacher, before they put an evaluation on paper. The teachers sign these evaluations if they agree with them. If they disagree, they can add their own comments. The Superintendent referees these cases.

In the end, specific dollar amounts are tied to specific ratings and matched to teacher's numbers and names in some secrecy by the principals. "We manage to get it done without dealing in personalities at the administrative level or in dollars at the evaluation level. Teachers can appeal, too, if they're not satisfied—but in six years we've had only three appeals."

Good teachers—and that's the only kind they want, and keep—move ahead much faster in Barrington. "But all we're doing, really, is paying them what we think they're worth—when they're worth it," said Finley. "For us, it works."

And I believe it would work for any other organization that had the same commitment to real merit and would devote as much time to the evaluation of each employee's performance. Frankly, I have never encountered anything like this in the public sector. In only one of the cities I worked for were the employees rated one or more times each year. And in that city the "evaluation" was considered a time-wasting exercise since little was done with the ratings and everyone knew that one's rating had nothing to do with one's pay. Salary increases were automatic and uniform in that system.

I MENTION THIS BARRINGTON SITUATION not just because it is interesting but because it offers some prime food for thought for library administrators. To start with, substitute the word "librarian" for "teacher" in the paragraph quoting School Superintendent Finley . . . "I don't see degrees making better teachers—or years of service," and complete the paragraph. It fits librarians just as well. Particularly the part about 'extra mile service.' We've all had staff members we've had to kick out of the library at night, as Finley puts it.

This is a concept that probably a majority of professional workers find hard to accept. If an employee has extra training or degrees he or she is pretty sure to feel that they should be given great weight in any staff evaluation program and that they should ensure that the person with them is rated higher and paid more than persons without this extra training. And similar thoughts are likely to be in the minds of those with the greater seniority. It is oftentimes difficult to get such people to see that the extra training and experience should make for better job performance and hence be reflected in their rating scores. In other words, their superior background or preparation should give them an advantage over others in the same job that should show up in higher ratings for them. If it doesn't, then perhaps these extra qualifications are not as significant for performance on that job as they thought, or there are some other factors that tend to hold them back.

Either way, performance on the job has to be the bottom line. It should be the No. 1 concern of both the employee and his or her supervisor. And what institution is doing a proper job of appraising the performance of its staff? What library, for example, is making an effort to observe and evaluate the performance of its professional employees comparable to what the school administrators in Barrington, Ill. have been doing?

As I noted once before, I worked in the main library of three large cities where the director and assistant director never came near our busy department. No supervisor ever talked to us about our work or seemed to notice how well we performed on the job.

For nine months I was head of a branch library where no supervisor or administrator ever came through the door or even called me on the phone. I can also recall working for six months in a small department where *no one* except a clerk-typist ever entered the office. The explanation for all this isn't that I had leprosy. It simply represents an all too common situation in our larger libraries. How can one have a true employee evaluation system in a library like that? How can you fill out a rating sheet on an employee you never see and whose work is never observed?

I JUST HOPE IN WRITING these paragraphs that it will lead some administrator, somewhere, to spend some time visiting and observing—and even talking to—some of the staff who work somewhere away from the administrative offices. I guarantee that the time will prove satisfying to the administrator and be much appreciated by the employees so favored. We all know library directors who have been concerned about the morale of their staff while, at the same time, they continue to ignore and stay away from most of their people. They know such a policy wouldn't work very well in their own home. Why do they think it would work any better in their business home?

When I was teaching a course in Supervision to engineers

at United Aircraft, the No. 1 rule they had to learn was: "Let everyone know how he is getting along." That was the most important thing for the employees. Much more than a raise, they wanted the opportunity to talk to their supervisor about their work, to hear what he really thought about it, and them. They wanted to know how they were getting along. They wanted to be told what the boss really expected of them, how they could improve their performance, and what kind of a future the boss saw for them with that company.

If anyone wants to know what is the most important thing to his or her employees, and always will be, that's it. I learned that years ago from talking to hundreds of professional and clerical employees. Nothing I've seen or heard in libraries since then has changed my thinking. People are the same everywhere. If it is important to Mrs. Smith to feel loved and appreciated at home by her family, how could anyone doubt that it is also very important to her to feel a good degree of acceptance and approval and appreciation at her place of work?

Many employees will not feel this, and may not feel that they know how they are getting along, without being told so by their boss. And how are they going to be told, and how are they going to experience the accompanying pleasure and feeling of security if the boss never comes near them and never takes the time to talk with them about their job performance?

.   .   .   .   .

JOB DESCRIPTIONS: The author of "Are Job Descriptions Necessary?" has produced one of the most thoughtful and provocative articles of the year. He has said a number of things that some people have felt but nobody has expressed before in print, to our knowledge, and it would indeed be interesting to know how many of his readers agree with him. How about you? Do you feel job descriptions are necessary? My one man's opinion is that they are not—although the personnel people are going to continue writing them anyway. I can hardly believe that's me saying that—since for 2¹/₂ years I was in charge of job evaluation and employee rating for a large engineering company. I have written a great many job descriptions myself, and used them in job evaluation and recruiting . . . but that was when I was in personnel work. When I think back on my 25 years as a library director, I can't think of a single occasion when I needed or used a job description. The only time I ever even thought of one was when the personnel office expressed an intention to review the various write-ups for library positions. This was done a number of times in the cities where I've been, costing a good deal of money but making no difference to the library.

Most libraries have the bulk of their staff in four positions—Library Assistant I and II (both non-professional), and Librarian I and II (professional). Everyone knows where a beginner starts, and if there is ever a vacancy to be filled on the staff, who needs to refer to a job description to know what grade job is to be filled or what kind of a person to look for? Personnel departments often distribute full-page job descriptions for positions they are seeking to fill but these broad write-ups often tell less about the particular job in question than one could say in a single specific sentence. A job description for a "Librarian I" doesn't indicate whether the opening is in the reference department, or in children's work, cataloging, or wherever. And it is of no value to the employer either, who is about to receive applications from several hundred hopefuls and is, or should be, concerned only with discovering which one of these people is likely to make the greatest contribution to the work of this particular department and be the greatest joy to both the public and the rest of the staff.

Mr. Britton is right again in saying that job descriptions

are unnecessary for proper performance evaluation, and likewise for performance appraisal forms. My own experience in industry was that department heads generally filled out the evaluation forms for their people and then adjusted them in order to get each person the amount of pay raise that they had already decided upon—but of course that was back in the days when a supervisor had many choices. Mr. B. is also realistic in saying that all the time spent on these programs could be spent far more profitably on supervisory training, that the job descriptions are so soon out of date anyway, and that the broad group of supervisors and executives feels no particular need for them.

All of which calls to mind the fact that public library directors in California are now (1975) being invited to participate in a large-scale project concerning "the design of selection, evaluation, and promotional systems. . ." The first of three phases in this project, to be conducted by the Selection Consulting Center, will concentrate on the analysis of librarian positions, and the budget for this phase is an unbelievable $154,121. Participating libraries will be charged from $500 to $5,000—with no indication what the total project will cost. . .

I have great respect for the top-flight professionals who are interested in this project but I can't for the life of me see how anyone but the SCC is going to profit from it. In the first place, people are selected and evaluated and promoted by people, not by selection systems, and the people we've all known who seemed to have no taste or talent for picking good people—and those who used to write to a library school and say "Send me a reference librarian," sight unseen, knowing and caring nothing about her personality or attitudes—will continue to suffer with poor people. The employer still has to talk to each applicant and try to pick the person who seems to offer the most in enthusiasm, imagination, openmindedness, interest, and a happy disposition. Given their equal professional training, what other more important qualities could this $154,121 study suggest? And in the second place, every city has its own personnel office, and they are likely to want to continue to do things their way, anyway. (6/1975)

·   ·   ·   ·   ·

CERTIFICATION OF LIBRARIANS: The California Library Association has recently authorized the formation of a committee of County Librarians to study the need for certification of Librarians. To be a County Librarian in California it has always been necessary to qualify for certification by satisfactorily passing the examination prepared and executed by the Board of Library Examiners, which has been made up of the State Librarian and the directors of the S.F. and Los Angeles public libraries.

Jean Davis, County Librarian in San Mateo County, has asked some of us for our thoughts on the three alternatives prepared by Barbara Boyd, Chairperson of the CLA Certification Committee. This, for me, is the easiest assignment of the week. Alternative 1 says: "Delete references to the Certificate from all relevant law and let the Certificate die." This would put County Librarians on the same footing as City Librarians, no more or less likely to be selected without regard for professional background. Alternative 2 would retain the Certificate, with CLA and the State Librarian providing certification using a mechanism yet to be established. And Alternative 3 would establish, with California Institute of Libraries, a Certificate in Library Administration, based on a procedure similar to that now used by the Board of Library Examiners.

I FAVOR ALTERNATIVE 1. I never could see why one had to obtain a certificate to become the head of a small county library but didn't need one to head a municipal library ten times as large. A Certificate doesn't stand for any more training or professional background than a Master's Degree in Library Science. If somebody wants to put it into the law that a County Librarian must have such a degree, that's all right with me—although I would then prefer that the statement wasn't limited to County Librarians but covered all types of Librarians employed by publicly-supported institutions. Although I don't think such a requirement is really necessary in the state law, at least it wouldn't require the giving of unneeded examinations and waste a lot of time and money. After all, non-professionals aren't likely to seek a County Librarian's position and wouldn't be seriously considered if they did. The cities and counties—as well as the school districts and colleges and universities—of this state, and the other states as well—have their own individual schedule of jobs, each with its particular requirements as to education, training, and experience. Each agency ought to be able to be trusted to select the best qualified person who meets these requirements—certificate or no certificate.

SOMETHING WRONG HERE: Certification may operate to keep well-trained people—as well as the untrained—away from these County posts. I well remember the case of an experienced librarian who came to San Francisco in 1958 to attend the A.L.A. convention and decided to take the examination for a County Librarian's Certificate, which was scheduled for that week. He failed to pass it. He never learned whether he flunked the written exam, or the oral part, or both, but wasn't too surprised as he recalled many questions on the written examination calling for authors and titles of books that he hadn't seen or thought of in 20 years, if ever. So many examinations like this are very difficult for the person who is long out of library school and has forgotten such items, few of which have anything to do with one's ability to manage a library. People just out of school—normally the least experienced and qualified for any administrative position—have a tremendous advantage in this kind of examination and generally come out ahead.

This person wasn't considered qualified to be the librarian of even the smallest of California's many county libraries. It meant nothing to the Board of Library Examiners that he had a Ph.D. in Library Science, had taught at a library school, been president of his state library association, a library consultant, the head of several public library systems (he was then in charge of a library serving a population of over 300,000), in Who's Who in America, etc. When I learned of this situation I put the Certificate requirement down in my book as a time-wasting impediment to the appointment of good County Librarians that could do as much harm as good.

I'm not saying that I am completely opposed to every type of certification for librarians. I just haven't seen anything yet in this area that seems to me to be needed, and at the same time, sensible and flexible enough to prove acceptable over the long haul. It's one of those ideas where the burden of proof should rest on its proponents. (4/1980)

■   ■   ■   ■   ■

"WE'RE TRYING TO GET LIBRARIANS THE HELL out of Civil Service." Linda Bretz, Director of the Monroe County Library System and Rochester Public Library (NY), is quoted as saying in the Mid-Hudson Library System's newsletter. I hope she succeeds. I'm sure she would be able to operate more freely, and get things done more quickly without Civil Service. There are things that can be said in favor of this system of personnel management, but most of them would be seen as benefitting other city departments more than the public library, clerical employees more than professionals, and the average and mediocre employee more than the ambitious and energetic worker. One wouldn't expect any good administrator to be favorably inclined toward Civil Service, and certainly not in the library field. An administrator is bound to view Civil Service as primarily a system and an agency designed to thwart, to delay, to restrict and hamper the things that need to be done, personnelwise. He or she feels that better people could be selected for library positions, and more quickly so, and that they could be better motivated and rewarded, and more effectively utilized, if the library could be freed from the constraints of Civil Service. I have always felt this to be so, though I'm sure there would be cases where the elimination of Civil Service would have no positive results for anyone.

I'VE ALWAYS FOUND the Civil Service people pleasant and as cooperative as the system will permit them to be. When the library has to replace a clerical assistant who has given two weeks notice of her intention to resign, it could quickly do so if left to its own devices. However, when the matter must proceed through the city's Personnel Department—which means a broad advertising of the vacancy, waiting for interested parties to respond, arranging for a written examination, scheduling individual interviews with the members of the Personnel Board for everyone who passes the written exam, and then, finally, certifying the top three scorers for interviews at the library—three or four months' time is easily consumed, while the library is left to make the best temporary adjustments it can. For instance, our local library is due to lose, in three weeks, a valued non-professional who for the past 35 years has performed a variety of duties that no one else has been involved with, except casually during vacation periods. The library director is anxious to appoint a replacement from the four people on the staff who are interested in such a promotion, in time for them to be trained for the job by the individual before she leaves for good. Unfortunately, the Civil Service system requires a promotional examination and that can't be held until an outside consultant conducts a survey of all the clerical jobs in the city, to ensure that they are all properly written and classified. I have no fault to find with that, but it would certainly help the library if it were free to make the simple selection of someone to fill the vacancy now, while she could be properly trained, and avoid having to wait several months and stumble around with insufficiently trained and temporary replacements.

FOR ALMOST TEN YEARS, this library had two openings on its staff for professional librarians, and couldn't fill them—thanks to the Civil Service system. These were years when most people coming out of a library school could pick from half a dozen job opportunities. Good jobs could be had with a single interview. No examination, no checking references, no waiting, no uncertainty. So whenever the South San Francisco Public Library tried to attract a new librarian it never got beyond explaining to the sought-after individual that he or she would of course have to first sign up to take the next examination for a Librarian I, whenever that would be given, then wait for and take the written exam. If he or she passed the exam, the next step would be an interview with the members of the Personnel Board on some future evening. The names of the three applicants with the highest scores on the written and oral examinations would then be certified to the library director who would then arrange interviews with these three people, and finally pick one of the three to fill the vacancy.

MOST OF US DON'T LIKE ways of doing things that make no sense, or that hurt the institution in a significant way without providing any compensatory benefits. If we are obliged to conform to some established practice, we want to understand it and see some merit in it, or some necessity for it. I don't mean to be critical of the entire Civil Service operation, because much of it is understandable and serves a purpose. I am only unhappy with the inflexibility and unreasonableness of it, and with the way it so often hinders and delays necessary actions, and frustrates administrators while lowering the morale of the bulk of the employees. It tends to be an impeding factor in all areas of personnel management—selection, staff organization, salary administration, personnel motivation, etc. Some may consider it a "necessary evil," and perhaps it is in many places. I must say that I never met a personnel officer that I didn't like or that I thought was doing a poor job. And I was one myself for 2½ years, but not in a Civil Service operation.

THE WHOLE THING WAS RIDICULOUS and was so considered by everyone we ever talked to, with the exception of the Personnel Board members. Needless to say, it never produced a single new professional employee for the library. After seven years of keeping the two positions in the budget and never being able to get an applicant to stay alive through all the weeks of waiting for the exam, the interviews, and the results, the City Manager decided it was hopeless and the two positions had better be scratched from the budget. We had to agree with him, after making a final and futile appeal to the Personnel Board to drop the requirement of a written examination. As we explained to them, the prospective applicants have recently completed four quarters of study in librarianship and have successfully passed written examinations in all their courses and been awarded a Master's Degree in Library Science. There can be no question that they are qualified to fill a beginning position on the library's professional staff, and no reason at all to require them to take still another written examination before being interviewed for the jobs at hand. They just couldn't consider changing the system or making an exception in this case. We asked how one could expect to interest any librarian in a job here, with all the hurdles we impose, and all the long waiting, and never knowing if one would get the job even if he or she passed all the examinations with good scores—when plenty of other jobs could be had by simply saying "yes" to the job offer. (1/1980)

■   ■   ■   ■   ■

JOB PERFORMANCE REVIEW: As some of you may recall, we have often mentioned that the greatest need and desire of employees is not more money, longer vacations, or better working conditions but, rather, to know how they are getting along on their job. They want above everything else to know what their boss thinks of them and their performance. They want to know whether their supervisor is pleased with them, whether he or she is happy to have them in the department, whether they are doing what they are supposed to be doing, and whether their work is considered average, or above or below average, whether they have made any progress recently, and what the boss sees for them in the future.

Only one person can satisfy this need and tell them what they want to hear. That's their immediate boss. It's the latter's job to see that all his or her employees know how they are getting along, at least in the eyes of their boss. But the sad fact is that very few bosses ever take the time to sit down with anyone who works for them and discuss the individual's job performance.

When I taught that course on Supervision to several hundred engineering supervisors, the No. 1 Rule that I emphasized above all others was, "Let every worker know how he is getting along." My "students" readily admitted that they rarely discussed such matters with their staff members. Most said that they didn't have the time to do it, but I never felt this was the main reason. Some didn't feel it was important, or didn't care enough about their people, but more often I felt it was a case of the boss not knowing how to conduct such a conversation with an employee and lacking the courage to be open and honest about his feelings.

A recent Cornell University study revealed that the number one stress factor among employees is not knowing what supervisors think of their job performance.

That is so logical and understandable that it is really surprising that schools of education, departments of library science, and every other kind of training program, don't give more attention to this matter. I never heard it mentioned in the two library schools I attended, although most of my classmates later became supervisors of one or more people.

ALL OF US NEED REASSURANCE that we are well thought of by the persons whose opinions most matter to us. Unfortunately, most people suffer a good deal of anxiety and insecurity in their relationships with others. Such concerns are particularly prevalent in the workplace. And because they are hurtful to the individuals involved, and detract from good job performance, they should be attended to. Everything possible should be done to satisfy the employees' needs and relieve any anxiety they may have. And the best way to do this is through an organized, systematic, and continuing program of job performance review such as outlined in the article by Mr. Oleskey.

I realize that one can set up the best possible system and still fail in the program for the reason that most of one's supervisors may not have the interest, the time, the ability, or the courage to talk to their employees in a forthright manner. I can remember too many department heads in this engineering company that I tried over and over again to get to sit down and talk with some of their staff who were insecure and unhappy because they had never heard from their boss before. They would often respond to my appeal with this question, "Why should I take the time to talk to my men when Mr. Brown never comes and talks to me?" Because the head man didn't care enough to let them know how he viewed them and their performance, they weren't going to treat their people any better.

Looking back on my career, I worked in three or four libraries, and as many business firms, and never once was told "how I was getting along." And in the four cities I was the library director I was never invited into the office of the library board president, the mayor, or the city manager to talk about how I was doing or what I ought to try and do better.

Apparently most of us operate on the basis of, "If you don't hear from me, you can assume you are doing all right." Which is the way many husbands and wives operate. "Why," they say, "is it necessary to tell one's mate that you love her (or him)? S/he certainly knows it by now." Perhaps the individual *does* know it, but why take a chance, and in so doing deprive the person of the pleasure of hearing it again. If you want to know what people most value and want to receive in life, you don't have to look beyond the letter "A"—acceptance, approval, affection, appreciation. What they have in common is that they can all be expressed, one person to another, and they have no price tag nor any limits as to how much one can give.

If you have a new employee, don't make him or her wait too long to feel accepted, approved of and appreciated. And the more that you can honestly give of these morale-building gifts, the more comfortable and happy the new employee will feel and the more positive feelings that he or she will have to pass on to other staff members and the library patrons.

And don't overlook all your older employees who may not

have heard an encouraging word about their performance in years. They may be tired of being taken for granted. Perhaps they *are* still doing the same job they did 25 years ago. That doesn't mean they aren't entitled to hear from time to time what a splendid job they are doing and how much it means to the whole operation of the library.

SO EMPLOY THE BEST JOB PERFORMANCE REVIEW PROGRAM you can, but regardless of what is accomplished here, never stop looking for the good things your people are doing and for opportunities to comment on them. They should be made to feel that you know what they are doing, that you are aware of their special efforts, and that you appreciate their contribution to the library operation. That is the way every employee wants to feel. Help them to feel that way and you will have the kind of happy and productive staff that will be a source of unending joy to you.

Actually, however, you will doubtless have to work with the employee rating system that your city or county or academic community has adopted for use with all its departments. Most jurisdictions that are large enough to have a personnel officer will have instituted some sort of program for reviewing the performance of their employees. It's a generally accepted idea in personnel management, and no one questions the need for it.

Yet it would be hard to think of a management tool or practice that falls down more or operates further below its potential than the whole job performance review system. As a former head of job evaluation and employee rating in industry, I'm not happy making such a statement. I'm inclined to think that it would take a group of supervisors of exceptional intelligence, integrity, courage and dedication to make an employee rating system work properly, and even then one would have to adjust the scores to take into account the tendencies of the various supervisors.

Most of us have probably worked with a rating sheet that lists from 12 to 18 factors down the left side and provides five columns to indicate where the employee is thought to stand on each factor. It would seem a simple matter to decide whether a staff member is excellent, above average, average, below average, or unsatisfactory, on a given quality, but nothing is easy when people and their feelings are involved. Frank Erwin, president of Richard Bellows, Henry & Co., one of the largest U.S. personnel research firms, says, "Job evaluation is the most difficult and sensitive area of employee management and relations."

A main difficulty is that supervisors are too lenient. Employees are given higher ratings than they deserve because the rater doesn't want to have feedback and defend negative ratings. It's admittedly difficult for most people to give a poor rating to someone they work with and want to be liked by, particularly when these employees are going to see their rating sheets, and it is even harder when the person being rated is a special friend, which is often the case.

I've worked with systems where the rating sheets were shown to the employees involved, and with others where the ratings were kept confidential. Likewise, I've had experience with evaluation systems where the rating scores determined the minimum salary one was eligible to receive, and with systems in libraries where there was no definite relationship between performance ratings and the pay of those rated.

The system I personally favored was the one I worked with as a salary administrator. It permitted all employees to advance automatically, with annual salary increases, to the midpoint of their individual salary range, but tied further advancement to their employee rating scores. An average performer couldn't receive a salary beyond the midpoint of the salary range for his or her position. That makes sense, and it keeps poor performers from making the same amount of money as the people who are working harder and producing more in the same job. That always makes for a lot of unhappiness.

To be eligible for a raise beyond this midpoint an employee would have had to earn a rating score of 85 or more. Each factor on the rating sheet had its own sequence of scores. The three most important factors—education required, quantity of work, and quality work—counted 0,5,10,15,20, according to the column the rater checked for each one. The least important factors progressed from 0 to 5. An employee rated Excellent on all factors would have a total score of 100.

Needless to say, some of the supervisors would cheat on their scoring in order to hold on to a valued employee who threatened to quit if he didn't get a raise. To keep everything as fair and honest as possible I would have every department head rank all his people for me in the order of their value to him. Every six months they would re-rank them, telling me who was the No. 1 person on their staff, who was the second ranking member, the third best performer, and so on. Then, when one of them wanted to give an employee a raise that would put him clearly out of line with his fellows and be unfair to some who were doing a superior quality of work, I wouldn't approve it. Wasn't the best way to make friends but it did save the company a lot of future headaches.

Those of you who have an employee rating system know that not all of your supervisory people check their sheets on the same level. Some have a tendency to put almost all their checks in the "Excellent" column, even in the case of their new employees. They offer the explanation that *their people* are all above average. But some of the employees know that they are really only average on most of the factors. And when one starts off being rated as almost perfect, he or she has little opportunity to show any improvement with the passing of time.

IN CONCLUSION, I would say that whatever system

you have for reviewing the performance of your staff members, try and decide what you want to accomplish with it, then make these purposes clear to all who will participate in the ratings, and from then on keep everyone's eyes on them. In most cases, the rating sheets are filled out in much the same way that one fills out the sheets in his or her income tax return. It's just something that is required, and the sooner it can be finished and done the better. Nobody looks forward to this particular assignment, and nobody is likely to profit from it.

But the administrator who looks at the pile of ratings sheets he or she receives as a means to a good end, rather than an end in itself, may realize some real benefits from their employment. Look at these sheets as a device and an opportunity for making a meaningful contact with everyone who works for you. You may long have wanted a chance to talk with some of your staff and about their work but it always seemed an awkward and embarrassing thing to do. But now, with the rating sheets to fill out, you have the opening that you wanted. Your people know that you are obliged to do and say something about their job performance, and they are properly receptive.

It is now an easy thing to invite each employee into your office to talk about his or her job. How's everything going, what does the individual like most, and least, about the work, does the person see any way the job could be done more efficiently, is there any other type of library work that the person would like to get into and is he or she trying to prepare in any way for a higher ranking position. What exactly does the individual see as his or her job (it may be quite different from the supervisor's perception of it), and how would this person rate him/herself as to the quantity and quality of the work that he or she is doing?

You might try filling out a rating sheet *with* each employee, inviting them to indicate how they would rate themselves on

each factor. Actually, I believe it is best for the library director to go through this process first with each department and
branch librarian, and anyone else who reports to the director,
so that these key people all understand the process and will
hopefully be conducting their own employee interviews and
ratings in the same manner.

In rating employees, as in raising money for one's library
foundation, or conducting an every-member canvass for
one's church, or doing anything else when many people are
involved, always start at the top of the organization or community. Contact the top people first, which gets the thing
started off on the right foot and provides the best results. And
it avoids the kind of situation that happens in many libraries
where the department heads and other supervisors fill out rating sheets on their staff members but never get rated by the
library director themselves, or at least never hear how they
were rated.

When an employee rates herself in one column on a particular factor and the supervisor feels she belongs in a different
column, it is fairly easy at that time for the supervisor to explain why he or she is inclined to favor a different rating. It is a
good opportunity for the supervisor to say what he or she is
looking for on this job and what might be considered a satisfactory amount and quality of work.

Which reminds me of a layout draftsman in that engineering company who was passed up for a raise three times in a
row because his rating score made him ineligible for one. His
supervisor rated him high on the quality of his work but very
low on the quantity factor, and the loss of 15 points here
knocked him out of consideration for a raise. I knew the
worker had no idea that his boss thought he was slow, and
urged that he be told. The boss would respond to my pleas by
saying, "I can't tell him that he is slow and doesn't turn out
enough work. He happens to be one of my best friends." My

reply to that was, "A fine kind of friend you are; you are keeping him from getting a raise." The worker finally came to me for an explanation and I explained the situation to him. He was much surprised and said he had no idea he was producing less work than the other draftsmen, or that his boss felt that way about his productivity, and felt sure he could increase his output now that he knew.

Most important, such job interviews should give your supervisors a wonderful opportunity to give each employee all the praise and appreciation that they deserve but haven't been receiving and the chance to encourage and inspire them to a greater performance in the year ahead and the attainment of some positive and specific goals in the future. All this while answering certain questions that some of the employees may have had about the job, helping them to do their work more easily and enjoyably, and possibly picking up some constructive new ideas from them at the same time.

In short, don't fill out rating sheets on your people and then file them away, or drop them on the employees' desks . . . just doing the minimum job that is required. Resolve to accomplish something worthwhile with this exercise and provide your supervisory staff with the direction and leadership to ensure that your goals are achieved.

■　　　　■　　　　■　　　　■　　　　■

SEVERANCE PAY: I was indeed sorry to read in the Chicago Tribune of last Sept. 15th that the Chicago Public Library Board had accepted the resignation of Library Commissioner Donald J. Sager for "personal reasons," but couldn't but be impressed with the fact that the Board had granted him six months severance pay, totaling almost $26,000. Critics of the board claimed that the unusual granting of six months severance pay was done to insure Sager's silence about the real reason for his being forced out—because he had supported G. Patrick Green, a deputy library commissioner and cousin of State Attorney Richard M. Daley, in Green's suit against Mayor Byrne.

I don't know or care anything about *why* the six months severance pay was granted. I'm just glad that Sager was given a full six months pay at the time of his termination. I believe every library director who is forced out of his or her job—and is not guilty of any immoral or criminal behavior—is entitled to six months severance pay. Such a person not only deserves such consideration but will definitely have need of it. Studies have shown that it takes six months for the average business executive to get relocated in a new position and it isn't likely to require less time for the head of a major library to find another acceptable position.

After all, how many jobs are there on the highest levels? Only a few dozen, with only two or three positions opening up each year. If the ousted director holds out for another position on relatively the same level, the waiting time is likely to be well over six months. Any job seeker can easily figure the odds against him.

Actually, most people who are obliged to leave a top-level position don't hold out for an "equally good job." They can't. They have bills to pay, to say nothing of the misery of being unemployed. The ousted library director normally receives only two or three months severance pay. He or she can't afford to be out of work very long. And one is conscious of the fact that a new position generally means a move to another city, which will entail extra expense. Hence a professional in this position normally accepts a lower-ranking position as soon as possible and is just glad to be back at work. A small minority will eventually make it back to the higher level, but almost none of them will do so immediately. My informal study over the years of more than 50 public library directors

who were ousted, showed only two or three who were fortunate enough to gain a better position on their first relocation.

School superintendents, university presidents, football
coaches, baseball managers, and other groups of top performers have contracts to insure a continuing income. If they
are let go, they still receive their salary to the extent of their
contract period. This often means a "severance pay" in six
figures. Contrast that with the $5,000-or-less that most library
administrators have been sent away with. In short, library
boards and city managers should offer more assurance in the
way of severance pay for their library directors—and the
same thing should be done in the academic field. I would like
to see a 6-months severance pay become an accepted standard for library directors in all jurisdictions. (4/1982)

    ■   ■   ■   ■   ■

THE KIND OF "MUSICAL CHAIRS" reported in
the article on the San Diego Public Library is one of the most
senseless practices ever conceived by civil service politicians
and/or union leaders. It is seem all the time now in the public
schools, but most of us have witnessed it in one or two large
libraries and vigorously deplored it. Just consider the tremendous waste involved in the following "bumpings" of SDPL
department heads. For example, Barbara Tuthill who headed
the art and music department is now in charge of history,
Dorothy Grimm was transferred from history after 14 years
to head social sciences, Rhoda Kruse, who built up a reputation in California and Mexican history as head of the California Room, is now in charge of art and music. Margaret
Queen, who spent nine years in the social sciences section
now oversees science and industry. That represents a total of
eighty years or more developing individual skills and knowledge in a particular subject field, lost to the service of the public.

That's as stupid as if "bumping" was required at the Mayo Clinic and the long-time head of Neurology was transferred to Pediatrics, while the head of Dermatology was switched to Geriatrics, and so on through the other departments. The result would be the end of the Mayo Clinic as the premier center of medical practice . . . And if "bumping" was prevalent in the sports world, just imagine what would happen to the world-champion Pittsburgh Steelers if quarterback Bradshaw was "bumped" to the position of center, while "Mean Joe" Greene, a tower of strength in the defensive line, was obliged to exchange positions with the speedy, pass-catching Lynn Swann. Such switching of specialists is indeed laughable in other fields; how can it be viewed otherwise in a subject-departmentalized library? (9/1979)

■   ■   ■   ■   ■

CHAPTER III

The Library Director

THE LIBRARIAN'S JOB: I was interested in the following paragraph from the latest newsletter of the Livermore (CA) Public Library:

"Your librarian is at one time or another manager, planner, system designer, leader and supervisor, mediator, resource allocator, writer, speaker, fund raiser, researcher, research colleague of the client, subject expert, database searcher, collection builder, budget analyst, proposal writer, statistician, consultant, telecommunications expert and entrepreneur."

Let anyone compare the above statement with what he or she would have thought or written about the librarian's job ten years ago. It is immediately clear that the job has taken on half a dozen additional facets that were not even known to most of us a decade ago. (9/1984)

.　　　.　　　.　　　.　　　.

THINGS ARE HAPPENING: It's a good time to be a library administrator. Everything is growing and expanding —library budgets, library staffs, library horizons and library ideas. We have been in a period of growth for the last 35 years, but the rate of growth continues to increase from year to year.

Those of us who were working in libraries before 1949 can really appreciate the changes that have occurred since then. We had a taste of that period from 1929 to 1949 (roughly speaking) when there was almost no growth in any aspect of library service. Library circulation in the big cities was at its peak in the Depression years, but everywhere budgets were at their lowest level, staffs were at bare minimum, book budgets were about one-fiftieth of what they are now, there was practically no library construction, and almost no new ideas to consider.

We were taught in library school how to order books, how to catalog them, and how to find information in them. But our instructors, as capable as they were, never suggested that there might be other ways of doing library work, or that libraries might possibly offer some new services in the future, or that we ought to try and develop our creativity and look for ways to improve existing library practices. We students got the idea that this is the way library work was performed and it would always be this way. The faculty clearly wasn't thinking of the possibility of change, and we never heard of a library that was doing anything innovative or operating in any way that was contrary to what we were being taught.

In many ways it was a very easy time for library administrators, despite the shortage of funds. Everybody did his job as he or she was taught to do. Nobody questioned the ways things were done or the way the library was operated. Neither the staff nor the library board had any thoughts about the library director acting in any other way.

The director in those days had relatively little to do. With library service confined to lending books and answering simple reference questions, there were few tough decisions to make and few problems for the director to handle. Library employees were loyal and contented, even though they never had a raise or expected to get one. Having been a Salary Administrator in industry where I continually heard requests for annual increases, it was surprising to me to later take over three public libraries where nobody on the staff had had a raise in fifteen years or any inclination to ask for one.

Studies show that librarians live longer than any other professional group. And I believe that library administrators who came through that relatively easy and serene period may outlive today's administrators who work in what may well be a more difficult and demanding time. The latter may experience more exhilaration and achievement but at the same time they may be burdened with more problems and pressures and perhaps a greater sense of insecurity. (3/1985)

■　　　■　　　■　　　■　　　■

STRIVING TO BE THE BEST: One of the most striking and effective ads that I have seen in recent months is the full-page ad for Chrysler Corporation in this week's *Time* magazine. I never look at ads but this one I couldn't miss. Large white letters on the black background announce "We have one and only one ambition. To be the best. What else is there." Underneath these 15 words is a photograph and signature of Lee A. Iacocca.

Over the years I have read statements by other business leaders that have said somewhat the same thing. Why is it that I have yet to come across such a pronouncement by a library administrator? I wouldn't expect them to make such a claim in a popular magazine, or through paid advertising, but a library director who truly shared Mr. Iacocca's ambition for his own organization might well express such a commitment in a convention speech or in an article in a library journal or newsletter.

As I think back over the last 35 years and of all the library administrators I have known or read about, I can think of only one or two who might conceivably have held the same thought. They may never have expressed the idea, even to themselves, that having the best library of their particular type was the one and only important matter to them professionally, but such an ambition wouldn't have seemed out of character to them.

We hope to see more Lee Iacocca types in the library profession. It is strong individuals like him, who are driven by a determination to excel, that make any business or profession move ahead. The library profession is steadily moving forward, and many of you reading this are heavy contributors to this progression, even though you may never have consciously set such a goal as expressed by Mr. Iacocca. (1/1985)

■　　　　■　　　　■　　　　■　　　　■

A SMALL TOWN IS THE BEST: So says Gordon Wade, director of the public library in Carroll, Iowa, who writes to us as follows:

"Your article on Gene Winn of the Bartlesville, Oklahoma Public Library was right on the money and gave me a special lift when I read it. I have been director of a small town Iowa public library for twenty-one years and expect to stay here for another eighteen. It's much more fun to be a big frog in a little puddle than the opposite. I can't think why I would ever want to leave Carroll: we fought the battle for a new building and won, our book budget is the highest per capita in the state, our Library one of the best in Iowa, and life in a small town is unbeatable!

"I've outlasted four city managers only one whom, by the

way, was pro-Library; I've even fought the battle of salary in proportion to qualifications, experience, responsibilities, and performance and I won that one, too! To move on to a larger Library would mean giving up a Library which I have shaped and molded into something far superior to anything I can hope to ever find again. Larger libraries tend to mean larger headaches and who wants to repeat on a grander scale the headaches one has already triumphed over?

"Thanks for the lift!"

THAT'S A GOOD CASE FOR STAYING in the small town, with the library that you have "shaped and molded." Now who wants to present the case for moving onward and upward, leaving one's wonderful small town?

The small city is the ideal place to start one's career as a public library administrator, just as a small college would seem to be the best place to start out as a library director in the academic field. And if everything is pleasant and one is happy with the people one works with and for, and has the money and the freedom to do the things that need doing, the temptation to stay right there will be great indeed. You thoroughly enjoy your work and are delighted by the progress that the library has made under your direction. Moreover, you and your family like the community and value the warm relationships you have developed with so many nice people. It's a great place to raise a family and you can't imagine yourself as happy anywhere else.

But then, for many administrators, the day comes when one begins to feel aware of a change in the job atmosphere. Things seemed to have slowed down. The intensity, the zing, is gone. One's ideas have been pretty well implemented. The library is operating smoothly and the need for change, for improvement, is much less than it was before. You feel relaxed and comfortable in your job now, but at the same time you miss some of the excitement and stimulation that you felt in the earlier period of growth and achievement.

The administrator may then begin to wish that he or she could have the best of both worlds, the stimulation and sense of accomplishment along with the peace and contentment. This is oftentimes not possible to attain. The administrator will generally then continue to carry on—working perhaps at 50 percent of his capacity—until an attractive job opens up in a larger institution. He or she is then faced with a difficult decision: whether or not to apply for it . . . or whether to accept the position if the offer is actually made.

Fortunately, there are always plenty of people interested in taking on a new and bigger job. In fact, the number of challenging jobs and the number of librarians qualified to fill them both seem to grow from year to year. To be sure, the applicants for these directorships aren't all coming from positions that are as pleasant and satisfying as Mr. Wade's in Carroll, Iowa. Some of them are out of a job, or faced with the possibility of becoming so, or are unhappy with their present staff or library board, or possibly just feeling that they have done all they can do with that library and are just anxious for a change of scene.

Whoever gets each new management position as if becomes open, I only hope they realize how fortunate they are. For there are probably 60 or more other applicants who wanted the job just as much but were disappointed. Some of them will apply for more than thirty library directorships and be turned down as many times before fate smiles upon them. Needless to say, there is a lot of luck and a lot of unhappiness in this job-hunting business.

Gordon Wade says, "Larger libraries tend to mean larger headaches and who wants to repeat on a grander scale the headaches one has already triumphed over?" Which would seem to invite such comments as: 1) The headaches of larger libraries aren't always larger or more unpleasant; 2) Headaches are of many kinds, as well as sizes, and you rarely meet the same type in your different positions; 3) Because they are different one isn't likely to be bored by having to undergo the same problems again. Facing different problems is invigorating and makes for a fuller professional life. But everyone has to decide for him/herself the best way to go. (9/1984)

．　　　．　　　．　　　．　　　．

THE FIRST YEAR IS THE GREATEST: An administrator's first year on the job is almost always the most exciting and eventful year that he or she will experience there. The innovative person is going to see so many things that can be added, eliminated, changed, streamlined, brightened, expanded, or promoted. If the new person doesn't see a number of things that he would like to change in some way, either his predecessor was unbelievably perfect or he is lacking the imagination that an administrator should have.

One wouldn't expect a housewife to take over someone else's furnished home and not make a number of changes in her first year there. So why wouldn't one expect a new library director to make similar changes in his or her new work home? Forty years ago the average new administrator made almost no changes in the library. In those days, librarians didn't think of change and there was so little in libraries to change—so few kinds of materials and services to think about—and almost no new ideas being talked or written about. Most libraries operated and looked as they had for many years, and as all other libraries did at that time. It was a wonderful time for a real library pioneer to come along, but few came along during the next fifteen years.

I have had four first-years as a public library director and they were the happiest, most interesting and rewarding years of my life. In each case we did a number of things that had never been done before, and the public was always appreciative, and the circulation always increased. Most of you have doubtless had the same experience. It's all been wonderful, despite some rough moments, and we all know we left our libraries far better than we found them. And we're generally right. But one must be careful not to get puffed up about that. For when I look back at the places I've been and think about the progress we made there, I inevitably get to thinking also of the tremendous progress that my successors have made. Several of these libraries now have eight times the budget that we worked with there, and the money has been put to good use. I'm sure some of my successors feel about their "reign" just as I do about mine. In short, everyone has his own ideas and efforts to contribute to each position, and it's in the accumulation of such contributions that each institution is built and continues to grow.

THE ABOVE PARAGRAPHS were inspired by an item in the newsletter of the Livermore (CA) Public Library telling about the changes there several years ago. It states: "Recognizing budgetary restrictions and the need to reassess the Library's goals and objectives in light of administrative changes, the new Director set about the following actions:
—evaluation of Library operations and procedures;
—identification of seven basic services;
—reorganization of staff positions;
—elimination of many labor-intensive procedures;
—reorganization of physical plant for client 'self-help';
—addition of client-centered changes such as curb-side book drop, automatic door, new signage, public announcements kiosk, among others;
—organization of Volunteer Associates program;
—addition of Thursday night and Sunday afternoon openings;
—tightened controls through a security checkout system, inventory of collection, and reissuing of library cards;
—utilization of gifts to the Library;

—encouragement to the Friends in the development of 'Friends Corner' where materials withdrawn from circulation are recycled."

That's quite a list of library changes. Whenever you come across a list of this kind, of such an impressive dimension, you can be pretty sure that the responsible party is in his first or second year on the job. There's so much to be done the first year. As many of these things are taken care of the first year, the total number of things to be accomplished the second year is generally somewhat smaller, and the same thing carries through to subsequent years. The number of new goals and objectives to be added to the list for any later year is normally smaller than the number of changes that have been effected and hence removed from the list of things to be accomplished.

Then too, many people have a tendency to slow up a bit after they have been in the same job for more than a few years. It's easy to get feeling comfortable and contented and somewhat complacent. Everything seems to be going well, with a minimum of problems and challenges. It's admittedly nice to feel relaxed and secure in one's job, but it may not be the best thing as far as library progress is concerned. Not many administrators who are working through that stage are going to be reporting a list of accomplishments like the one from Livermore. We all know a number of library directors who never seem to run out of either ideas or energy, but the number who have slowed down on the job and probably ought to move on to a new job with all its new challenges, is probably greater.

. . . . .

THE FIRST FOUR MONTHS: Listening this morning to a tape of my talk to new library directors I see that I narrowed down the one year mentioned earlier. I said there:

"The first four months in a new directorship is generally the happiest time in one's life. When new to the library, one is likely to walk around the building thinking to himself/herself, 'All this is mine to do with. Wow!' And then there's the fun of exploring the inside, looking into every room and closet, meeting the staff . . . and then sitting behind your big desk and feeling like the boss. Feeling free to go and come as you see fit, with nobody to check on you.

"You will be introduced everywhere around town as 'our new city librarian.' You will be invited to join churches, give talks to clubs, perhaps write a column for the paper, be invited to join in community activities that your friends on the outside will rarely have a chance to participate in. Your job makes you a personage, somebody known and respected, and gives you opportunities for serving the public and enjoying its satisfactions that few people have.

"Enjoy the freedom you have in your job . . . If you like to read your library journals on a comfortable lounge under that shady tree behind the library, do it! I often did.

"Nobody other than yourself knows what you should be doing, or how you should be doing it. You have no quotas, and few deadlines, and nobody demanding that you produce certain results in a certain period. I remember a library school student coming to tell me that he'd been asked to be the librarian in a small town. He wanted to know if I thought he could hold the job. I assured him that if he did nothing scandalous, and didn't rock the boat too much he could stay there for 50 years. Nobody there, I said, had any expectations of what he should do, or any standards of performance to judge him by, so he had nothing to worry about. That was over 30 years ago but it's still in large part true.

"You might take some comfort in that fact even though we know you want to do much more for your community and will definitely do so.

"So relax a bit. Resolve to do everything that needs doing

in and for your library but don't take yourself or your work so seriously that you lose that nice smile and start worrying about things and forget to delegate all the work you can.

WORKING EFFECTIVELY: "The average administrator doesn't delegate sufficiently. You ought to delegate everything that someone on a lower level can handle. Why should you handle any paper work or do anything else that someone at a lower rate of pay can take care of? Follow the 3-D rule: Do, delegate or dump. If it's a job that only you can do properly, do it. If it's something that needs doing, but not necessarily by you, delegate it. Everything else . . . dump.

"In visiting other libraries I always used to want to peek into the head librarians office. After some years of this, I gave up doing this. It made me feel guilty. Almost all these directors had desks piled high with reports, catalogs, and paper of all kind. I'd return to my own office with almost nothing on the top of my desk to indicate I was a busy person, and feel I wasn't working as hard as my colleagues. To be honest with you, I wasn't. I know I shouldn't say this—I'm always getting into trouble this way—but most of my years as a library director I didn't have enough work to do. To be sure, there was more than enough paperwork to keep anyone busy but when one works by the 3-D Rule (Do, Delegate or Dump) and questions the necessity of everything that makes a demand on his time the job is simplified and the pressure is gone from it. However, I'm speaking about the years before computers and automation; the new technology has increased the demands on the time and thought of library directors.

"A friend of mine had a nervous breakdown running the same kind of library operation as mine, and I tried to understand why. All I could see is that he loved detail work and did a great many little jobs that I never bothered with. I see library directors doing this all the time.

"At the same time I see them handling the same paper over

and over again. They'll look over their mail and instead of making decisions and dispatching each item with a single handling they'll put much of it aside for future consideration. I know this for a fact because every time I send out sample copies of the *Library Administrators Digest* or promotional letters about it—with business reply cards enclosed—the recipients don't act on the matter right away. One might think that all the cards that were coming would be returned to me within 16 days. Actually, no more than 5 percent of the cards will appear in 16–18 days. The rest arrive at a fairly even pace over the next 14 weeks. It amazes me every time I do such a mailing. Apparently, the average administrator doesn't get around to acting on such mail for some 50 days.

"At the same time, remember that it's more important to work effectively than efficiently. Being effective means doing the right things; being efficient means doing things quickly—and sometimes this includes things that don't need doing. Do the most important things first each day, rather than handling things in the order of their arrival on your desk.

"Really cut down on your paperwork. Throw away much more incoming material, delegate more of the rest, and what's left, take care of more speedily. Answer 95 percent of your letters by simply writing your response in a few sentences on the bottom of the letter and putting it in a return envelope. It's much more helpful to the person who wrote to you, and far faster than dictating or typing a separate letter in response. I've done this for years and almost never made a copy of the letter to me. Never found a need for such copies.

"When I started *Administrator's Digest* my accountant advised me to keep all purchase orders and three different sets of books. I found the first year that this was completely unnecessary and just wasted hundreds of hours. Since then I've thrown out all PO's after writing the one-line renewal note on the single card that I keep for each subscriber.

"File a bare minimum of material coming to you. Most of the paper in your VF cabinets you will never look at, or need, again. Save the cost of cabinets and the filing time. A few hours of weeding every few years will eliminate the bulkier material and keep the VFs from growing on you.

"When you need to write a letter yourself, leave off the name and address of the recipient at the top and just begin 'Dear ——.' What earthly good are these three lines of type, except in a few instances where it's important enough to keep a copy of your letter. In the majority of cases you shouldn't need to keep a copy.

"If you are making copies of all your letters, you are just not thinking. You are guilty again of doing something just because that's the way you were taught.

"And if you do what I'm suggesting, you won't need a secretary. I love secretaries. I've had four or five that I picked most carefully and that were a complete joy. One of them was instrumental in getting me chosen 'Boss of the Year' by the Nashville Secretaries Association. But in So. San Francisco I transferred my secretary to the circulation desk and got along beautifully for 13 years without one. I might add that when I asked the directors of our 200 largest public libraries if they really needed a full-time secretary more than a third said No." (12/1983)

■　　　■　　　■　　　■　　　■

A ROUGH TIME: Just before I left for the ALA convention I had a call from an unemployed librarian asking about two director's jobs in California that had been advertised. It turned out that he had recently been fired as City Librarian when he apparently tried to move his library ahead faster than his staff were prepared to go, thus incurring their wrath and opposition (an old story). As I listened to him tell of applying for every possible opening and waiting for the right response which never came I could feel his fear and sense of hopelessness. Losing a job is a traumatic experience for anyone. But it is particularly rough when one has no unemployment insurance or any other money coming in, and when there are so few openings in his type of work and most of them are normally filled before an outsider learns about them, and the few that are advertised are likely to draw 60–90 applicants—most of whom have never been fired and so have a great advantage over my caller.

The chances of his winning another appointment now as a library director seem so very small. I tried to encourage him by remarking that so often when one has a door closed to him, another door opens up down the line that offers something even better . . . and also quoted the title of Dr. Schuller's latest book: "Tough Times Never Last, But Tough People Do!" Most people go through some tough times in their life, but the great majority emerge from them and go forward again. My main piece of advice was for him to take a job, any job, as quickly as possible. Don't wait for another top position but take any library job that he can get. The important thing is to get back to work, to be busy again, to have some money coming in, and to feel like a human being again rather than an "unemployed freak."

Seeing thousands of librarians rushing around downtown Los Angeles, all seemingly busy and happy and blessed with employment, I couldn't forget my caller. If only there could be one more job—one out of many thousands—for this individual. What a difference just one makes!

A JOB IS A WONDERFUL THING. Particularly one that is enjoyed as much as most library directors say they enjoy theirs. I hope everyone with such a position appreciates having it and realizes how fortunate he or she is to have been given it. I say this because I believe such realization adds to the joy of one's work. I've found over the years that one of the best ways to be happy is to cultivate "an attitude of gratitude." If one is continually recognizing the good things in his life and work and feeling appreciative about them he or she is bound to feel happy and enthusiastic. It's impossible to feel grateful and unhappy at the same time. Willard Scott, the popular TV weatherman, said he never goes before the cameras on his morning show without thanking God for a job that he so greatly enjoys. Jimmy Stewart said the same thing the other day about his acting career. Call it positive thinking or just plain appreciation, it helps to put the sizzle in the steak. And we need all the enthusiastic library administrators we can get. They are the ones who step out and achieve things; negative thinkers accomplish very little.

Since then I have learned of a library director long in his job who was suddenly fired because he was thought to be too slow and unexciting and the board wanted to bring in someone more dynamic who would move the library ahead farther and faster. Also heard about another director who was let go because she didn't seem to know how to deal with her staff. She drove many of the older members of the staff to early retirement by her unkind and insensitive treatment of them. Some members she wanted fired but the city council said this was out of the question. When a new supervisor joined the staff she is said to have presented her with what she called her "Hit List," saying that "these are the members of the staff we want to get rid of," and seeking the new person's help in this cause. The latter replied that she hadn't come there for such a purpose and would have none of it. Needless to say she found another position in half a year's time. I checked this story out with the most reliable sources and only tell it here to show that the blame in such troubled situations isn't always on the same side and I don't hold the opinion that the administrator is always without fault. In this case the fault was entirely the library director's. (10/1983)

■   ■   ■   ■   ■

IT'S "VERY TOUGH TODAY": "Your common sense administration is badly needed today," writes Don Dresp, director of the public library in Las Cruces, N.M. "The 3D rule certainly made me take a look at myself and the steps in my job. I will frequently send you materials so that you will know that New Mexico does exist. Public library administration is very tough today, even in Las Cruces with 50,000 population."

We know many library directors who feel just the way Don Dresp does. We always hope that they are still able to enjoy the job as much as we did. There's nothing really bad about having a job that's "very tough." Political leaders, business executives, top athletes, astronauts, and most successful people have jobs that are tougher than yours or mine, but they still love what they are doing and as long as they have a sense of accomplishment and can feel that they are doing something worthwhile they are likely to be fairly happy in their work.

We often wish our readers would write and tell us more about their jobs and their problems. What part of your job do you find the "toughest?" I'm sure the answer has a lot to do with people. Books, buildings, etc. aren't capable of causing real unhappiness or making one's job seem truly difficult. I've never seen a librarian cry over such matters, nor have I heard of one who couldn't stand these material elements and so gave up his or her job. It's only the people you work with and for who can make you that miserable.

Except for very rare acts of nature, it could be said that all problems, all failures, *everything*—good or bad—in libraries is people-caused. If the job is tough, someone is making it that way. It might be the library administrator, or some member(s) of the staff, or some Board member(s), or someone at City Hall. You may say, "No, our problem is nothing like that; we just need more money." But that's also a people-problem. Your budget is determined by the people who meet in the City Council chambers, and if they are not giving the Library its proper share of the total city budget it must be because they are not persuaded that the Library needs or deserves a larger portion of the pie.

When your budget is seriously cut, you may say that it's the 15 percent cut in dollars that is making your job "very tough." But one could argue that, again, it is the people involved who are causing the trouble for you. And not just the people at City Hall. It's much more a matter of the library staff members whose jobs are affected, and some of the public who are upset over an anticipated reduction in library service.

Everything comes down to a matter of the kind of staff you have, the quality of the relationship you have built with them, and the kind of person you are yourself. I've known staffs where anything out of the ordinary would create a lot of negative thinking and cause trouble for the administrator, and I was blessed for many years with two groups of employees that nothing seemed to upset. The great majority were happy dispositioned people who enjoyed their work, liked their fellow staff members, and had positive feelings about their employers and the public they served. There is nothing that can make an administrator more happy and relaxed than that.

If your job is tougher than you think it should be, try to figure out what, or who, is causing the trouble and what you might be able to do about it. There will sometimes be people and situations you can't change. But, fortunately, you can change how you think about these obstacles and how much attention you permit yourself to give them. Like any roadblock in life you can try and fight it and be completely miserable and blocked by it, or you can accept it as an unchangeable fact of life and go around it as best you can and move on ahead. Don't waste any emotion on the problem; that's just the way he, she, or it is. Nobody promised you a rose-garden . . . and if there weren't such difficulties in the job they wouldn't need an administrator of your capabilities. (4/1984)

■   ■   ■   ■   ■

"WHY SOME AIRLINES SUCCEED" is the title of a newspaper article that I've just been reading. We have all been hearing so much about large airlines, such as Braniff, Continental, Pan American, World, and Republic that are in real trouble and are desperately cutting fares, laying off workers and making deals with bankers and labor unions to stay alive, that I was curious to learn what the minority of successful airlines are doing differently. To be honest about it, I thought the answer would have some implications or some educational value for libraries—and I believe it does.

Libraries have always been in the very fortunate position of not having any competition and not having to show a profit. Whether their management is wise or stupid, capable or ineffective, the individual library will continue to operate. Its leadership can make poor decisions and waste a lot of public money, but they will continue in office and the taxpayers will continue to pay all the bills. In a large percentage of cases, the city fathers won't even be aware of this poor management.

We all know libraries—both public and academic—that would be run out of business if they operated under the free enterprise system and had another library competing with them for the favor of their patrons. The same thing might be said of many post offices, other city departments and publicly owned utilities. After the War I went to work for the Cleveland Electric Illuminating Co. in northeast Ohio. Our competitor in Cleveland was the municipally owned light and power company. It was so inefficiently run that the private utility, despite having to pay $25 million in taxes each year that the other company didn't have to pay, had 92.5 percent of the business. We had far fewer outages, better service, and, of course, better PR. If the MUNY had been obliged to show a profit it doubtless would have gone out of business.

I NEVER FORGOT THAT PICTURE. I always tried to keep my public library moving ahead so that it was continually serving more people and doing so more fully and more efficiently. Though we never had a competing library I often imagined one and wondered what they could do to attract some of our "business" that we weren't doing. In short, were there some new services that a competitor might think of and attempt, that we ought to get into? I recommend this line of thought to our readers. I daresay most of them have a number of new library ideas in some stage of consideration. Our minds are continually bombarded by thoughts of things we might do. Most of these thoughts are quickly forgotten or passed over. A few of the more choice ones are filed away in the back of our minds . . . for possible implementation when we have the necessary time and money and staff. They are good ideas but there is no need to do anything about them now. Nobody is thinking about such action or will miss it if we don't do anything about the idea. Under such conditions it is so easy and inviting to do nothing, and a difficult task may be postponed indefinitely.

Every time you see yourself in that situation, imagine another public library system in your service area, one that you must compete with for your very survival. If you are a county library administrator, just imagine that the Baltimore County Library has moved into your area from Maryland, or the Hennepin County Library from Minnesota, and you are go-

ing to have to match ideas and services with the Robinsons,
Rohlfs, & Co. to hold on to your patrons and stay in business.
Just think about that for a minute or two. You may decide
that some of those good ideas that you have stored away on
your back burner ought to be put to work right now. Good
organizations just don't seem to dilly-dally around, waiting
for their competition to get their act together or to make the
moves they have long been procrastinating about. Some good
competition might do wonders for a lot of public organizations.

■   ■   ■   ■   ■

HOW TIME FLIES: Last month I received a letter
from Gene Winn, the director of the Bartlesville Public Library (Okla.), announcing his retirement after 30 years of
service there. I couldn't believe it. It seems only a short time
ago that Gene came to my office in the Nashville Public Library looking for a job. I liked him at once and when I learned
that he was a fellow Phi Gam I became doubly interested in
helping him find a suitable career.

I talked to him about the pleasures and opportunities of
public library work and was pleased when he enrolled at Pea-
body Library School. He made a good record there and upon
his graduation accepted the directorship of the library in
Bartlesville. What an ideal job for one just out of library
school. That has always been one of the great attractions to
me of the library profession . . . that one has the possibility of
starting at the top. What matter if it's the top of a small organization. I always thought it better to be a big frog in a small
puddle than the other way around. And there are not many
lines of work where one has the chance to "start at the top."

I've never talked to Gene about his life in Oklahoma and
haven't seen him since he went there, but book salesmen have

told me some glowing things about his life in Bartlesville. He seemed to fit right into the community and found the life of a city librarian in a small Southern community was everything we'd pictured before he went there.

I might add that I've told a number of young librarians about him—"one librarian who was smart enough to realize what an ideal situation he had and to stay right there with his pleasant job, nice home and seven acres, and good friends, rather than give up all that for a new and distant job, simply because it was bigger and better-paying and had more prestige.

Most of my generation grew up believing that we ought to be ambitious and try to advance in our work as far as possible. It wouldn't have seemed right to turn down a bigger job, and most of us never did. I can extol the wisdom of people like Gene Winn and Johnny Hodges, my old classmate at Illinois Library School who went directly from there to the Librarian's office at the University of the South, atop that beautiful mountain in Sewanee, Tenn., and stayed right there (he loved that spot and was smart enough to know that he couldn't be as happy anywhere else), but am not sure that I could do the same thing myself. (5/1984)

• • • • •

THE WAY TO FEEL: Alan Woodland, the director of the New Westminster Public Library in one of those nice suburbs of Vancouver, sends us a copy of his latest annual report with this comment: "NWPL is 116 years old this year and we think we are blessed with the best library, best library Board, best library staff and best and most supportive public in the whole of Canada. (I was going to say North America, but I guess that's fighting talk south of the 49th.)"

I truly like to hear a librarian talk that way about his or her library. I felt that way about "mine" throughout most of my working years and sincerely hope that the majority of the readers of this column feel as Mr. Woodland does, regardless of their position or rank in their library. If one can't honestly believe that his-her library is "the best," one can always maintain that "it *will* be the best before I'm through with it," or "it is improving all the time and we are determined to make it the best."

Realistically speaking, no library is actually going to be the best in all departments—any more than an individual university. In my years in Nashville, we thought we had the best children's department to be found anywhere, but realized that some of the other departments were only the best that they could be expected to be with their small staffs and limited materials. Still, I felt and talked about the library just as Alan Woodland and most of you people do. That's positive thinking and it's pretty important in building any organization. (3/1982)

■   ■   ■   ■   ■

OFFICE AT CITY HALL: Chris Albertson writes from the Orange, Tex., Public Library to "toot the horn" for North Texas Lib. School grads, enclosing a clipping telling of David Price being moved into the City Hall in Aurora, Colorado, where the library director can hobnob with the other city officials. Price will become coordinator of all department head meetings and is responsible for general information services to other city departments. Chris says, "I'm not sure of the pros and cons of leaving the library to work up on 'the Hill,' but with an invitation like that who'd refuse?"

It's my guess that most library directors would prefer to have their office in the main library, though the directors in Tucson and San Diego seemed to prefer to be located outside the library and saw no disadvantage in this arrangement. For myself, I wouldn't want to be separated from my staff, or from the book collection or the library patrons, or from the sight of the library building in use. They could go all day, or all week, or all month, without seeing me, but I couldn't be removed from them and enjoy the same pleasure and satisfaction from my job. Without these elements that attracted me to the profession in the first place, I'm afraid the job might seem a bit tasteless, as it might be for the average school principal if he were removed to an office at school headquarters. He would probably get more work done there, and live longer but something would be missing from him, or her. Of course, the director can visit the library at any time but I can remember my first job in a public library; the library director had his office three miles away and I never saw him in the library. He was a nice, friendly person and a capable administrator, and the location of his office may have made no difference to him. (6/1979)

·   ·   ·   ·   ·

RISING HIGHER: The job of Library Director is no longer the absolute end of the line as far as one's career advancement is concerned. In the past we have had a few college and university library directors, like Eugene Wilson at the University of Colorado, who were promoted to a vice-president's position . . . and a small number of public library directors who were moved up to a new position as manager of a number of city departments including the public library.

The most recent member of this group is David Price who has served for a number of years as Director of the Library, Television and Convention Services for the City of Aurora, Colorado. He has just been appointed to the position of

Deputy City Manager for Administrative and Information
Services in Aurora. The library is one of several line departments under his direction. Among other departments he will
oversee are Data Processing, Personnel, Budget, Convention
Services and Community Media Relations. A new library director will be appointed at a future date.

"I PERCEIVE A GROWING CHASM, indeed a con-
flict, between the interest of library administrators and grass
roots 'desk' librarians," writes James Chaffee in his independent newsletter of fact and opinion concerning the San Francisco Public Library. "As a member of the public I want the
person who helps me at the desk to be a professional. To be
told that the professional is in an office somewhere is simply a
version of irresponsibility . . . I expect every librarian, if he
or she is a professional, to take responsibility not only for my
service as an individual but the efficacy of the system as a
whole. That is what professionalism is after all. When librarians and library administrators become two different species,
it will be a serious setback for public libraries."

I don't believe this young San Franciscan has ever worked
in a library, or studied library science, but few people have
written more pages of readable material about the operation
of a library or evinced a greater interest or concern about the
state of libraries today. His insights are oftentimes quite provocative and his readers would do well to give them some
careful thought. For example, his remark about librarians
who are "in an office somewhere" may hit home with some
professionals—and not just librarians. He says he wants the
person who helps him to be a professional. So the college student wants the person instructing him to be a professor—and
not a graduate student. Some of us tend to want to get away
from our public when we move up in the ranks. Some of this
withdrawal can't be helped, but much of it can. A library ad-

ministrator doesn't have too many callers, other than his own staff-members, so I've always spent some time every day in the main public areas of the library, talking with the public as well as with the staff, seeing and being seen. If I had to confine my activities to an office—as many administrators prefer to do—my pleasure in the job would be seriously diminished. Incidentally, I was reading a newspaper article Saturday about a college president who was being criticized by both his faculty and the students because he remained in his office all the time. "We never see him on the campus," they said, "and he never shows up at any of the social or athletic events." (2/1980)

■   ■   ■   ■   ■

HOW MANY PUBLIC LIBRARY DIRECTORS have a day named after them? Well . . . Sarah Long, past director of the Fairfield County District Library in Lancaster, Ohio, just did. County Commissioner Donna Crist Cook, at an informal going-away party for Long (she became director of the Dauphin County L.S. in Harrisburg, Pa.), declared February 20, 1982 "Sarah Long Day" in Fairfield County. An official PROCLAMATION was drawn up, full of complimentary "Whereas" statements, and signed by the three county commissioners.

We think every library employee ought to have his or her own day—even if it's just a day at the library, instead of in the whole city or county, and without any proclamation. Whenever an employee left the South San Francisco Public Library, besides a luncheon or other party, he or she got the day named after him/her. From 9 to 9, every member of the Staff wore a ribbon badge that said "Mary Miller Day," or whatever the name might be. This of course brought many inquiries from the public as to who the person was. When told that

she was one of our nice high school pages that we were sorry
to lose, many patrons commented, "What a nice idea."
(6/1982)

■   ■   ■   ■   ■

HOW THE CITY LIBRARIAN RATES: It is always
interesting to see how public library directors are paid in comparison to other city department heads. It tells a good bit
about how difficult and important the city council members
feel the City Librarian's job is in comparison to that of the
police chief, the director of the P&R Dept. and the other city
officials.

In three of the cities I served as City Librarian my salary
was about on a par with that of the head of parks and recreation, and only a thousand or two behind the pay of the fire and
police chiefs. In the fourth city, my salary was ahead of that of
almost all the city department heads—and the school superintendent, as well—but that was an unusual situation in that the
library board could pay its executive any amount they wished,
completely independent of City Hall.

In recent years, the other city departments have grown
more in staff and total budget than the library, and the salaries of these department heads have increased more and
pulled away from that of the library director.

The magnitude of this salary differential was impressed on
me this morning when I read in the *Peninsula Progress* of the
pay hikes just approved by the City Council in South San
Francisco. The City Manager's salary was increased to
$64,480, and the Director of Public Services went to $57,449.
That is a new position that they didn't have a year or two ago,
and it is hard to understand why it is needed now. All the city
department heads are capable people and don't need any direction or other help from this new coordinating official imposed between them and the city manager.

Next come the City Attorney at $53,713, the Chief of Police at approximately the same amount, the Fire Chief at $49,712, and the Assistant City Manager, Director of Community Development, Director of Finance and Director of Parks and Recreation, all at $48,360. The Personnel Director is now paid $42,099, the Asst. City Attorney $41,850, and the City Librarian, $39,270.

I might add that the population of So. S.F. is now 50,000 . . . so you can compare these salaries with those prevailing in your own area. But anyone doing this should remember that housing out here costs twice as much as in most parts of the country and that most salaries and living costs are just a lot higher out here. (3/1984).

■   ■   ■   ■   ■

LIBRARIAN'S CAR: Lee Brawner, Executive Director of the Metropolitan Library System in Oklahoma City/County, has just been given a 1983 Oldsmobile Cutlass Supreme to replace the 1972 Plymouth sedan that he has long been using on library business. Reading about the retirement of "Ol' Blue" really reminded me of the wonderful little Henry J coupe that the Nashville Library Board permitted me to get some thirty years ago. I couldn't have been more pleased to have that tiny bright yellow automobile to drive to and from work and wherever I needed to go during working hours. The Library provided the three or four hundred dollars that the car cost, and then took care of the insurance and maintenance costs. My only expense was for all the gas (about 20 cents a gallon) and oil that went into the machine. Almost nobody had two cars in those days, so having the use of this library car—which left our own car at home—was a tremendous fringe benefit for the whole family. I hope many of you reading this are equally blessed today. (6/1984)

■   ■   ■   ■   ■

"WE WERE DISAPPOINTED WITH your editorial approach and philosophy," explains a Midwestern librarian who is cancelling his subscription after one year. "Particularly distressing was space taken with the 'Who's Got the Largest Circ.?' issue.

"Sophisticated Administrators and Boards are only beginning to learn that 'bean counting' is not a measure of satisfaction or quality service. Those who would pass this data on to the rest of us are like the corporations that issue profit statements but don't adjust for inflation. What's really going on behind those gorgeous data curves?"

I am not sure I understand this analogy but I do appreciate his honesty and his taking the time to share his thoughts with me. We want and need all the feedback we can get.

We are always cognizant of the fact that many librarians do not share our feelings about "bean counting," but statements that a library's circulation "is *not a measure* of satisfaction or quality service" will always surprise me. It may not be the only measure but certainly it is *a measure.* And we believe that for the time being, it is the best single measure that we have in public libraries. In the same way, circulation may not be the only measure of satisfaction with a particular magazine or newsletter, but it is the best one that we have. In both cases, the circulation normally goes up when people are satisfied with the quality of service, and goes down when the quality drops off. The correlation between the variables here is quite high. When the expected relationship is not there, one can be fairly sure that the answer lies in outside economic conditions that are beyond the control of the librarians.

We have given a lot of attention to circulation figures over the years because we have found that librarians who think about circulation and are concerned with circ. figures generally increase them. Far more than librarians who don't seem to care whether their circulation goes up or down, and can't tell you what their library's circulation was last year. Administrators should be competitive-minded, which normally means they are out to compete with—and better—the record they made the year before.

THINK OF THE LIBRARY ADMINISTRATORS you have known. If you try to put them into two groups—Competitors and Non-competitors—I believe you will find that most of the ones you consider as having improved and expanded their library's services are in the first group (Competitors), and you will recall that they were always concerned with their circulation and almost always increased it. It is hard to think of any topnotch library administrators who didn't particularly care whether their figures of library use went up or down as long as the quality of service was maintained. It would be just as hard to think of a good golfer who didn't care what his scores were as long as he was playing well.

Treat the public nicer at the front desks, make the library more attractive and inviting, increase the number of interesting new books, offer some helpful new services, do more work with and for the public, or make any other significant improvements in the quality of your service . . . and you can expect to see an increase in the use of the library. And this increase will not be limited to the particular department or service improved. A study of library annual reports indicates that increased activity in one area of the library is more often than not accompanied by increased use of other services. When you read about a sizable increase in circulation the picture presented is generally one of library progress overall. If this is all pretty much true—and I can't recall hearing or reading any statements to the contrary—then how can anyone say that circulation is not a measure of library performance? And a good one at that. It may be the oldest and the simplest measure, but sometimes the simplest way IS the best way. (5/1982)

■   ■   ■   ■   ■

CHAPTER IV

Relationships With the Staff

GIVE THEM RESPONSIBILITY: We heard the other day about a chief reference librarian who won't let her new professionals answer the telephone until they have been on the job for six months. If that is true, I would be surprised if any of the young people were still on hand at the end of this probationary period. It is indeed sad to think of students coming out of library school, all rarin' to go and eager to show what they can do, and then finding that they must prove themselves for six months before being trusted to handle a simple reference question. This is of course an extreme case and we really needn't give it any further attention other than to comment that times have changed and young people today want a real job and to be given interesting and meaningful work and some responsibility almost immediately. If an employer can't provide this, he or she had better pass up the best of the library school crop, and the same thing applies to every other professional field.

A department head or administrator's responsibility in this area doesn't end with seeing that every staff member has a significant job to do; it is also an important part of every supervisor's job to see that his or her staff have every opportunity to try out some of their better ideas. When I taught Supervision at United Aircraft, I would endeavor to bring this idea in under Rule No. 4 which was "Make the Best Use of Each Person's Ability" . . . and I believe it is equally pertinent today. Do let your people know that you expect them to be creative, contributing members of your team, and that you want them to question everything they do and see if it is necessary, and, if so, how it can be done better. Librarians—and everyone else, too—should be continually experimenting, observing, analyzing, seeing what works and what is popular, and what isn't. But how many do? I got to talking with a young children's librarian at the Las Vegas convention who was full of ideas and enthusiasm but never has been given a chance to do anything, as her boss apparently doesn't believe in change. What a waste!

If someone comes to you and wants to move some sections of books, or try arranging or displaying some material differently, or anything within reason . . . be thankful for her interest and initiative and say YES. Don't say you'll have to think about it, or talk to someone else about it. Just say "It sounds like a good idea: why don't you try it?" You both know the books can be put back later if the idea doesn't work out, and no harm can possibly be done. Even if you have tried much the same thing before yourself and know it probably won't work, don't say no. Let the person try it and learn for herself; her next idea may really pay off. At least, she'll stay a contented and thinking member of your staff, and that's what you want.

The important thing is to give your people all the responsibility you can, and as much freedom and opportunity to be creative as possible. Most people are more competent than one thinks they are, and you can be certain that the busier they are and the greater their sense of accomplishment, the happier they will be. And nothing makes an administrator's job more pleasant than having a happy and energetic staff. And when I say that I am not just thinking of your professional people. There are—or should be—three non-professionals on a library staff for every librarian, and if this majority is not encouraged to contribute to their fullest capacity, the library is bound to miss out to a considerable degree. Let me cite just one case which really brought this fact home to me. You may remember my telling you last month about the two branch assistants in South San Francisco who decided on the spur of the moment to take paperback books and magazines to the people waiting in the long lines for gasoline, and received such an enthusiastic response from both the motorists and the news media. These young ladies are both non-professionals, though college graduates, and one works only 15 hours a week. Yet, in the three months since they made this big move—learning something of the joys of real achievement and recognition up the line—these two have really stepped out on their own and done a great many interesting and useful things. They (1) organized a "book wagon" service to take books to shopping centers distant from a library building, (2) published the first issue of a most interesting branch newsletter, (3) collected maps, tourist brochures, calendars of events, and other travel literature from all the states, most of the countries, and all counties in California, and started advertising a special new library travel information service, (4) started a branch collection of college catalogs, and (5) took steps to rebuild the branch's collection of books in Spanish. Every one of these projects was conceived and accomplished in this 90-day period by these two employees, who still carried out their regular assignments in the branch. And none of them cost more than $20, though the Spanish collection will of course occasion a greater expenditure. Last night when the library director invited Mrs. Hansen and Mrs. Patrick to come to the monthly meeting of the library board and tell the members what they were doing, the trustees couldn't have been more pleased and impressed by their presentation. It just goes to show what staff members can do when given the chance. (5/1974)

■   ■   ■   ■   ■

GIVE STIMULATING ASSIGNMENTS: Reginald Jones, the retiring board chairman of General Electric Company, was quoted in *U.S. News & World Report* as saying:

> "You have to manage people differently nowadays. When I went to work for General Electric Company in 1939, I spent one year checking holes in punch cards for business machines to be sure they were in the right places—as a college graduate. You would not think of giving that kind of job to a college graduate today. If you give people stimulating and rewarding assignments, and if you let them participate in the decisions, they're very happy, very challenged. Feed them special assignments, and it's like raw meat."

I expect that statement will register strongly with many readers of this column who had similar experiences in their first library job. I well remember my first professional position—in the Reference Department of the Rochester, N.Y., Public Library. Almost every morning I would be given some sort of book list or catalog and asked to check 150 or more titles in the public catalog to see which ones were already in the Library's collection. It was a boring job and a great waste of time. I certainly hope that no librarian in 1985 asks people—whether professional, clerical, or volunteer—to check long lists of titles in the catalog preliminary to book selection. Most of these were new books and not likely to be already in the catalog, but even so it is far more sensible to select the titles you want and then have this much smaller group checked.

However, being new to the business I did whatever I was asked to do and never questioned the need or good sense of any assignment. I figured that all low-grade jobs required a good deal of laborious work, that everyone had to go through this sort of experience, and that one would rise above this sort of assignment when no longer on the bottom rung of the totem pole. I didn't stay on the bottom rung very long, but when I did reach the level where I was on the giving rather than the receiving end of such assignments, I never would ask a professional librarian to perform such low-grade work. In fact, I made every effort to limit the need to perform dull tasks, even by clerical people. I've always tried to make library work interesting and challenging for the clericals as well as the professionals. After all, they are basically the same kind of people, both wanting interesting and satisfying work to do and both reacting the same way to boring assignments. One group has just as big a need and desire for personal satisfaction and fulfillment on the job as the other, and is equally entitled to experience it.

SO TRY TO MAKE NEWCOMERS JOBS interesting right from the start. Don't make them go through dull probationary periods before they are given a chance to do the kind of work trained to do. Try to think of some special project or study that you can assign the new staff member, something that clearly needs doing and will require some real thought and imagination on the part of this person. The immediate supervisor should be thinking along these lines, as well as the library director. The latter should at least make it a point to visit the newcomer at his workplace and contribute

something to his or her feeling of welcome and acceptance in
the new position. An invitation to lunch is always nice, as is an
invitation to accompany the director on a visit to some branch
libraries. It is very encouraging to the new person to feel that
the big boss knows he or she is alive and is happy to have him
or her on the staff. I'd like to have a dollar for every librarian
who has joined a large library staff and gone an entire year
without any sort of contact from the library director. This is
indeed a sad thing—for the director as well as the new staff
member. (2/1986)

.   .   .   .   .

BEING A NEW LIBRARIAN: All of us were at one
time a new librarian in some library, much like Sherry Crow
of Englewood, Colorado. At least I hope many of you were
like that new librarian who was "determined to make a good
impression and bursting with new ideas." I expect I fell in that
group, too, though it was never a problem until I became an
administrator and started changing things before I'd been
there long enough for the staff to know and feel comfortable
with me.

Still, I would have liked to have Sherry Crow on "my
staff," and believe that people like that with imagination and
enthusiasm are the best possible recruits for any library.
Those are the particular qualities I always looked for in seeking new people and I would never take anyone who didn't
seem to have them. I've known librarians who were primarily
interested in the grades that candidates made in college and
library school and would always take the person with the best
record. That's a senseless policy and is guaranteed to bring
you some people that you won't always enjoy working with. I
don't believe anyone has shown a convincing correlation between good grades in school and satisfactory job perform-

ance, any more than good grades have been proven a guarantee that one will be a pleasing husband or wife.

Some of your new staff members will suggest adding or changing something before you are prepared to entertain any new ideas from them. Just thank your stars that you were lucky enough to draw a live, quality person this time. People like that with spirit and ingenuity will always be the greatest assets that you and your library will have. If you don't have many ideas of your own, how wonderful for you to have some Sherry Crow-types on your staff to provide them for you. And if you are blessed with imagination and enthusiasm yourself, how even more wonderful for you to have an additional staff member who will accept your ideas and support them, rather than resisting them, and help bring about their implementation.

So the new person comes to you with his or her positive suggestion . . . comes with eagerness and hope, mixed with a good dash of fear. I do hope you will stop and listen and be patient, and appreciative. Please don't react like most human beings and simply say "No." That is of course the easiest answer. You don't have to do anything and nobody else will be upset.

Even if the idea seems ridiculous to you, you don't want to squelch a possible future source of many good ideas, nor do you want to cause a lot of unhappiness. I couldn't ride over a person's feelings with an abrupt No any more than I could drive my car over a bed of flowers. One can always say, at least, "That's certainly an interesting (or original) idea and one I'd like to think about a little more. I do thank you for bringing it to me and hope you will keep thinking about how we can improve our library service. It's wonderful to have someone with your imagination and enthusiasm on the staff and if we don't ring the bell on this particular idea of yours I am sure that we will on many others in the future."

That might be an adequate response in the case of a clearly impractical suggestion. But in reality, most employee suggestions are not in this category. They are normally sensible and worthwhile. They are rejected in most cases simply because the boss is resistant to change and doesn't even like to talk about a new idea. Its the natural inclination of most people to oppose any change that is likely to affect them. And bosses who have no interest in seeing anything changed have the additional negative of not wanting to do anything that will upset or impose a burden on any of their employees, because that means trouble for them.

In the case of Sherry Crow, her suggestion for a videotape library was a good one and there is no reason in the world why it couldn't, and shouldn't, have been encouraged. Such a collection would be a positive and appreciated addition to the library and it would have been so easy to say, "That's a great idea. We *ought* to have a videotape collection, and there's no reason we can't get started with it right now. Of course we will have to start small, with perhaps only fifteen or twenty tapes, but I am sure that will please a lot of our patrons and be the start of a new service that will quickly grow as we find more money for it and people give us money and tapes for the collection."

While there is understandably no money in the budget now for videotapes, it certainly ought to be possible to find $125 in the book budget (buying ten less books) or some other account, just to get started with this new service. And with a slight effort it should be possible to interest outsiders in donating a similar amount or more for this purpose.

Starting any new collection in your library should not be a big problem. I'm always sorry when I hear of someone who has been holding off starting something that should be started, waiting for the time when the library will have the funds to do the thing right. That's a big mistake. It's as senseless as waiting to get married until you can have an $8,000 wedding or have your own house.

As I've been saying for many years, it's far better to "think small" and get going on a small scale with the little money you have, than to put off doing something until you can afford a big splurge. I've started a great many new collections with less than $100 to spend (perhaps $300 in today's money), and they all bloomed in size and popularity. The important thing is to "get on the board" and then you will quickly pick up interested users who will help ensure the continuance and growth of the new service. (12/1986)

·   ·   ·   ·   ·

HOW DO YOU TREAT THEM? An article on education in the March 1st issue of The New York Times asks this question: "Because virtually all supervisors are former teachers, why do many of them appear insensitive to the way teachers would like to be treated? The cause may be the 'Peter Principle,' " which maintains that people tend to rise to the "level of their incompetence." L. J. Peter cites as an example the outstanding nursery school teacher who, after being promoted to supervisor of nursery school teachers, talks to and treats them as if they were 3-year-olds.

"Similarly, many principals deal with their teachers in weekly staff meetings as if they were addressing a group of students. They talk at them, not with them . . ."

Some of you reading the above question doubtless substituted the word "librarians" for "teachers," as I did when reading the original article. It then asks: "Because virtually all (library) supervisors are former librarians, why do many of them appear insensitive to the way librarians would like to be treated?"

Librarians—being human beings—want to be treated as

individuals, and with the proper courtesy and respect. They want to be communicated with—to be told how they are getting along, to hear in advance about all changes that affect them and their work, to be informed of library board and city hall deliberations and decisions that have implications for them, to receive credit and praise when it is due them, and to be treated in general as an important and appreciated member of the library term.

There isn't a library supervisor who didn't want to be treated that way when he or she was a librarian in the ranks. And there are not many who didn't at some time or another feel that their supervisor wasn't treating them with the consideration that they deserved. If this is true, why are there so many supervisors and administrators in our libraries today who appear to some of their staff to have forgotten how librarians would like to be treated?

In many cases, of course, it's not so much a matter of forgetting how other human beings like to be treated as it is the fact that the newly-promoted supervisor is now operating on a higher level, with additional responsibilities and concerns and demands on his/her time, and it is not always possible to give each staff member all the time and attention he or she might like.

Yet it is a rare supervisor who couldn't be a little friendlier, kinder, more appreciative, more interested, more helpful, to some members of their staff. No supervisor has the same regard for all his/her staff. Some of them work harder than others, some work more pleasantly or more cooperatively or with greater effectiveness. Some of them are a joy to have around, and are loyal and completely dependable. A few may be just the opposite. So it is only natural for the boss to like and appreciate some of the staff more than the others.

While this may not make the job of the supervisor more pleasant, it does make it more challenging. A supervisor gets his results through people. And while he or she may not particularly like one or two of his/her people, they are still performing essential work for him and it is definitely in his interest to see that they are as happy and well-motivated as possible. As the Bible says, it is easy to love those who are lovable, but that's not enough. What really counts is to show caring for the gloomy, grumpy, colorless or downright unfriendly people on one's staff . . . and do it in a sincere, convincing manner because you really do care. As someone put it the other day: "I love you not because I need you, or want you, but because you need me." The sad part is that those who need caring the most, get the least amount of it. Some time you might like to pick out the seemingly most miserable member of the staff—your current biggest headache—and for three months shower her with all the attention and caring and appreciation that you can muster and see if she doesn't become a bit nicer. It will surprise the rest of the staff as much as it will this particular individual, but if the effort does no more than make you feel better about this person it will prove to have been time well spent. (6/1984)

■　　　■　　　■　　　■　　　■

SOMETIMES THE NEW CHIEF LIBRARIAN becomes so involved with the changes he is trying to make that he loses sight of the bulk of his staff. He is too busy to really communicate with them. He goes ahead, doing his thing, completely wrapped up in the improvements he is bringing about, while most of the staff is left alone to wonder what he is going to do next, to second-guess what he has already done, and to worry about how everything is going to affect them. The more they imagine and worry, the more apprehensive and upset they become, until the administrator is awakened to the fact that he has a big problem on his hands.

As disturbing as this is for the new executive, it can turn out to be a good thing if it happens in time for him (or her; most library directors are of course women) to turn around and start giving more of his time and attention to his staff. He needs to share his dreams and his plans with his people, explaining why he favors each proposal, what it will mean for the library and, above all, how it will affect the person(s) he is talking to. His task is to calm fears, to make people feel relaxed and comfortable again, to build trust and confidence and open-mindedness. To do this, he is going to have to show honest approval and caring and consideration for his staff, individual by individual.

Some people can't be won over. They just can't tolerate change, or they can't accept the particular new ideas that the new administrator has brought with him. If they can't block the changes, they can do their best to make things unpleasant or impossible for the person responsible for them.

FORTUNATELY, MOST LIBRARY STAFFS are made up of predominantly pleasant people who will make the new director feel immediately welcome. I had two library staffs like that and I enjoyed them all the way and stayed 13$\frac{1}{2}$ years in each library. But I encountered a completely different group of people in the library I told about in an earlier editorial column. There was just no welcome at all. My first few weeks on the job, I sat at my desk in the big Librarian's office, looking up whenever a department head or branch librarian came into the outer office to turn in material or visit with my secretary. I could see them well enough, and they could see me. But not once did anyone wave a greeting or come into my office to say hello or to introduce herself. Nobody knew a thing about the new man on the fourth floor, and it seemed as if everyone was content to keep it that way. Nobody took the new director around the system to meet the staff. After the warm friendliness of my previous staff, I just couldn't understand my new associates. It certainly wasn't a good omen for the future.

THE DIRECTOR IS ALWAYS OUT FRONT, taking whatever is thrown the library's way. Most of the time, of course, there's nothing. But sometimes there are words of praise and appreciation, and occasionally some criticism. Whatever comes, the staff is in the background. They may never be singled out for favorable attention in the local newspaper, but neither will they be the recipient of any public criticism, nor will they suffer anxious moments about the permanence of their employment. This seems like a fair exchange, and it is.

But unfortunately, some employees may not like it if the boss gets "too much attention." They may feel that they had a lot to do with the progress that he is being praised for and may feel some resentment that they are not getting any of the plaudits. In short, they may want to share in the positive recognition while still being shielded from the negative. It really isn't fair that one should have the gains without the pains—they normally go together—but since some people are inclined that way it would seem highly desirable for the administrator to spread the glory around and share the spotlight, as much as possible, with his board and staff. He or she doubtless knows that he will stand pretty much alone come serious trouble, but by lowering his profile in the good times and letting his staff raise theirs and be recognized, he will do much to avert such trouble.

This is not always easy to do. It's difficult to share credit for a well-received library improvement with department heads who were opposed to the idea and resisted it all the way, and still seem to resent the change. It is sad that the people who most need some praise and appreciation in their lives are the ones who make it the hardest for others to give it.

YOU WILL DOUBTLESS FIND that some employees are easily hurt, offended, aggrieved. It doesn't take too much to make them suspicious, fearful, critical and hard to deal with. If left alone to feed on each other's fears and complaints, they are capable of real hate and resentment, manifested in disloyalty, trouble-making and plain nastiness. Feelings rarely develop to that point, but it does happen.

Administrators should always be alert for signs of such unhappiness so that they can straighten things out—not only to avoid trouble for themselves but, even more, to give comfort to a fellow worker who may be suffering from an imagined slight or a needless fear.

Any considerate boss wants his people to be happy in their work. He would do well to have someone on his staff—generally his secretary—who would advise him whenever someone on the staff was troubled. I had a secretary like that. She would inform me of personal problems that individuals had, where I might be of some help, as well as the job-related situations that could be improved with a little further explanation, or encouragement, or schedule adjustment that the director could easily provide. Sometimes she would just say, "I believe Ms. So-and-so could use a little extra attention."

Everyone probably has his own way of communicating with his staff, though it's surprising the number of large-library directors who do almost no communicating on an individual basis, except with the middle-management people they must see. They pretty much confine their staff contacts to an annual meeting where they speak to a hundred or more people seated together, and then leave, I've worked in four libraries where the lower ranks only saw the director once a year. However, I can't recall any staff problems in the short time I was in each place. Perhaps the explanation for this lies in the fact that all of the directors had been there for quite some time, and none of them made any changes that upset anyone. The staff went about their work and the secluded boss attended to his. He seemed so remote a figure, at least to us library assistants, that nobody would have thought of blaming or resenting him for anything. Perhaps if these directors had attempted some changes—such as transferring some people to a branch, or requiring more weekend or evening work, or streamlining some pet library operations—they *might* have aroused some opposition. Who knows. Disloyalty was just as unknown in those days as change.

I believe administrators communicate better with their people these days. They've seen the need to do so. And there is so much more to talk about in the '80s. And the professionals on the staff want to be kept informed, and want to discuss and be heard. One of the best public libraries for Librarian-staff communication was the Vigo County Library (Ind.) under Ed Howard, who retired several years ago. They held frequent and regular staff meetings and before each one, each department head received a packet overflowing with material bearing on the topics to be discussed at that session. Those people worked hard, and they worked together.

The only consistent thing I did in this area was something I truly enjoyed doing: taking about ten minutes every morning to visit with the staff at the main library. I didn't always get to all the departments but I never missed the circulation and cataloging departments. We talked a lot more about sports, politics, families, etc. than about their work, but it gave me real pleasure and it perhaps let them know that the boss cared about them as individuals rather than just part of the library machine. And since we could talk freely about anything on one's mind, there was no chance for any negative feelings to develop, and none did. That went on for 13$\frac{1}{2}$ years in each of two library systems. I'm sorry it never seemed a good or possible idea in the library I'll tell you about later.

■　　　■　　　■　　　■　　　■

TRY ASKING THEM: We have often urged supervisors to ask their staff to suggest improvements. From our experience in business and industry and in working in public libraries we are inclined to believe that few managers ever think of asking their people how a particular operation might be done more efficiently, or whether they think it might be eliminated altogether. I had half a dozen employers who never talked to me about improving anything we were doing, and I never heard of anybody else being asked to suggest better ways of getting the work done.

To be sure, most supervisors don't spend much time thinking about making changes in established ways of doing things. They have no particular interest in change of any kind, even if they saw the need for greater efficiency of productivity. Most of them wouldn't recognize such a need, and a sizable portion of those who came to see the need for improvements in their work area would leave it to someone else to make the changes.

Every supervisor or manager should look at his or her workers not just as people who do the work in that particular office or department, but as the best source of information and ideas about every job that is performed there. If these employees have been well selected for their individual jobs they ought to be intelligent enough to think seriously about the work they do week in and week out. They should occasionally have a feeling that something they do really serves no purpose at all, or perhaps duplicates the work of someone else. Or it may be a growing conviction that some routine or process could be accomplished in much less time if a few simple changes were made in it.

Such possibilities for improvement are in the mind of the particular low-ranking staff member who actually performs this work. The supervisor is unaware of them. He or she has his or her own work and special concerns. Needless to say, it's to the supervisor's advantage, as well as the library's advantage, to acquire this employee's ideas. Provided, of course, that the supervisor is receptive to change, able to recognize the value of this employee's suggestions, and willing to make the changes called for.

Such suggestions for improvements too often don't reach the supervisor. The main reason for this is that nobody asks workers for such suggestions in most work places. In many of them the boss stays in his or her office and is so busy most of the time that there is very little communication with the staff. I've known many employees who wouldn't say two words to their boss in a month's time. When their paths did cross, the boss had no time or inclination to ask for suggestions on how to improve anything.

WHAT PROMPTED THE ABOVE was my reading the following two paragraphs in the July 15th issue of U.S. News & World Report. It was part of a conversation with Tom Peters, the co-author of *In Search of Excellence.*

". . . time after time when I'm wandering around a plant I talk to somebody who has been employed at the same machine for 12 years. I don't understand the machinery, but I have a 20-minute conversation with them, and they tell me 97 things that could be slightly improved and wouldn't cost more than a few nickels' worth of capital. You say to that person at the end of the talk: 'Why don't you tell somebody about it?' You get this unbelievably pathetic answer: 'Nobody asked.'

"A guy who retired a few years ago who ran quality control in a sizable division of a Big Three auto company said that in a dozen years in that job he was never visited by a member of the corporate staff and only once by his division general manager. That says to me that the company didn't care about quality. What can you recommend when that's the case?"

SO START TALKING to your staff members, and ask them for their opinions and ideas about various aspects of the work they do. And be sure your mind is wide open so it can really hear and consider whatever is said. And when an employee suggests a possible improvement, don't just let the matter drop without any response on your part.

Any employee suggestion deserves a response from the supervisor. The worker shows that he or she is thinking, and trying to improve the performance of the work in that supervisor's area, and the latter should be happy about this and express appreciation for the suggestion that is offered.

But one can't stop there either. When a person suggests an improvement he or she wants to hear whether it will be accepted and implemented or not, and if not, why not. Too often, the ideas and suggestions of staff members are "taken under advisement," and nothing more is ever heard about them. Do this a few times and staff morale may never be the same.

I recall the time last year when a golfing partner told me of an idea he had for improving a situation at our golf club. It sounded good to me and I encouraged him to write a letter to our elected board of directors. He has yet to hear a word of response to his suggestion. He may have some even better ideas that could be helpful to the club in the future, but you may be sure the board will never hear of them. This lack of feedback may be perfectly normal, and it probably does happen more times than not, but I hope our readers will never treat their staff members that way. (10/1985)

■   ■   ■   ■   ■

ANONYMOUS: In the 17½ years that we have been publishing this newsletter we have never had an anonymous letter. I am happy to report that we are now the recipient of such a communication and am pleased to present it to you here:

> "While I realize your publication is intended primarily for library administrators, who would presumably be in agreement with policies beneficial to library directors, I think you are sometimes too kind to library directors and do not give much credit to other library employees. For instance, you frequently mention the benefits to be derived by firing "disruptive" library employees. You also suggest rallying to the side of an embattled library director. Have you never come across a situation in which the library director was the "disruptive" employee. Do you have any idea how discouraging it is to employes working for such a person to take legitimate grievances to the library's board of directors, only to be told, in essence, that they should do as they are told, because the director is the boss? I suppose that in any organization there must be a very few persons who must be dismissed within a few years time. When the director considers 10–20 percent of the staff at any one time to be inadequate or "disruptive," I think the problem lies with that director, rather than with the staff. Furthermore, I think that you, as an influential resource in the library field should stop advocating the knee-jerk solidarity response from fellow administrators, when an administrator is in a jam. Maybe he picked the fruit.
>
> "Since I know that my library director looks to your publication for justification for much of his behavior, I'll just sign myself,   Troubled in Texas"

THAT'S A GOOD LETTER and I certainly wouldn't dispute anything in it. Perhaps I don't give enough credit to the non-administrators. I try to, whenever the story that comes to me mentions the staff people involved. Generally, the reporter simply states that the local library is now offering such-and-such new service, or is scheduling a particular event of interest, or has increased its circulation 9 percent, or whatever. Most of the credit for all good things at the library is bound to go to the library director, which is perhaps only fair as he or she is the person who catches all the flak when anything goes wrong there. But of course this is true in every organization, in both the public and private sectors. The person at the top always has his neck on the line. If the business goes down or if the organization is made to look bad in the public eye the axe is more likely to fall on the head man than on the employees who may have contributed to the sad picture. And unlike the employees, the boss has no protection and no appeal.

While this publication is admittedly "intended primarily for library administrators," most of what I write is designed equally for department heads and all others who have supervisory responsibilities. From the mail I get I am convinced that the majority of our readers are in this group for the simple reason that they outnumber the director on the staff of most of our subscribing libraries.

As for "disruptive" employees, I've only had two people that I would put in that category. These were real crusaders, out to get their director fired for the reason that they couldn't or wouldn't accept the changes that he was making to modernize a library that hadn't even considered a new idea in the 30 years before when these two top department heads actually ran the library. It was hard for them to give up the power they had had for so long. They were intelligent, skilled workers. The only thing wrong with them was their attitudes— which bears out my contention that one's work-attitudes are more important than anything else. Or to put it more simply, they were completely disloyal to their boss and harmful to their institution. They constantly "bad-mouthed" the new director to library patrons and misrepresented most of what he said to their staff people. As I said before, I should have fired these crusaders. And if "Troubled in Texas" had been in my shoes I'm sure he or she would have considered such action quite justified.

Have we ever known a situation where the library director was the "disruptive" employee? Of course. In some of these cases, the director was asked to resign. In others, the disruptive director went on seemingly forever. I've known a director who would never listen to a new idea from one of his staff, another who communicated with most of his department heads only by letter, most of them quite insulting—whether intended so or not—and another who drove out all the older staff members that she had inherited.

DIRECTORS ARE JUST PEOPLE: I couldn't sympathize more with this Texas librarian but I can't think of anything that one could say that would be helpful . . . other than to quote King Solomon, who was certainly one of the wisest men who ever lived. "When someone does you wrong," said the King, "it is good virtue to ignore it." This may not fit the Texas situation too well, but I would still urge this librarian to try and accept what she or he cannot change, and try to be as tolerant of the boss' behavior as possible.

One must always avoid thinking of administrators, or employees, as "the other side," or as a different kind of people. They are all librarians, and they are all just people. Meaning that they all want pretty much the same thing out of life and they all react the same way to given stimuli.

My two detailed surveys of about 400 library directors showed—among other things—that most directors didn't want to be an administrator and had no intention of being one. The job was just dumped in their lap. Somebody had to replace the retiring chief librarian and the library board picked them. They had no training for the job, and most of them no particular inclination for it. It's perhaps surprising that in view of all this so many of them perform so well.

When I was a personnel officer I was continually told by department heads that they had no desire to be a supervisor, and no particular aptitude for it either. They much preferred concentrating on their own work, but because they had been the top draftsman or engineer in their group when a new leader was required, the unwanted responsibilities were given to them.

That may or may not be the case with the Texan's boss. But this one thing he or she can be sure of: The boss knows that he is disliked by a person of his staff, and doubtless also knows that they have gone over his head to the library board. And that is enough to make any administrator both unhappy and insecure. If our anonymous friend is unhappy that she/he can't get the desired support from the board, let him/her take satisfaction from the fact that she/he is making the boss every bit as miserable as he is making him/her.

WE ALL HATE TO HEAR ABOUT such troubles and disaffections in a library, just as we hate to hear about them in a marriage. They just cause too much unhappiness. If I do tend to spring to the director's defense it is simply because he is the one being judged, and being hurt, and not his anonymous attackers. He is the one who is spotlighted and publicly embarrassed, the one who is on the defensive, the one who may lose his job. The average citizen won't even know the names of the employees who claim their boss is a poor administrator. But there will be no question as to the identity of the person attacked—and most people are not inclined to think well of anyone who does not seem to be liked by his employees. In short, it's just not a fair fight!

In conclusion, I'm not questioning our anonymous writer's opinion that the fault of the trouble in Texas lies with the director. It well could be. Who knows? I just hope that our letter writer doesn't get embittered or do anything unkind or unprofessional in this situation. A disloyal employee is no better than the boss who offends her.

As for me, I will "stop advocating the knee-jerk solidarity response from fellow administrators, when an administrator is in a jam," when fellow professionals, in whatever field, stop their knee-jerk judgments of the person in trouble before they know of the facts in the case or give any consideration to what the person accomplished there and what he had to contend against to do this. (11/1983)

.   .   .   .   .

WHAT'S A GOOD BOSS? Those bosses wanting to turn over a new leaf might want to consider the results of a recent survey about the attributes of a good boss, says the newsletter of the Baltimore County Public Library. The survey was conducted by Padgett-Thompson, a management training firm in Overland Park, Kansas.

More than 1,000 respondents were asked to name the three qualities of a boss that would add the most to individual on-the-job satisfaction. The more frequently mentioned responses:

Provides freedom to work without interference and lets employees make independent decisions; 27 percent.

Is fair, consistent and honest with employees; 22 percent.

Optimistic, friendly and personable; 19 percent.

Respects employee opinions; 17 percent.

Gives recognition for work well done; 15 percent.

Teaches and helps employees; 13 percent.

(That is indeed a fine list of the qualities that every employee wants his or her boss to have. But I was interested to note that it makes no mention of two of the things that all employees want as much or more than anything else. They are: (1) To be told how they are getting along; and (2) to be told in advance about changes that will affect them.

Supervisors fall down in this area more than anywhere else

and thereby make a great many problems for themselves. An employee who isn't ever told by his or her supervisor how s/he is doing, is apt to become an unhappy and insecure worker. Even an animal needs to be patted and made to understand that he is an appreciated member of the family and that the latter are happy to have him. Every member of the library staff should be told at least every six months that the boss is well satisfied with her work and delighted to have her on the staff—whether it's a branch, department, or the entire library.

And as for letting people know in advance about changes that will affect them, I could write a whole column about the unhappiness and general trouble that I have seen caused by bosses who made changes in their organization without bothering to tell the staff what was going on and why . . . and telling them in advance, before they got excited, fearful and resentful). (2/1986)

.   .   .   .   .

TRAITS POSSESSED BY 'SUPERLEADERS': Professor Warren Bennis at the U. of So. California's School of Bus. Administration set out four years ago to determine what makes a "superleader." He interviewed 90 of them, including chief executives of some of the nation's biggest corporations, university presidents, public officials, newspaper publishers, and winning coaches, and identified five traits his superleaders had in common.

• Vision: the capacity to create a compelling picture of the desired state of affairs that inspires people to perform.

• Communication: the ability to portray the vision clearly and in a way that enlists the support of their constituencies.

• Persistence: the ability to stay on course regardless of the obstacles encountered.

• Empowerment: the ability to create a structure that harnesses the energies of others to achieve the desired result.

• Organizational ability: the capacity to monitor the activities of the group, learn from the mistakes and use the resulting knowledge to improve the performance of the organization. (10/1986)

■   ■   ·   ■   ■

AN EXAMPLE OF THE KIND of item that we looked for in the management journals but never found there, is the following contribution by Edward C. Schleh that appeared in the February 1966 issue of *Dun's Review and Modern Industry*. It is headed, "8 Basic Elements of Supervision":

1. The first responsibility of any supervisor is to set goals for his people—in terms of results, not just actions. This is very rarely done consistently.

2. A supervisor should be responsible for training his people.

3. He should check, or follow-up—to make sure things are going right.

4. A supervisor must discipline.

5. A fifth duty is one that supervisors often neglect, especially at the lower levels: that is, to stimulate subordinates. All of us "drag" from time to time and need encouragement to regain our enthusiasm.

6. Another responsibility is the installation of new methods—no matter where he gets the idea. A common error is to give the supervisor more credit if he thinks up the idea, but this is a basic mistake—much more serious than most people realize. There are thousands of good ideas available. The trick is to latch on to them and get them installed. Recogni-

tion of this requirement usually leads to more innovation all the way down the line.

7. Like it or not, a company must rely on a supervisor to develop his subordinates for future promotion. This is a basic responsibility of every supervisory job.

8. Finally, it is the responsibility of any supervisor to call his people to account. Obviously, employees must be straightened out if necessary. But the most valuable aspect of this responsibility is emphasizing the positive; in other words, complimenting someone for an accomplishment.

(That's our kind of management item . . . completely understandable and significant, and as helpful and true in 1986 as in 1966. We are always looking for such material and will run anything like it that we find. Ed.)

■　　　■　　　■　　　■　　　■

GOOD ADVICE FOR NEW SUPERVISORS: The 6/25/85 Staff Newsletter of the Prince George's County Memorial Library System (Md.) carries some ideas from Anthony M. Micolo, Group Health, Inc., N.Y., that should be helpful to anyone moving from the rank and file to a supervisory position. Here are some ways to ease the move into management while building up respect for one's self in one's new position as supervisor:

RELATING TO SUBORDINATES: Always be receptive to your subordinates. Be quick to listen to your workers' problems, comments, feelings, and criticisms—weigh them accordingly. They may see situations in a different light than you in your supervisory role. If you ignore feedback from your subordinates you will find that it will dwindle and eventually disappear.

SET A GOOD EXAMPLE: Get to work on time, preferably a half hour early. It will help get a head start on the day. Do not take long lunches. If you do, why shouldn't your subordinates? Avoid gossip and rumors; they are unprofessional. Give credit where credit is due—your workers expect it, deserve it, and will appreciate it. Criticize only for just causes and only in a one-on-one setting. Criticize with the intent to educate and foster change, not to demean. In short, be the kind of worker that you expect your subordinates to be, practice what you preach. Only then can you recommend changes or improvements in their behavior, attitudes, and work performance.

GOOD MANAGEMENT SKILLS: Make yourself available to other supervisors. The more you help your peers fulfill their needs, the more valuable you make yourself. Remember that you may need a favor or some help from them at some time.

STRIVE TO KEEP THE PROMISES THAT YOU MAKE: If you promise a project's completion by a certain date, make sure it is done by then. The most important promises to keep are those that are meaningful to others: timely reports, fair performance appraisals, and the like.

KEEP TRACK OF WHAT YOU WANT TO ACCOMPLISH: Maintain a weekly diary: meetings to attend, people to contact, and projects that must be started or followed up. Always know where you are in terms of your responsibilities and accountabilities.

INSPIRE CONFIDENCE IN YOUR ABILITIES: Do your job as comprehensively as possible. Every extra hour after work, each lunch hour, and all the Saturdays you devote to your job help gain the reputation of being a hard worker. Few supervisors who do not put in extra time, effort, and energy ever advance beyond their present position. Do not build a career plateau for yourself by being a nine-to-five worker.

NEVER COMMUNICATE WITHOUT ACCURATE BACKUP DATA: When you are a part of a committee, or must submit a report, be sure to have valid backup material. Your contribution will count more if you can prove that what you say is true. Facts are rarely disputed; opinions and feelings are easily discounted or overruled.

WHEN YOU ARE WRONG, DO NOT TRY TO PASS THE BUCK: Nothing irks a boss more than pointing out an error you made and getting a feeble excuse in return. Accept responsibility for your actions and learn from your mistakes. Few new supervisors readily admit they goofed. By admitting errors you might make yourself vulnerable, but you will definitely gain respect from those people who count.

ACCEPT RESPONSIBILITY FOR YOUR SUBORDI-NATES: There will be times when your subordinates make mistakes which reflect negatively on you. Ducking responsibility and claiming that it is not your fault is not good enough. Go to your superior and accept responsibility for the mistake, even if you did not do it. Remember that as a supervisor you are accountable not only for your actions but also for the actions of your subordinates. By the same token, if one of your workers is falsely accused of an error, be sure to come to that worker's defense. You expect your subordinates to work for you; be aware that they also expect your loyalty and support.

.   .   .   .   .

ON STAFF READING: Elsie Heitkemper, director of the public library in Two Rivers, Wis., writes us regarding our June editorial item about restricting staff borrowing of the most sought after new books:

"You wonder how a person can read a dozen books a week. Does seem impossible doesn't it. Perhaps she speed reads.

"Our staff, 7 full-time and 7 part-time take their turn with reserved books, first, middle, last, whatever. They must observe the dates if book is reserved and then there are no renewals.

"Staff members denied reading new books for 6 months is hazardous to our profession! Ever hear of Reader's Advisory? And on our staff, EVERYONE is a reader's advisor!

"P.S. In larger libraries one could limit the number of best sellers, new books, etc. staff members may have at one time."

I'm not going to criticize any of the practices of this Wisconsin library. Too many librarians feel and operate the same way. But I can't resist making a few comments to explain why I, for one, always felt obliged to pursue a different policy, as related in that June editorial column.

According to Ms. Heitkemper's letter, 14 of her library employees "take their turn with reserved books." That must really cut down on the chances of a library patron finding a popular new book on the shelves. This is tremendously important. Most people enter a library hoping to find one of these most-sought-after titles on the library's new-book shelves. They are disappointed every time they fail to find a really interesting new book, and it doesn't take many such disappointments before these people become soured on their public library. The most common complaint or criticism that the public makes against libraries is that, "I can never find anything that appeals to me on the shelves."

Generally, the complainers will go on and say that they see the same old books every time. "Why doesn't the library get more copies of the books everyone wants to read," they will often remark.

If a library is going to be judged so greatly on its ability to provide the titles that the public comes looking for, and the library's supply of such new books is so very limited at best, how can library administrators permit their employees to take "best-sellers" out of circulation for a week or so at a time?

The suggestion is made above that in larger libraries one could limit the number of best sellers that staff members may have at one time. To my way of thinking, one best seller taken home by an employee—who has such an unfair advantage over the public in getting her hands on the book in the first place—is one too many. The thought of more than one in that library employee's home—benefiting no one all day while their borrower is at work—is rather appalling. If I was a councilman in that city I would certainly ask the library director whom the library is trying to serve: the public or the library staff.

Many librarians have always felt that it was essential that they have a chance to read all the best sellers while they are still new. When I have asked them why, they have replied that otherwise how could they talk to the public about these books.

In the first place, most librarians are seldom asked for reports on popular new books. The people who seek such titles already have read or heard of them. they want them and can recognize them, and need to know nothing more about them. If one should ask about a particular title, the request would normally be made at the circulation desk, to a non-professional who may or may not know the book. I might add here that I have never found any difference between the professional and clerical staffs in their desire to read the appealing new books. If anyone were to tell me that the desk attendants in his or her library don't read as much as the librarians I would say that someone is doing a poor job of staff selection in that library. (12/1984)

■   ■   ■   ■   ■

READING THE NEW BOOKS: Skimming through one of the many library newsletters that we are always happy to see, my attention was caught by the following paragraph in a brief profile of the head librarian of a new branch library. It stated:

"Besides her work, her passions include sailing, cooking and reading. She estimates that she devours 12 books a week on the average and for that reason alone she is happy to be a librarian. Admittedly, she enjoys going over book reviews, 'so I can find my reading for the next month.' "

Sounds like an excellent librarian. My first reaction was

envy. I wish I could read that fast! Then if I could learn to write faster so I would have some time left for reading, I might be able to average a book or two a week.

But as I read the above paragraph I had the brief thought, "When does she take these books home—before they are processed, or while waiting to go to the shelves, or after they are placed on the shelves of "New Books"? And are all the other 21 members of her staff free to do the same thing? Just my native curiosity again.

For years we had an unwritten rule in our libraries that no staff member should take out a new book during its first six months in the library. We would explain to new staff members that it just didn't seem fair to the public for us to grab the new books for our own pleasure since we had so much greater access to them. It was no problem for a staff member to put aside a popular new novel as it was returned by a previous borrower. But what chance did that leave for all the people who came from a distance, perhaps once a week or less often, hoping to find that title or one like it on the shelves?

At any one time there may be some fifty new books that are particularly sought after. The average patron would be surprised and delighted to find one of these titles on the new-book shelves at the particular moment he or she landed in the library. If it was a best-seller that they hadn't read and wanted to read, they would probably go home and tell their family and friends about their good fortune. We have all been in many public libraries where we couldn't find a single book in this special best-seller category. And we have heard many patrons complain that they can never find a best-seller on the shelves.

When you figure the mathematical odds, it isn't too surprising. Just multiply the number of best-selling titles by the number of copies you have of each one and divide by the average loan period. The result might indicate that the average library can expect to have only one such volume returned to it each hour that the building is open. And when you consider that these plums are plucked off the shelves fairly quickly, and estimate the number of patrons that visit these special shelves in an average hour, it is certainly not surprising that a good percentage of one's patrons are disappointed by what they find, or don't find, on the shelves.

Becoming aware of this situation many years ago, and seeing staff members putting aside the choicest new titles for their own enjoyment, I decided my first year out of library school that some kind of restraining order might be a good thing. I'm sure that this unwritten law has been violated many times, but I believe that it did increase the public's chances of finding something they wanted on their brief visits to the library. I took home many new books myself but I would generally borrow them from the catalog department for reading over the weekend, where it could make no difference to the public. I'm not criticizing the librarian who reads 12 books a week—which is certainly admirable—but I would be interested in knowing whether any of you have any "unwritten rules" of your own covering this situation, or whether you feel that it is not necessary to have any. (6/1984)

    ■   ■   ■   ■   ■

CHAPTER V

Relationships with Library Board and Community

THE ETHICS OF LIBRARY TRUSTEESHIP: "It required some effort to restrain myself from writing to you when I read your November issue with its letter from 'Troubled in Texas,' " writes a library director, "but now I think an explanation might be in order. I will be very surprised if the author is not our locally-famous 'Disgruntled Trustee,' or a member of our staff who is greatly influenced by her. This is a Trustee who has done nearly everything she could in recent years to undermine the work of the library administration and the Board of Directors. She has had some noticeable success working through a handful of our employees.

"For years this Trustee has been demanding the Head Librarian be fired (at the annual meetings of the Trustees) because of an imagined slight which occurred in 1971! When, in the January, 1983 meeting, she was again rebuffed by her 19 fellow Trustees, she declared the Library would be unionized by the time the Trustees would meet in January, 1984.

"Enclosed is a copy of an article from last Saturday's local newspaper, explaining that, after a year of turmoil in the Library, the N.L.R.B. has declined to exercise jurisdiction over this library in the latest of a series of attempts made this past year to unionize our staff. We hope this will put an end to the episode, but I suspect it's only an intermission. Meanwhile the Library has been forced to spend a great deal of money in legal fees at a time the Board was sincerely trying to find resources to improve the employees' salaries and fringe benefits. Incidentally, the Library has not used *any* public tax funds in defending itself in this case.

"My reason for bringing this to your attention is that, in searching the library literature, I find little that could be considered definitive in any way in regard to the *ethics* of library trusteeship. The museum field is somewhat better provided for, but not in a way that could be considered directly applicable to the problem of a Trustee who will not accept the decision of the majority of her (or his) colleagues and causes chaos in the institution by trying to force it to take a different direction than the one dictated by the majority of those responsible for it.

"Throughout all this experience I have often been reminded of the situation Arless Nixon faced at Fort Worth when, about 1960, he and his Board passed a bond issue for the construction of library branches over the strong and vocal opposition of one member of the library's Board of Directors, who publicly swore he would see Arless Nixon run out of Fort Worth if the bond issue passed. The bond issue passed, but the crusading Trustee was later elected mayor and appointed a library board which finally gave him his pound of flesh.

"It seems to me there must be some way that we can encourage those Trustees who want to give more than is required in service to our institutions in a helpful and constructive way, without at the same time opening the door to those who will misuse their position to satisfy their own personal goals or carry out vendettas, as sometimes happens. It may be that the time has come when the profession must, for its own preservation, work on the problem of Trustee ethics—if only to make sure we are all playing the game according to the same rules."

Situations like that are not uncommon in libraries, as in museums, school management and other areas of public service. It's of course equally true of the private sector. One wonders why the disaffected member of the board doesn't resign, when he or she is so unhappy in the library relationship. Particularly so when he or she is so completely outnumbered by the rest of the board members.

It happened to me once and I wondered both why the person didn't leave of his own free will and also why the other 8 members of the board didn't make a joint request to the mayor to remove the recalcitrant one and give them someone they could work with. Library board meetings had been pleasurable events for years until this young man joined the group. They never were the same again. And it was all my fault, as I had got him appointed to the Board. A newcomer in the city, he had attended library programs and shown a real interest in the library. I thought he would be a good library trustee and so recommended him to the Mayor. Shortly thereafter, he started calling my secretary to find out when I came to work.

I don't think it would do any good for the profession to work on the matter of Trustee ethics, as our letter writer suggests. I don't think it would prevent the appointment of the kind of unusual Trustees such as she or Arless Nixon or I had to contend with, nor would it provide a solution to such problems. The troubled individuals would continue to serve, and the negative effects on the Head Librarian, the other Board members and the staff would continue to be felt. Having such a person on the Board is certainly no way to build public support, board member interest or staff morale. But does anyone have an answer to this problem? (11/1984)

■   ■   ■   ■   ■

"HERE'S SOME MORE ON LIBRARY DIREC-
TORS," writes Marv Scilken, enclosing a Feb. 18th item
from a New Jersey newspaper that is headed "Library President Sues Directors." Since it reports a unique situation I will
excerpt some of it for you:

"Three Verona library directors, each of whom has re-
signed during the last four years, have been hit with lawsuits
for a joint statement that blames the actions of the library
board president for the frequent turnover in the administrative post.

"Complaints were hand-delivered to Mitchell Martin, Judy
Matz and Paul Miller for what the suit claims to be the 'false
and malicious' statements publicly presented to the Library
Board about Board President Carol Stafford . . .

"The statement charges Mrs. Stafford with undermining
their authority as administrators by contradictory orders, demands and instructions to the library staff. The statement also
charged that library funds had been used improperly.

"It alleges library monies were used to purchase gifts for
board members on occasions such as illness, and the withdrawal of library cash to pay for babysitting expenses incurred
during a library-related meeting . . .

"The directors noted in the statement, 'Few situations are
more destructive of a director's effectiveness than that
wherein individual library trustees are allowed to infringe
upon his authority by regularly issuing contradictory orders,
demands and instructions to the staff. Yet, for several years it
has been the practice of the board president, Mrs. Stafford, to
frequently confront various staff members directly with demands for services, projects, tasks thus circumventing the position of the director and undermining his authority. Such
two-boss situations, with their inherent ambiguity concerning
command, harm staff morale and lessen the ability of the executive officer to direct activities.

"The directors also stated that attempts by them to build up
the library book collection have been repeatedly blocked by
demands for more library programs."

Mrs. Stafford has requested a trial by jury. Her attorney

states that she "has suffered, is suffering, and will continue to suffer from severe physical, mental and emotional distress, in addition to the injury she has sustained to her reputation."

Anyone reading this newspaper article is likely to feel that Mrs. Stafford brought most of this trouble on herself by filing this lawsuit and giving all this publicity to the matter. The distress she has suffered so far is nothing to what she will experience before the case is finally resolved. She would do better to give some thought to the distress she has caused the three library directors. They have been hurt far more than she, since they have had their whole careers upset; her career, if she has one, has not been affected.

My only reason for running an item like this is to indicate again that everything is not peaches and cream in the area of public library administration . . . that one can get into troublesome situations through no fault of his/her own . . . and thus one should always be as kind and understanding as possible and not feel superior or pass judgment on a colleague who is going through a bad time. Far nicer to send him/her a note indicating that he has your understanding and support and continued high regard. You can be sure that he or she is really suffering—from shock, from loss of self-esteem, from fear about the future (both financially and career-wise), and from concern about what his fellow professionals are saying and thinking about him. And when the latter keep their distance and let the person suffer all alone—perhaps for the same reason that most people stop communicating with those who are suddenly reported to have a fatal illness—he or she is convinced that nobody cares. (2/1983)

■   ■   ■   ■   ■

"FACULTY-LIBRARIAN RELATIONS in the Academic Library" is the title of an article by Robert C. Brown in the Rhode Island Library Association Bulletin. Let me just quote two paragraphs from it:

> Competition is one cause of tension between faculty and library staff, according to Robert T. Blackburn. Since faculty have a strong desire to own books, they resent the librarian who actually possesses and controls the books which they consider to be rightfully theirs. ". . . the librarian gets to order thousands of them (i.e. books) every year, gets to unwrap them when they come, and is the first to have journals and magazines in hand . . . Faculty cannot even find time to read all that they want to, and obviously the librarian, sitting quietly and undisturbed in her office, just reads, and reads and reads." The librarian, on the other hand, harbors a secret jealousy against the professor because he determines what his students read; the librarian feels that she knows better than the professor what the best books are and what students really should read.
>
> Librarians, among whom order and neatness are prized traits, Blackburn goes on, take exception to the more anarchic ways of academics, while faculties find distasteful the librarian's avidity for status. Faculty members hold the more powerful positions in the academic hierarchy, while librarians are in a position of servitude and have to accept more or less whatever the faculty "dishes out." Describing one aspect of this situation, Blackburn states that "Professors complain about librarians to the Dean more easily than librarians can retaliate. Ordinarily, librarians cannot use the power of the Dean even to recover a book the faculty member will not return." (2/1983)

.   .   .   .   .

NATIONAL COVERAGE: The Pawtucket Public Library (R.I.) may have received some by the time you read this. Their local P.M. Magazine asked them to put on their 2nd Annual Amateur Dog Show on August 16, to kick off their fall season with a full half hour show on nothing but the

PPL's crazy dog show. The production crew will go to people's homes the night before the dog show and cover the people getting the dogs ready for the show, etc. The producer told the Library's Lee Eaton that his crew is going to work on this as a show they can "sell" to the national P.M.—so it could be that we will all have a chance to see this fine event.

I hope Mrs. Eaton had a chance to rest a bit in San Francisco. The day she got back from the conference she had to make arrangements for a party for the mayor, a farewell party for which she had to solicit free food and wine from most of the caterers, restaurants and liquor stores in the area. The party was for the next Sunday evening, and from 600 to 1,000 people were expected to attend.

This is of course extra work for the Library's community services director, and quite apart from anything learned in library school, but it is a real compliment to Lee Eaton, showing that the people at City Hall recognize her considerable talents for planning and staging all kinds of parties and programs, and a fine opportunity for the Library to make some extra points with the City Fathers. It is easy to understand why the PPL has increased its budget so considerably in the past few years. Many public library directors seem to feel that the farther removed they stay from the folks at City Hall the happier they'll be. That may be so—and I have been guilty of that approach myself—but one often pays a price for not mixing more with the local politicians. I always gave top priority to responding to any request from the mayor, city manager, or a Councilman. If they wanted to see any kind of report on the library, or obtain information regarding some matter of city concern, they always had it on their desk the next morning. If one of their wives mentioned that her grandson was deeply interested in some particular subject, she was certain to immediately receive some new books that would be of interest to him. I was never particularly close to any of these local officials, but, on the other hand, I never had a problem with any of them or heard any personal criticism from them. Many of them at one time or another expressed appreciation for the fact that I never caused them any problems. I never criticized them or caused them any public embarrassment, I never complained about their treatment of the library at budget time or any time thereafter, and I never dumped any library problems on them.

Fortunately, the library always enjoyed excellent public relations so City Hall never had to get involved in anything in that area. I can recall only two real problems that we had in this 30-year period, and neither of them went beyond the library board. There was a great deal of change and new development, not always without some upset, but the four city library boards and I always felt that it was our duty and responsibility to handle everything involving the library ourselves without burdening City Hall with any of it. The mayors and city managers seemed to be continually involved with troublesome situations arising in the other city departments but I can't recall a single instance where one of them was called on to help straighten out a library matter. It was never necessary to do so, but more than that I always felt that these officials had more than enough on their hands and I was ever careful to see that I and the library didn't add to their problems. I never went near City Hall except when I had to—for budget sessions, meetings of the department heads, and the like. Unlike some of the other city department heads, I stayed away from all meetings of the City Council except for the relatively few occasions when some library matter was scheduled for discussion. Perhaps I was wrong to stay aloof to this extent from the non-library business of city government, but I never could see how anyone was the loser from this behavior of mine. And perhaps I made up for it by being active in many community organizations.

I expect most library directors have experienced pretty much the same thing, though many of them seemed to have maintained a much closer contact with their mayor or city manager. I have known several who called on their city manager at least once every week. (10/1981)

■   ■   ■   ■   ■

COMMUNITY INVOLVEMENT: Art Goetz, the Administrator of the Wicomico County Free Library (Salisbury, Md.) has sent us a memorandum he distributed to all his Board members as a position paper on his community involvement, which he deems of importance in furthering the goals of the library. "I thought you might be interested in my position on this topic and I'd be interested to hear what you have to say about it," he writes.

The position paper, "Role of Library Administrators in Community Service," starts off:

"One of the important functions of an administrator is to be active in both the political environment and the voluntary leadership in the community. He/she must be visible, and visibly effective, to all who are leaders in the community volunteer structure and to those who are politically influential in the community. How better to accomplish this function than to demonstrate one's ability and willingness to work hard for community improvement than by accepting a leadership role in the United Way Campaign or to organize and run a leadership awards banquet for the Greater Salisbury Committee? While proving himself/herself capable, the administrators are also creating indebtedness to the library that can be called upon as needed in the future. When we must call on influential community leaders for help for the library, people that an administrator has worked with and helped will be willing to help the library freely.

"Some of the benefits accrued to the library in this way are subtle but long term in nature . . . Membership, whether passive or active, in community oriented organizations enable him/her to educate community leaders about the ability of the library to produce hard relevant data that helps enrich the economic base of the community . . .

"It takes time to do these community activities and even though a good bit is accomplished during evening and weekend hours, some daytime hours are necessary . . . It is necessary though to realize that community involvement is one of the unwritten tasks of a public service manager in a political environment. The politically isolated manager is an ineffective manager without needed contacts or trust.

"However, all community involvement is not always useful for library relations. A request for a library administrator to become involved in community service ought always to meet three equal criteria:

1. Is the task of substantive benefit to the community?

2. Will it build a productive relationship between the library and the organization?

3. Will service in the organization reflect favorably upon the library?

"Finally, let it stand as a rule that a library administrator who does not demonstrate that he/she cares about the community will find himself/herself in a community that doesn't care about that administrator or that library!"

ART HAS SAID IT ALL so well, that there is little that one can add to his position paper on community involvement. I expect most library administrators are in hearty agreement with him. Not only because they are similarly involved in the volunteer work of their community and realize the importance of their being so engaged, but because of the pleasure and satisfaction that such service provides them. The average library director would see relatively few people during a given week if it weren't for the various meetings that he is called upon to attend and the other outside activities that he/she gets involved in. I dislike staying in any meeting for more than half an hour, but I have always enjoyed going here and there in the community and encountering so many active people that I know, and am known to. It gives one such a nice feeling of being a real part of the community. And because the library director is ordinarily better known than most citizens, and represents an institution that is generally well thought of, he/she has a real advantage over the majority of newcomers trying to make a place for themselves in the community.

I recall that in my first few months on the job, in my first library directorship, I was invited to participate in two very active fund-raising campaigns. One was for the YMCA, and I believe the other was for either the Red Cross or the Community Chest. Such participation was a completely new experience for me and I truly enjoyed it. I met many people in a hurry and immediately felt a warm sense of belonging to this new city. I believe the experience was good for both me and the library, but I don't think I would have had these opportunities if I had been just another new salesman in town rather than the new head librarian.

The position makes us all stand out, so we have far more than our share of opportunities to assume leadership roles in the community. When a civic organization needs a new head, who would be a more logical person to try to enlist than the library administrator. He/she is fairly well known, and ought to be fairly intelligent, and certainly can't be too busy in his job to undertake this outside assignment. So if you are inclined to accept such invitations, you will have plenty of opportunities. I can count a dozen organizations that I was elected or appointed to head during my years as a library administrator, and most of you will be able to do the same thing when you come to retire. I was never made president because I was especially popular, but rather because I was well known as the head of the public library and because people knew I would work hard at any assignment I accepted. I might add that in the six years that I was in the business field—and out of library administration—I didn't have a single invitation or other opportunity to participate in volunteer community work.

In short, community involvement is a wonderful opportunity that is made available to library administrators far more than to most people, and it should generally be accepted with zest and appreciation. Provided, of course, that the opportunities for community service meet the three criteria listed above by Mr. Goetz. The administrator and his/her organization are so closely associated in the minds of the people who know them that any contribution of time and effort to a good cause by the administrator is bound to rebound to the benefit of the organization. If you work hard in some public campaign or play an important part in some community effort, the public is going to have a warmer feeling about your library and the city fathers will be more inclined to treat it favorably at budget time. If you live outside the city and try to avoid involvement in community affairs outside the library you may someday feel it was a mistake to pass up the opportunities that were there to play a more active part in the life of the community. Looking back on the various organizations that invited my involvement, I must say that life there would have been much less interesting without them. (1/1983)

■   ■   ■   ■   ■

CHAPTER VI

The Director's Insecurity

"LIBRARY CREWS TELL DISCONTENT" is the headline of a long article in today's newspaper reporting the unhappiness of some staff members at one of the two largest public libraries in a bay area county. Among the series of complaints is that cuts are being made from the bottom, not the top . . . that degree-holding employees are doing less work and shifting the burden onto part-time or CETA people . . . and that the head librarian is not open to staff suggestions and is determined to get a new $50,000 computer at the expense of jobs.

One library employee said, "The library is top heavy with administration and professional librarians." Others agreed that library service hours could be increased if some of the "deadwood at the top" was pruned.

Others complain that the Children's Room is staffed with "two top-level professional people, not those at lower levels who could do the job equally well," or that money is wasted in providing reference service at branches where they may only get a dozen questions a day and the hard ones are referred to the main library.

AT THE OTHER LARGE LIBRARY in that county, a number of staff members signed a letter to their director's employers, recommending his dismissal. I can't think of a more unkind, disloyal, unprofessional act. It infuriates me to think about it, and to consider the pain and mental anguish thus imposed on the poor man and his whole family. I'm sorry that I couldn't do more than write and let him know that his fellow administrators understood what he was up against, knew that he had to make many decisions that were bound to be unpopular with his staff, and wouldn't change their good opinion of him because of any such staff reaction.

Both of the library directors mentioned above are fine librarians and likable human beings. But one can have all the finest qualities in the world, and be loved by all his or her staff, but that means nothing when the time comes that the director must make a decision adversely affecting one or more staff members. This is something that librarians all over the state of California are sure to find out, it they haven't already done so. I know one librarian who dreads having to tell one of his senior department heads that she will not only have to discontinue her habit of many years of taking Monday off but will also have to put in hours at the loan desk and work one evening a week. He knows it will be the end of their close friendship.

Dr. Robert Hutchins, the former president of the University of Chicago, once wrote that every manager has a choice to make. He is either going to be an administrator or an office-holder. If he's the former, he will make many necessary decisions. And every decision will be sure to displease as many people as it will please. There is just no way an administrator can please everybody, or be popular. An office-holder, on the other hand, can go on for years, being loved by everyone. You don't step on anyone's toes standing still, nor do you antagonize anyone by making no changes.

BUT THE GREAT MAJORITY of library directors in California are now (1978) having to make more tough decisions in a 3-months period than they've probably had to make in their professional lifetime, and all are more upsetting to the staff members involved and more trouble-and-pain-producing for the directors than anything they've done before. Not only are the directors saddened and depressed by what they are obliged to do to people with whom they have had a close relationship for years, but they are subject to whatever resentment and enmity their decisions to lay off, or reduce the hours of, veteran staff members may arouse. And when their complaints reach the attention of library board members and the city council, the library director may be put in the position of having to defend himself or herself and will be lucky to come through this questioning period with no loss in reputation or employer-confidence.

IT IS ALWAYS TO BE HOPED that members of governing boards will be understanding and supportive and will always judge their directors and superintendents on the basis of the kind of public service they operate and on what they have accomplished on the job, rather than on how they are viewed by their subordinates. But unfortunately, too many of us rate our fellow human beings—our doctors, our ministers, our bankers, our library directors, school superintendents, college presidents, etc.—on their personality and their popularity with their patients, parishioners, or staff. A library director, for instance, who is thought to be loved by all his staff, will generally be rated higher in his community and in his profession and normally preferred for a higher job over a director who has accomplished more in every way but has expressed opinions and taken action that made some of his professional staff uncomfortable.

SO WE MAY WELL SEE A RECORD LOSS in library directors in California this year. Some will be forced out by the loss of the support of their departments heads, which is the most common reason for the firing of the public library director (and 13 percent *are* fired), and others will resign because things have changed and the old job is just no fun any more. A few of these people may simply retire earlier than they had planned.

IN THIS TIME OF BUDGET QUESTIONING and cutting, a library needs the best "image" it can build for itself. It needs to be well thought of not only by its users but by many non-users as well. Perhaps 90 percent of city council people and county supervisors and magistrates are non-library-users. In other words, the fate of the library is each year in the hands of people who rarely go near a library facility and only know about it what they hear from members of the community who do use its services. This may be practically nothing or it may be a good deal, mostly critical. Some of these decision-makers may still feel that all a library does is circulate books, and "certainly that doesn't take a great deal of intelligence or training." Maybe you don't know just how some of your city fathers really feel about your institution. However, it would probably be safe to guess that most of them are unaware of anything new or startling that their library has done in the past few years, and that any distinct and positive thought placed in their minds regarding the library at this time would be bound to help the cause of libraries in that community. (9/1978)

■　　　■　　　■　　　■　　　■

" 'HOW TO FIRE SOMEONE' (AD, November, 1981) has to be the worst piece of advice on this subject ever offered a public sector employer," writes Jay Wozny from Baton Rouge, La. "I suspect it is equally dangerous for private employers as well. Firing someone at 4:45 p.m. on a Friday without offering the individual in question the least reason is the surest way to a grievance proceeding or civil suit. Most organizations have written procedures covering discipline and termination of employees, including previous notification and warning regarding the nature of the problem involved. Surely, such precautionary measures are legitimate and beneficial, providing the employee with both a basis for improvement and notice that disciplinary action may be imminent.

"The AD item was culled from *Nation's Business* with the original piece being a chapter in Wareham's *Secrets of a Corporate Headhunter* (Atheneum, 1980) where the 'Firing' chapter implies previous warning and discussion. Not so in the abbreviated version. Perhaps a bit of editorial comment was called for."

Well, I must agree with Mr. Wozny that you couldn't fire anyone in the public sector without giving good reasons and ample warning in advance . . . and maybe not even then. Perhaps I *shouldn't* have run this article. On the other hand, it does have *some* good advice in it, it stimulates some thinking and it makes interesting reading. And the "Friday 4:45 p.m. shuffle," as Wareham calls it, does happen in the private sector. I saw many instances of it when I was a personnel officer in a large manufacturing company. I don't believe I could operate in the manner suggested by Mr. Wareham, but I'm not obliged to agree with every idea and policy and activity reported on in these columns.

I HAPPENED TO READ the Wareham book before receiving Mr. Wozny's letter and don't recall much said about "previous warning and discussion." At least, not as an essential element of the termination process . . . I did, however, make note of two short paragraphs from his "Firing" chapter that weren't included in our November article. It might be interesting to present them here:

"The essence of the 'Friday p.m. Shuffle' is summarized in four words reportedly uttered by Henry Ford II when he was stopped late at night driving with a lady apparently not his wife and advised that he was violating the speed limit, and also that he seemed to have imbibed a little freely. Did he have anything to say? he was later asked in his prison cell by reporters. Ford's answer was to the point, and memorable: 'Never complain—never explain.' "

I'm sure these four words—and many will recall reading them in the newspapers at the time of the event in Southern California—made a strong impression on many people. It's one of those statements that the more one thinks about it the wiser it sounds. Most administrators learn early that it never helps to complain when something goes wrong personally or institutionally. Most are slower, however, to learn that it generally doesn't help to explain, either. Explanations, like complaints, aren't normally welcomed and they only serve to keep one in the spotlight when it would be better to be out of it. This is particularly true in the case of administrators who are asked to resign their posts. The ones who leave as quickly and quietly and amicably as possible have the easiest time getting relocated. Those who refuse to resign and "complain and explain" in the public press only bring out more negative comments about themselves from their employers and arouse the animosity of individual library board members so that they are far less likely to say something positive about the person when asked for their opinion. And the more that is said about the termination, and the longer the thing goes on, the more people over the state, and throughout the country, know about it—which makes it that much harder for the person terminated to secure another job on the same level. Whenever interviewed for a job, he or she will have to spend most of the time explaining what happened in the last position, which is a negative and self-defeating posture, instead of being able to focus on what he or she is prepared to bring to the new post.

In short, if there is ever any complaining or explaining that needs to be done, do it while you are still in control of the situation and can employ it constructively. Once you are stopped by the police (in Mr. Ford's case) or the library board (in the case of many fired librarians), it's too late for complaints and explanations. They can do no good, and they can do much harm. Henry Ford II doubtless learned the hard way that one should, "Never complain—never explain." And the person who wrote the recent popular biography of Mr. Ford was so impressed by these words that he made them the title of his book.

THE OPENING PARAGRAPH of Mr. Wareham's "firing chapter" is equally quotable. He writes:

"I remember asking the president of an advertising agency on the day he went broke, after seven years in business, whether he had any regrets. 'Yes,' he said, 'Two. I should have followed up on more of my client prospects. And I just wish I'd been quicker to fire some people. I was always too slow. I procrastinated, hoped, prayed they'd improve but nobody ever did.' "

Wareham goes on to say, "I have never yet met an executive who didn't procrastinate over a firing. The reason for the delay is threefold. It's an unpleasant task, it involves an admission of your own earlier poor judgment, and you tend to worry about how it will affect other employees . . ."

I daresay many of you reading this have been guilty of the

same procrastination. You are probably wishing, just as the advertising agency president did, that you had gotten rid of one or two people who were a real problem to you and the library, serving to block much of the progress that might otherwise have been made.

I could belong in that group. I once harbored a strong regret that I didn't fire two department heads when I had the chance. These two people had been running the library for a great many years before I came along, successfully blocking even the thought of any change. When I started doing the things that were long needed, it was hard for them to accept it. They fought every change, both before, during and after it was made, even though they knew the library board unanimously approved each one and they heard every day that the users of the library couldn't have been happier with the "improvements." They continually stirred up the other department heads and badmouthed the library director with the public. When after eight or ten months of this, two board members suggested that I fire these people, I replied that this wasn't necessary, that I had a thick skin and it didn't bother me what they said about me since the public could easily see what I was doing in the library and everyone well knew that they were delighted with what they were seeing and experiencing. I stated that as long as the behavior of these women didn't hinder or slow our progress—which it never did—and as long as I had the support of the board members, I could put up with the troublemakers. I explained that they performed their work well enough and reminded the board that the library was their life and they would be lost without it. I was exhilarated over what the library had accomplished in such a short time and disinclined to do harm to these people.

MY TALKING TO THEM never accomplished anything. They were on a crusade—to rid the library of the new director's ideas and person—and who listens to reason at such a time? They just kept talking to anyone who would listen. The board continued to approve and be pleased with the further progress of the library and I never had any inkling that the crusaders were really getting anywhere. So when I got home from a library convention to be met by a request for my resignation, I couldn't have been more surprised. Those department heads just never stopped working at their crusade until they finally wore the board down. The members just got tired of hearing their complaints and wanted harmony at the library above everything else.

Sometimes—perhaps most times—you can't have both harmony and major change at the same time. The library board had agreed 18 months earlier that a choice had to be made, that there was no possible way of accomplishing any one of the many needed improvements without arousing heated resistance from the department heads who had never been obliged to accept a new idea in thirty years. They had encouraged me to go ahead and stick my neck out and do all the things that we all saw as essential to the modernization of the library, in accordance with the desires and needs of a very active and vocal reading public. Then, after all the tough decisions have been made and the "dirty jobs" done, the board complains about the lack of harmony at the department head level and wants a change.

I RELATE THIS STORY TO YOU, as I would to a class in library administration, simply because I believe it is both interesting and instructive. There are enough lessons to be learned in this case to provide the basis for half a dozen good library school sessions. There was a time when I didn't want to ever think about what happened there, but that is long past. This is perhaps the first time I have reviewed the situation in over fifteen years, but that's not because of any emotional hangups. I believe now that I should have given both department heads a short period to shape up and then fired them when they failed to do so. However, the matter is too long dead now for me to have any regrets about it. Actually, I'm rather glad that I didn't fire these people even though I would recommend to anyone else in a similar situation that they waste no time in firing the offenders. In the first place, there's no pleasure in kicking someone off the team when yours is the only game in town. But more than that, if I had done so, I might still be there. And I'm sure that I have been happier in the years since then than I could ever have been in that city which has never been known for its contented library directors.

PERHAPS THAT IS THE SECOND THING to be learned from this episode: Do not be too afraid of losing a job or anything else in life, nor too upset should such a misfortune actually happen to you. As the minister remarked to us last Sunday, "When the Lord closes one door for us He generally opens another one for us down the road, and the second one is oftentimes better than the first. Closing doors is just His way of steering us where He wants us to go, in the working out of His plan for our lives." Yesterday's sports-page listed some of the professional football players who had been let go by other teams only to be picked up later by the Oakland Raiders and go on to star in the Superbowl. This sort of thing happens all the time. One loses what he or she considers a wonderful job, or wonderful mate, is completely depressed and defeated, then wakes up a few years later to the realization that the new position, or husband/wife, or whatever, is truly superior to the one that was lost.

The *first* thing to be learned of course is that one *can* be fired or otherwise eased out of his or her job. It can happen to anyone, at any time. The axe is always there, even though most librarians never see or think of it. After all, such a thing was never mentioned in library school, at least not in all the classes I attended.

AS I MENTIONED ONCE BEFORE, it's not hard for an administrator to be completely safe from the axe for any number of years, if that is his or her top priority. Just don't do anything to rock the boat, to arouse opposition on your staff, to attract unfavorable attention. I can't recall a single library director who was ousted for incompetency or for doing nothing. *Officeholders* never get fired in the public sector; only *Administrators*. Only people who make decisions, institute change, and make demands on their staff. These are the big achievers.

Another lesson from this story (actually, they are no more than reminders, for we all know them well) is that most people can't be counted on to stick with you when it seems the easier thing to abandon you. When they say, "We're behind you, we support you all the way," that really means that you can count on them as long as everything is going well. If you can bring about major change and keep everyone whose job is affected happy at the same time, supporting you is a pleasure. But suppose, as is more likely, some of the department heads aren't happy, and are vocal in expressing their displeasure, and the board members have to take some of the flak. This is most embarrassing and unpleasant to them and one can't expect them to put up with it for long.

The board members in this case were good people. Intelligent people. It would be hard to find better people to serve on the library board. I liked them from the first meeting with them. And while it might be said that they brought me in to do all the things that they realized were needed, and then after 22 months when all these new services and facilities were successfully achieved, didn't need me any more . . . that wouldn't be quite fair to these people.

They didn't become a library trustee because they were

looking for work, or for public controversy. It was an honor
to serve on the board, and they doubtless expected everything at the library to be as serene and uneventful as it always
had been. A library administrator can select the wrong kind
of books or the wrong kind of staff members (and we've seen
instances of both these things) or he or she can waste a lot of
money and make poor policy decisions, and nothing is likely
to be said or done about it. The library board may not be
aware of any of these things, and nobody else outside the library is likely to be sufficiently informed and interested to be
concerned about the matter.

AS IN THE CASE OF MOST public institutions,
something has got to happen there before one gives any
thought to it. One has got to see, or hear, or experience something bad before one feels any concern. The sort of mistakes
and failures mentioned in the paragraph above are not going
to be noticed or felt by anyone—at least not to the point of
embarrassing the board or jeopardizing the position of the responsible party. But when a few staff members badmouth the
ideas or performance of the director, that is something else.
Words are easily heard and recognized, and when they are
unexpected and malicious they make quite an impact and are
readily transmitted from one person to another. Library
board members are obliged to answer a lot of questions as to,
"What's going on down at your library?"

The longer this goes on, the unhappier the board members. They may even come to resent the administrator who is
indirectly responsible for this situation, forgetting that they
had been in favor of the changes that had upset these librarians and still felt they were highly desirable moves. They feel
that any indication of disharmony in the institution under
their control is a reflection on them personally and they feel a
responsibility to put an end to it. Perhaps they should feel a

greater responsibility to provide the best possible library service to their community, but then that poses no problem or embarrassment to them and nobody is judging them for what the library is or isn't doing in that area.

WHICH SUGGESTS THE FOURTH point of which we are reminded in this case. And that is the considerable difference between the public and private sectors as to what they most value in their executives. In private enterprise owners and managers want people who can get the job done and who will help the company realize the greatest profit. If they are producers and money-makers, the board of directors isn't going to be overly concerned with their popularity index. If some of their employees are unhappy with them and show it in their behavior or job performance, there is no question as to who should and will leave. The top man doesn't have to worry about his job security as long as he is moving his company forward and making money for the owners. Nor does he have to slow his pace to a walk in order to avoid upsetting some middle management people who may prefer to see things stay as they have been.

All of this is quite obvious, but I can vouch for it from my own experience. Some time ago I took over a private country club in the Bay Area that had failed three times before, at considerable loss of money. I felt I could put it back on its feet as I'd organized some successful swimming and tennis clubs in the South. I was able to do this but it was a long and hard struggle. During these 28 months I hired two managers and two golf pros that I didn't particularly like simply because they could do the job and protect my investment. We always needed more members to provide the dues' income that operated the club. In all personnel decisions regarding these top jobs, the main consideration was always the relative extent to which the person in question could help attract and keep members in the club. That was the bottom line as I couldn't afford to lose the money I had borrowed to get into this business.

Things aren't that simple in the public sector. You don't have the same clear standard for effective and desirable management, and you have to be concerned about the reactions of many thousands of not-too-well-informed outsiders (yet also owners) who can get disturbed over a relatively minor matter that has little to do with the goals and purposes of the institution, and perhaps bring about a major change in management that will impede the attainment of these goals.

ANOTHER REMINDER IS THAT the library administrator doesn't enjoy the same job security as his or her staff. It's so difficult to terminate a public employee that most administrators rarely even consider the possibility of such action. The price is just too high. The bulk of the staff who are under Civil Service have little to worry about, no matter how poor their performance or their attitude and disposition. The employee who is not popular with his or her supervisors and fellow workers is doubtless more secure than the administrator who is unpopular with some of his employees.

One wouldn't even think of terminating a staff member without a number of warnings to this person and a full file of documents specifying the reasons for the action to terminate and supporting each claim that is made. How different it is with the administrator. We have seen that he can be asked to resign without any warning or opportunity to get in step with the new thinking of the board. I say this not in complaint or even to suggest that library trustees should not have the privilege to act in whatever manner seems expedient or desirable to them. However, one can hope that they would be considerate enough to give their chief executive a chance to straighten things out before they dropped the axe. He might accomplish this simply by calling a halt to all unusual activity, announcing that there will be no further change for at least a full year, and let the dissidents know that they will be free to do their own thing. That should allow him ample opportunity to find a more congenial location. And it wouldn't hurt the board to do this. They should realize that when it comes to terminations it's much easier to give than to receive. It may mean no disruption at all in their lives but it may mean the professional's whole career.

A FINAL LESSON TO BE LEARNED from this situation is that the administrator ought to go slower and watch out for himself more, rather than going all out to get things done for the library and for the reading public. In this particular case, it was quickly apparent to the library director and his assistant that the department heads' minds were completely closed to any new ideas or the possibility of change. This became clear in the department-head meetings I instituted—a disturbing new idea in itself. So in my fourth month on the job I brought up the matter at a meeting of the board, suggesting the possibility of postponing all moves in our new "game plan" for a revitalized library until the department heads became more relaxed and comfortable with the new administration and changed their thinking so that they could entertain some new ideas. I admitted, however, that I really didn't believe they would ever change, whether we waited nine months or nine years. Particularly so since my very nice predecessor there had told me that whenever she came downstairs with an idea for something new, their reaction was always, "It's stupid. It's ridiculous. We don't want to even think about it." And that was always the end of it. Apparently, working with someone for many years is no assurance that minds will be opened in the process.

After some discussion, it was the unanimous judgment

of the board that the people in question would *never* change, hence there was nothing to be gained by sitting quiet and waiting for such a miracle to happen. From then on, in the phraseology of Cape Canaveral, all systems were go.

All in all, it was a truly wonderful and satisfying time, despite the final outcome . . and it's nice to be able to talk about such an incident in one's past, without any feeling, as if it had happened in another lifetime or to someone else. My main reason in talking about my own experience in this way is my hope that it will elicit some real response and invite others of you out there to write us about your experiences. (2/1982)

　　　　■　　　■　　　■　　　■　　　■

"IN RESPONSE TO YOUR COLUMN in February," writes a library director, I didn't see the November article Jay Wozny responded to, but you started right off with a number of statements that were so relevant that it was spooky. Such as, "Explanations . . . only serve to keep one in the spotlight when it would be better to be out of it."

"My situation was similar to yours, apparently. Actually, I wasn't asked to resign (although I'm sure no one would ever believe it)—my key board members and I discussed the situation and agreed that there was little that could be done to retrieve an impossible and exceptionally bad political situation, and I told them that I had applied for several positions and would be willing to resign. We hadn't planned to release that information as early as we did, but the Board was told that if I would announce my resignation on the following Monday (this was Friday), the Chairman of the County Commissioners would see that the library got the $56,000 in construction and renovation matching funds that it had been denied for 10 months. I had put my house on the market (quietly) three weeks previously, and had four job interviews lined up at that time. I moved at the end of September and have been thoroughly and completely convinced that I did the only right thing. My lawyer wanted me to sue, and I probably had grounds. I won't go into the details, but it was messy and gossipy and I was tried by the grapevine. Criminal accusations were made, although I was never officially informed, and the Board chairman presented evidence proving those changes false. Of course, that part never made it on the grapevine!

"I did have the complete support of my Board of Trustees; they just were not prepared for the kind of attacks that the library and I personally received, and failed to take a stand when they should have.

"I should have said at the beginning that this all started because the library board and I decided that we wouldn't have enough money to continue seven positions in the new budget because we got $58,000 less than we asked for (in a $400,000 budget). Three of the people who were laid off were determined to get me fired and get their jobs back. Two of those have hired a lawyer and have written the Board that they intend to sue the library for back pay and their jobs, and the board has decided to fight it in court.

"YOUR PARAGRAPH ABOUT THE 'CRUSADERS' I could have written myself. Likewise your comments about getting fired and fear of losing jobs, etc. and about the trustees and their reasons for being trustees. I guess what I'm trying to say, Bob, is that your longsighted comments about your experience, your feelings, the philosophy you developed through that experience, were helpful and meaningful to me. It is reassuring to realize that the philosophy that I have developed about my experience in the short run is almost identical to what you have developed in the long run.

"I cannot say right now, though, that I can talk about my experience with no feelings. For one thing, it's not over yet, because of the lawsuit. But my feelings are not bitterness, particularly, and certainly not hate for the people responsible. It's more amazement that the public will sit by and let these things happen; that they will believe everything they read in the newspaper; that (if you will) women in the public sector jobs will attack other women out of spite (yes, I know it can happen with men, too); that trained, professional-level librarians will go to the lengths of a lawsuit to 'get' a boss they didn't like, for whatever reasons . . . I found out that I still have a lot to learn about people!

"I wish my successor the best; he is a nice, competent young man and should be a good peace-maker. I guess I'm not a peace-maker—I'm too anxious to improve my libraries and offer the best possible services to my patrons, so I probably push a little harder than I should, on occasion. That's my style, and there are times and places where that is what is needed. I'm in one of them now, I didn't become an administrator to be loved, but I do hope for some degree of respect—at least for my motives and efforts. It's really nice to be in a library where the board encourages me to go ahead, I don't read ugly lies about myself in the paper three times a week, friends don't call nightly to tell me what gossip they heard about me today, and I have a fine, supportive staff. Money is tight—where isn't it? But we are doing a good job here, all of us, from Chairman of the Board down to the page. And people appreciate us. For now. I'm sure the time will come when the honeymoon is over and people will not accept me bag and baggage without question. That's okay, too. I'm in this business partly to communicate, and every chance I get to practice that, I will.

"I WOULD LIKE TO SEE SOME COMMENTS from some of the instigators of such 'get the director' movements who act outside of the formalized procedure. I can't help wondering how they feel. Do they think they have done something wonderful for mankind? I, too, have worked for a director with whom I had a personality conflict. I stayed as long as I was willing to work for her, found another job, moved on, and have never gossiped about her or her methods. We have worked together successfully on several occasions since, and we have both been adult, mature, and big enough to recognize that there is work to be done and it is a waste of time and effort to cut down one another. I have followed, here, a young man who was fired. He is still here, trying to find another job. I wish him good luck. He has behaved in a very professional manner, never taking his 'case' to the public or trying to gain support through gossiping about what he, I'm sure, thinks is wrong with our Board. I will do my best to see that he receives nothing derogatory in a reference concerning his professionalism.

All of us have talents, and all of us have failings. Wouldn't it be nice if we were all a little more tolerant and willing to work through the system to accomplish the things we want?

"In case you think, after that, that I'm a 'softie,' I'd probably better add that I have fired people for poor performance, but only after giving them an opportunity to improve. I don't like doing it, but I can. I didn't enjoy one bit telling seven people that their jobs were being eliminated. I suffered over it, but I did it because I was the director and had been instructed by the Board that that was the route we had to take."

THAT'S A TRULY GREAT LETTER, and one I was most happy to receive and am proud to run. I have never had the pleasure of meeting its writer but would certainly like to. She has courage and a strong positive spirit. She has learned that what's important is not what happens to one but, rather, how one reacts to what happens to him or her. She is looking ahead, and letting the past take care of itself. There is much in her letter that I would like to comment on, but I'm not going to. She has said it all too well. But I would hope to hear from others who have experiences or thoughts relating to it.

Some of you may feel that we shouldn't give so much space to a single letter. Maybe so. But where else in the literature of librarianship can you find such a letter—one with as much reality, humanity, honesty, and downright educational value? And where else can one find a medium for the communication of such experiences? In my more than three years of studying at a library school I never heard a professor talk about such problems nor did I run across a library journal that published such material. (5/1982)

■   ■   ■   ■   ■

"I THOROUGHLY ENJOY reading *AD*," writes a library director in Virginia. "The February issue on firing was especially interesting. May I purchase five additional copies for my Trustees?"

Another comment on this issue comes from a Librarian who writes: "I too am an administrator not an officeholder. My job hangs by a thread everyday, but I have survived more than six years here so far. I know my Trustees would sometimes rather I be an officeholder, but my conscience does not permit that luxury. I feel my job is a public trust to do what is best for the whole library community not what is momentarily popular. When the axe finally comes (tomorrow or perhaps quite a few years in the future), I will go quietly, with understanding for my Trustees' action."

■   ■   ■   ■   ■

CHAPTER VII

A Case History

"LIBRARY WORKERS LASH OUT" is the heading of an article in the Pawtucket Evening Times of January 18, 1982. It came to us in a plain envelope, with no indication of who sent it or why—though the answer to both questions is obvious. Someone, probably one of the lashers-out, wanted to spread the unhappy news about the subjects of this article to a wider audience while remaining anonymous themselves. Not a very nice person, and one with a real problem herself, or himself.

The newspaper article reads (and I will skip over most of it):

"This is a tale of two men and their wives—and of the flip side of the weekend euphoria at the Pawtucket Library over the sale of celebrity shoes which brought national attention to the city.

"The story's principal characters are Library Director

Lawrence Eaton and his wife, Lee, and Roger Viens, president of the city workers' union, and his wife, Kathy.

"Until two weeks ago, Kathy was Lawrence Eaton's secretary at the library. Mrs. Eaton was hired last year as the library coordinator of community services.

"While the public has been reading about John Travolta's shoes and seeing and hearing heaps of good publicity about the library on television—last Friday's celebrity shoe sale raising well over $2,000 for the library—a large majority of the fulltime employees of the library seem on the verge of a rebellion.

"Nineteen of the employees signed a strongly-worded letter to Mayor Henry S. Kinch complaining about the way Eaton treats them—and complaining he gives his wife special privileges as a library employee . . .

"The current turmoil was brought on by the firing of Mrs. Viens as of Jan. 4. Eaton said the library trustees ordered the position eliminated. Because Mrs. Viens, part of whose job was to act as secretary to Eaton, had nine years' seniority, she did not lose her city job but was transferred to a different job at City Hall.

"The dismissal of Kathy Viens clearly galvanized the employees to unleash resentment which had been building toward both Lawrence and Lee Eaton for some time . . .

"The letter accuses him (Lawrence Eaton) of dismissing four other employees and causing the resignations of more than a dozen others over the five years he has been director. His actions as director have morale at an all-time low, according to the letter . . .

"I admit the atmosphere is extremely charged," Eaton said.

"He said much of that is due to the 'heavy union involvement' in the Kathy Viens incident, the fact his own wife was hired for a supervisory position and the many modernizing changes that he says many long-time employees do not want to cope with."

  I CONSIDERED AT LENGTH throwing out this article and saying nothing about it. I generally try to avoid publicizing other people's problems, just as I try never to say anything critical of an individual. But I concluded that the matter is probably already known to the librarians in that area and has perhaps been mentioned in the national library journals (which I haven't had occasion to see in the past 18 months). I recall that in two similar cases—involving previous librarians in Tucson and Santa Barbara—where almost the entire staff signed complaining letters to the city fathers, someone also wrote a nasty letter to the *Library Journal* stating that the poor man under attack was believed by his staff to be totally unfit to run a library. Can one imagine anything more cruel and unkind, more unprofessional and totally despicable than that! To be termed incompetent by fellow professionals before the whole library world . . . and this on top of losing a choice job and having to leave the library and community that has come to mean so much to one. It seems incredible that human beings—probably as nice as can be in other areas of their lives—can treat a fellow human in this shameful way.

Signing such a letter is such a cowardly act. The signers are protected by almost complete anonymity. Each is just one of many unknown names that will be remembered by no one. Their jobs are perfectly safe, and nothing in the letter is aimed at them. The mud is all going in the other direction, hitting at a single individual who is caught in the spotlight with no way of extricating or defending himself. No person seeing the letter will fail to recognize or remember who it was who was so demeaned. The signers of the letter can go home and forget the whole thing. Not so their victim.

NO ONE CAN GO THROUGH LIFE without hearing or reading about one or more letters of this kind. They are common to every vocational field. Most letters complaining about a supervisor are treated in a confidential manner so that nobody is embarrassed before his peers. Generally it is possible to keep the matter out of the public press. But when the complainants are so full of resentment that they just turn plain nasty, they want the object of their dislike to be publicly humiliated and will see that the newspapers get the story. That is going too far, and of course writing to the library journals is far worse still.

I have known a number of men who have been subjected to such treatment, and can honestly say that I never knew one who really merited it. Some were business supervisors, some were library directors, one was a fire chief. Most of them were innovators—and some of you may remember that broad study of innovators that reported that the average life of an innovator on a job is only two or three years; most of them are fired. These particular men all seemed to be above average in their ability and performance, if performance is measured by the quality of service of their department, rather than by their personal popularity.

The recipients of such complaints in the private sector seem to behave better than those in the public sector. In the first place, there is less publicity and the top people are far less subject to outside pressures. But more importantly, they know the supervisors and their work much better than library board members and the people at City Hall know their library directors. They are closer to them physically, have known them more intimately and over a longer period of time, and have better measures of their performance. They know what they have actually contributed each year to the company, and how indispensable they are. That's the bottom line for them, not their popularity with their workers. And if they decide that the offending supervisor is worth keeping, they are better able to straighten out the situation. One solution might be transferring the supervisor to another department or company office—something that isn't possible in the case of the library administrator. And then I remember the vice-president who told the workers that they would work in harmony with the supervisor or not work at all. Again, not something you can carry out in the public sector.

THE MAIN REASON I FEEL I CAN talk about the Pawtucket situation is that the principal characters have done nothing wrong. The professional qualifications and capacities of the Eatons are beyond question. The two of them have expanded the facilities, services and programs of the Pawtucket Library far beyond what they were a few years ago, and doubtless well beyond the expectations of the people and the officials of that community. One might ask the signers of the letter to Mayor Kinch why they said nothing about the considerable and so obvious improvements in the Library, accomplished under the leadership of Mr. Eaton (whom, incidentally, I have never met). I've always felt that one should tell the good things about a person or an issue to provide a fair balance to whatever is to be said on the negative side.

Any impartial observer would have to say that these people have done an excellent job. I'm confident that the reading public in that community is well pleased and appreciative of what they have accomplished for them.

To achieve this, they have conducted one of the finest continuing PR campaigns that we have seen in the library world. This has inevitably brought a lot of public attention to the Eatons, and doubtless a fair share of praise and "glory." Such publicity may not be sought, or welcomed, by the recipient because he or she knows that it carries the seeds of trouble with fellow professionals—both inside and outside the library—but there is little that can be done about it. It just "goes with the territory."

THE PAWTUCKET LIBRARIAN SIMPLY HAD too many strikes against him. In the first place, he made a lot of good and needed changes, and anyone who does that is bound to upset a good percentage of the older employees who prefer to see things remain as they always have been.

In the second place, the Eatons brought the quiet old library into the mainstream of community life and got it reams of publicity . . . and many older librarians have sincere reservations about this sort of thing. They don't think it quite professional to get an "unreasonable" amount of publicity even though the recipient didn't seek the extra attention, and it was primarily directed at the institution rather than at the individual heading it.

In the third place, the library director was known to fly his own airplane. To me, that's great . . . but to some staff members in any organization that is just something to make the boss more "different" and apart from the rest of the team. Like being the only city employee to belong to the country club or the only Librarian to have a little business on the side, or anything else that gives someone an opening to believe that you probably think you are superior to the rest of the herd. Until someone outlaws jealousy and envy, the person who lifts himself above the crowd in some particular, or is perceived to have done so, is likely to earn more resentment than approval.

Fourthly, Mr. Eaton employed his wife as a department head in the library. To be sure, he did so at the suggestion of the Library Board who had been impressed by her performance as a volunteer worker in the Library's successful bond issue campaign. But that couldn't satisfy all those who had never heard of such a thing being done before. They were bound to watch her every move to see that she wasn't shown any favoritism by her husband. Some of those who would be furious if anyone kept track of *their* actual working time have pointed the finger at Mrs. Eaton in this regard.

LEE EATON IS THE LIBRARY'S COORDINA- TOR of Community Relations, and anyone who is familiar with the tremendous number and variety of library programs that she and her staff have put on would have to agree that she is one of the most energetic and effective program and PR people in our profession. Some of the Pawtucket staff claim that she took off time that she wasn't entitled to, but I'm afraid that they neglected to count all the extra time that she put in. Nobody who has seen the amount of work she turns out could believe that anyone could do that in less than 40 hours a week, no matter how much help she has. I couldn't do it in twice her hours, even if I were capable of doing it at all. Sometimes we don't realize how much time writers and other idea people put in away from their office.

A fifth factor working against Eaton is the feeling on the part of some of the staff that he is responsible for the depar- ture of a sizable percentage of their group, either through dis- missals or forced resignations. I just can't believe that. I haven't heard a word from the Eatons so I don't know the facts in this matter but I do know what sounds right, and what doesn't, and I have never heard of a library director who was able to accomplish such a feat. Getting rid of a staff member that one doesn't need or want isn't all that easy. I am sure that any administrator who felt it necessary to oust 16 or more people—a majority of his staff—would soon decide that it would be a lot easier if he took his own departure. There is no doubt in my mind that the bulk of the staff separations in Paw- tucket were for personal reasons that had nothing to do with Mr. Eaton. Some may have moved away, or gotten married, or decided to go to college or graduate school, or whatever. But it serves someone's purpose to lump them all together and drop them at Eaton's doorstep.

Any administrator could at least understand what he was trying to do, if he had actually attempted this. How did Coach Bill Walsh turn the San Francisco 49-ers completely around and take them all the way to the Super Bowl this past season? In one sentence, he got rid of two thirds of the team that managed to win only two games two years earlier and replaced them with the best players he could find for each position.

One can't do things like that in the public sector, and perhaps it's just as well. Still, administrators can dream, and doubtless the great majority would like to see it made easier to terminate the small minority of "impossible" employees who contribute nothing but trouble. Some of you may recall that when I asked the directors of more than a hundred large public libraries if they had anybody on their staff that they would like to get rid of if they could, they all had somebody in mind. The average number was, "Ten percent of the staff."

In the sixth place, there is that factor of heavy union involvement, which is always touchy, and in the seventh, the fact that he eliminated the job of his secretary. In my book, that is a very commendable act. I did the same thing in my last library and got along very nicely for 13 years without one. Yet, at the same time, I recognize the fact that the secretary is a key figure in most organizations of this size, enjoying a close relationship with almost everyone. Any boss who tampers with this special individual can count on arousing a lot of animosity.

PERHAPS THAT'S ENOUGH TO INDICATE that Larry Eaton had a lot of things working against him at the Pawtucket Library. I can't, however, see that he did anything wrong—whether in his deeds or decisions. He did stick his neck out more than is commonly done, but one can't fault him for that. Many administrators make it a point not to stick theirs out at all. But then their institutions don't show the progress that the Pawtucket Library has made the last few years.

I believe that Eaton is most perceptive in diagnosing his problems as due in large part "to the heavy union involvement" in the Kathy Viens incident, the fact that his own wife was hired for a supervisory position and the many modernizing changes that he says many long-time employees do not want to cope with. Certainly these things are true, and they would be enough to cause havoc in any organization.

In short, this would seem to be just another case of a fast-moving library director interested in building and promoting library service and giving his community the most modern and helpful library possible, and a much slower-moving staff that would like to stick to the type of service they have always known and not be bothered with any change or new ideas. The director and his staff are so apart in their points of view—their thoughts and desires and attitudes—that there is no way they can get along harmoniously unless the director is willing and able to slow his motor down to about the speed of his staff. Which means that he must put aside his dreams, his hopes and his goals for the time being, and let the community continue along without the improved service they would so welcome.

If a director finds that he inherited such a staff—and some do—he must face up to the fact that some friction and unhappiness is inevitable. I am assuming, of course, that the person has some imagination and the desire to make the improvements that appear needed. He may have to decide how much he wants to do what is pleasing to the staff and how much he wants to do what would be pleasing to the public and, generally, his library board. He wants to do the best job possible—which means benefitting the public which supports and uses the library—but he knows that if he greatly displeases the staff (which normally means his department heads) he may not be around very long to accomplish for the public what he would like.

THE MORE I THINK ABOUT the Pawtucket situation the more convinced I am that it had to be the Community Services Department that was primarily responsible for the trouble in the library. Whenever one hears about a library staff becoming upset the first question that comes to mind is, "What has the Librarian proposed, or instituted, that is non-traditional or contrary to what the staff learned at library school?" There almost always is something new in the picture that the department heads never heard about at school and so are disinclined to accept on the job. And the more years they have gone along without this new thing, the more resistant they are to change.

You take a group of people who have always firmly believed that a library was a place for reading and study, that library service was book service, and service given inside the walls of the library, and then open up a new major department in the library that appears to go against all these staff convictions. How can they be expected to accept it or be content with it. The answer probably is that one doesn't really expect them to be happy with the situation but just hopes that they will come to accept the idea in time.

I expect some of you who have read in these columns about certain of the stupendous events that the Community Services Department has staged for the library in Pawtucket have wondered what a dog show or a sale of the shoes of movie stars have to do with library service. Perhaps you would not be in favor of your library spending a similar amount of time and money on such programs. That's fair enough. Everyone is entitled to his own opinions and no one requires that others

agree with any of his ideas. The trick is to separate the unpopular idea from the person(s) espousing it. The sad thing is that
so many people find this seemingly impossible to do. Our best
friend believes differently from us on some important public
issue, and he stands a chance of no longer being our best
friend. We think our boss is a wonderful person—until he
proposes a change in our work program that we don't think
we'd like. Instead of confining our opposition to the idea, we
lump the idea and the person together and end up disliking
both. Even though the boss has a perfect right to propose
such a change and certainly did not wish to cause us any unhappiness.

Ideas and their possessors will always be linked together. If
one can't block or kill the idea one can certainly make the person pay who proposed and implemented it. If the staff in Pawtucket (to take the most recent case) can't abide the library's
new community programs, they can tell the city fathers how
the library director and his foolish ideas are ruining the library and making things impossible for the staff, all to the end
of running him out of town and thereby, hopefully, getting rid
of this strange idea of library service that they find so abhor-
rent.

WE COULD QUOTE ANY NUMBER of experi-
enced administrators, all saying pretty much the same thing:
It's impossible to be a good administrator and liked by all
your employees at the same time. To give you just one
for-instance, listen to this writer that I just stumbled on in the
Jan. 22, 1979 issue of Purchasing Magazine. He writes:

> "As a manager, you must realize that you can't be popular
> with all the people, all the time. But this may be just as well.
> Consultants say that if you're too popular with your subordi-
> nates you may not be doing your job effectively enough to at-
> tain hard profit objectives.

"A good manager should always be prodding his people to think and work harder. It's his job to make tough decisions that often favor one subordinate over another. And it's certainly no way to win a popularity contest.

"Generally the trick is to avoid extremes and pinpoint behavior that provokes antipathy in your employees . . . But resign yourself to the fact that if you manage people you will be disliked by a number of them."

Most people don't want to be disliked by anyone, which is part of the reason most individuals don't want to be managers, or even the lowest grade of supervisors. They are apt to say, "I just don't want the responsibility. I'd rather do without that kind of hassle."

I hope the non-administrators reading this will not get the idea that all library directors are subject to the kind of unpleasantness that we have been talking about here. Some experience such staff problems once or twice in their full career, and others never do. It all depends on so many variables both in the library situation one inherits and in one's own makeup and what one attempts to do to bring change to the organization.

THAT PAWTUCKET NEWSPAPER ARTICLE, that I almost decided to ignore, has really unloosed a lot of words on my part. I'm surprised to see how much I've written, and yet I'm not surprised. I have deep feelings about such matters and I would like to help people better understand how trouble sometimes arises between the administrator and his staff, and why they shouldn't hasten to pass judgment on the former.

It is indeed sad that the beleaguered Librarian is too often abandoned by the library board and city fathers who should instead be praising and thanking him or her for the improvements that he or she had the imagination, the ability, and the courage to effect in their library. It's too bad they don't realize that it's the new administrator who accomplished all this. He's really the indispensable part of the equation, not the individuals who constitute the staff. The leaders of the revolt in Pawtucket have probably been on the staff for years, but they never brought about the doubling of the library's space or the other major improvements there.

A final thought about letters of that kind: Don't give too much weight to the number of signatures on it. It's a rare staff—in business or the professions—where the great majority of people agree and feel that strongly about anything. Generally you find a few strong personalities who deliberately try to make their fellow workers as aggrieved and unhappy as they are. Ask the younger staff members in Pawtucket why they signed the letter to the mayor and I would wager that some would say, "What are you going to do when your department head wants you to sign something? After all, she is the person I have to live with and satisfy, not the director." (4/1982)

    ■   ■   ■   ■   ■

POLICY AGAINST NEPOTISM: "Although I do not know any of the details of the Pawtucket Library affair," writes Louise Nelson, director of the Wyckoff Public Library (N.J.), "I believe it is obvious that a policy against nepotism would have prevented most of the problems of that troubled library.

"Our library policy forbids the hiring of any person in the immediate family of present staff members or trustees. This is an excellent policy and I recommend it to any library."

MORE OF THE SAME: Jack Ramsey, director of the Glendale Public Library (CA), writes: "Regarding your long consideration of the Pawtucket problem in the April issue, you miss the main problem.

"I too am concerned about the direct contact with the Mayor made by 19 staff members. However, as a good manager, Lawrence Eaton should never have hired his wife. You as editor of a periodical for administrators must realize that. It's wrong to hire your wife in that kind of organization. It's also wrong for Eaton to say that she was hired at the suggestion of the board. Surely he does the hiring, not the board. If the board has taken over that responsibility, the action adds one more reason for my position that, in this age and in modern well-run cities, library boards should be abolished."

I HAVE ALWAYS HAD THE SAME FEELING about nepotism as the two writers above have expressed, and I'm sure Mr. Eaton felt the same way. but they say that there are exceptions to every rule. I don't believe it's *wrong* for someone to hire his wife, or anyone else, under special circumstances. Perhaps "ill-advised," or "chancy," but not "wrong." If the person is willing to risk it, for what he believes are worthwhile and probable gains, it's all right with me . . . More important, however, in this case, is the fact that the Eaton appointment was approved in advance by the Mayor of Pawtucket.

We have been hearing about more cases of this kind in recent years and they seem to have occasioned no serious problems. I believe that the acceptance of this practice in any institution depends on the position to which the family member is appointed, and what he or she does on the job. A staff officer might be better accepted than a line officer. Anyone with outside skills is going to arouse less concern than one with the standard background for that place of employment.

A library director, for instance, could expect less trouble appointing a member of his family as the library's Business

Manager, or as, say, a Systems Analyst, than as the head of the Reference Department. Most of the staff would feel they have no qualifications for or interest in these special positions so there would be no ego involvement on their part, nor any feeling that the new appointee would be competition for a higher post.

I'm thinking of the head of a scientific organization who appointed a female member of his family as their Head of Publications. No problem! Nobody else would have wanted the job and nobody felt threatened. He also employed and promoted sons and grandsons without any serious trouble.

In privately-owned businesses one can appoint family members to high positions with little difficulty. A friend of mine has just appointed his son as the No. 2 man in his company. A member of my family has appointed his wife as president of their company. If such appointments aren't considered wrong in privately-owned businesses, should they automatically be judged wrong in every other type of institution? Clarence Sherman, the distinguished director of the Providence Public Library, employed and promoted his son Stuart to the assistant directorship of the PPL, from which position he was appointed to succeed his father as director. If any of this proved seriously upsetting to the staff, I wouldn't know.

I honestly don't think Mrs. Eaton was upsetting to the Pawtucket staff because she was the wife of the library director. If she had kept a low profile and hadn't done any more than the average librarian in such a capacity she would doubtless have offended no one. But no non-relative that Eaton might have appointed could have come in and done an equally effective job so that she was getting more public attention than the rest of the staff combined, and her programs were made to appear more important than the book collections that everyone else was involved with, without upsetting and antagonizing the staff to an equal degree. If the Director of Publications that I alluded to earlier, had somehow made a similar splash with and for her particular service department, most of the scientists in that organization would have been working to get her fired. I don't doubt that for a minute.

If yours is an engineering company, you can be sure your staff expects that any glory or publicity will fall to the engineers. If it's a medical clinic, the doctors will insist that any and all public attention will be theirs. And in a library, many of the staff still feel that only a professionally trained librarian working with books is deserving of whatever few spotlights might sometime be turned the library's way.

If you want work performed, and you want it done to the library's greatest benefit, then hire the best-qualified person available. If this happens to be your wife, or your husband, then so be it. Hire her, or him. But plan to spend a lot of time and effort on seeing that your mate doesn't get isolated from the rest of the staff, that the latter aren't given any reason or opportunity to dislike or resent her, and that everyone understands the importance of her program to them and has a chance to share in the spotlight, to the extent possible.

No director should enter into such a situation unless he understands and is prepared to make the continuous efforts required to keep such an appointment on a harmonious basis. But this would be the same whether this special post went to his wife or a total stranger.

Regardless of who is appointed to such a position, and no matter how hard the director and his appointee work to keep everybody happy, it is just not always going to be possible. The feelings of professionals regarding what is right and proper about the work of their organization are pretty strong and not subject to manipulation. So we should never judge an administrator on the basis of how popular he or his decisions are, or have been, with his staff, but, rather, on the basis of what he has accomplished and how well his decisions have worked out as far as the library's service to the community is concerned.

THAT'S ENOUGH SAID ABOUT the Pawtucket incident. I don't particularly enjoy writing about situations where people are hurting, or where something I say may offend one party or the other; nor do I feel comfortable talking about anything I haven't seen or experienced myself—though I have seen copies of all the significant documents in the case.

I would have preferred writing about it as a simple case history, without identifying the library, but gave up that idea when the story broke in the *LJ "Hotline"* and it seemed likely that many would know whom I was talking about anyway.

Once I knew about the situation I was doubly motivated to say something about it; first, because there seemed to be so many aspects that invited comment and so much that one might learn from it, and secondly, because of my continuing interest in helping build a climate of greater understanding and tolerance regarding the difficulties that administrators often have with their personnel. Innovative directors are always going to upset some of their staff from time to time and I'll probably always try to help people to understand how and why this happens. I have seen too many administrators who have been badly hurt by the common tendency of people to judge others not on the basis of what they have accomplished but on the basis of how popular they are with their subordinates and what happens to them on their job.

Perhaps I was too rough on the Pawtucket staff. But of course they brought that all on themselves by sending me the newspaper clipping quoting their letter to the mayor about their boss. I do wish they had kept the matter out of the newspapers and strictly between the library and city hall. I know they felt they had been treated badly by their director and had ample cause to complain. Listening to their side of the story, one is tempted to agree that they did have some real grievances. But then I think of my good friend, the school superintendent, who was hounded by the teachers in the school district—even to the extent of their dumping garbage on his front lawn. They said he was "insensitive." But many of us non-teachers found him one of the nicest and warmest human beings we'd ever met. He just wouldn't stand for any nonsense in the schools. So we learn that no one is perceived the same way by everyone and that we mustn't pass judgment on people we don't really know . . . and the same policy is recommended for those we *do* know.

We gave ample praise in our April issue to the Pawtucket Library director for his considerable accomplishments there in the past five years. But in working on our index to the AD we have been reminded that we found cause to compliment this library more than once on things that they had done before this time. No public library staff in Rhode Island has had a greater reputation for innovation than this one over the past dozen years. It has been consistently a strong library, with leadership to match, and such institutions normally weather storms of this type and stay in the forefront of their profession. The person at the top will of course have to make some changes and set a new tone, and then the rest of the staff will have to put the past behind them and set to work mending the fences and helping build a new spirit and an even better library service in that city. And that's just what they'll do, too! (5/1982)

.   .   .   .   .

SPEAKING OF THE PAWTUCKET PUBLIC Library, we are happy to hear that the audit of library records has exonerated Director Lawrence Eaton and his wife, Lee, of charges of misuse of funds. And Mayor Kinch said he hopes to resolve the problems at the library by improving communications between the library administration and employees.

We certainly share the Mayor's hope for an improvement in the situation there, but don't believe the problem is a lack of communication. That's too simple. The real problem seems to be a difference in philosophy. The librarians do not think the library's programs for adults are viable library services. Even though the public loves them, the staff would prefer to stick with books. As their letter to Mayor Kinch stated, "A library is by definition, 'a place set apart to contain books and other material for reading, study, and reference.' " The Eatons' conception of library service is so much broader that it will take a good deal more than mere communication to straighten out that scene.

It has got to be a difficult situation for the Eatons. They have apparently known for some time that the staff has hated all of the noise, excitement and glitter of the library's community programming but really thought that the staff recognized that the programs were cultural and informational and thus of value. How wrong we can all be at times!

It is hard to give up a public service when you know how much the public loves what you are doing, and it is doubly difficult when one has spent three years working very hard to get all kinds of favorable publicity for the library. But it might be a helpful move by the library administration to slow the programming down to a walk—until the staff can accept it in good spirit.

This may take awhile as some people's feelings seem to have gotten a bit high. Take the person who called Debbie Waldman, a singer doing a concert for the Pawtucket Public Library, and told her, "If you sing, you will be shot." Detectives are trying to learn whether the threat was in any way part of a pattern of activities to harass the library or its officials. The library has already had two bomb scares and a couple of false fire alarms, according to the article in the Pawtucket *Evening Times*.

Cases like this have so many common threads. For example, the staff told the mayor the other day that the last thing in the world they wanted was bad press for the library and that they are saddened by all of the recent media coverage; they forgot to mention the clippings they sent to me and the Library Journal, and doubtless others, too. Which proves again that people don't behave very well when they are upset.

I DON'T MEAN TO BE particularly critical of the Pawtucket staff for their unwillingness to accept or support the various fine innovations of the PPL under Mr. Eaton's Administration. I know a dozen others who were no more loyal or supportive. One might think that the Pawtucket librarians would have just been proud and contented that their Library has received 3 National Awards in the past 4¹/₂ years, as well as being declared the grand winner of the New England Library Association's 1980 PR contest. But, alas, human nature doesn't seem to work that way.

We all know by now that winning a lot of awards and getting a lot of attention is not calculated to increase one's popularity. It is no surprise to hear that Pawtucket's community programs have resulted in a certain amount of envy and hostility on the part of some of the library directors in the region who have not been able to replicate their services. If anyone has any difficulty understanding this, let him/her read the article, "The Marva Collins 'Scandal'," in this issue. It tells the story of the schoolteacher who got a lot of publicity on a national TV program, and how this aroused the envy and resentment of other teachers who then set out to get Marva Collins. You see, teachers are just like librarians. They have the same human nature with all its problems and frailties. (5/1982)

■　　　　■　　　　■　　　　■　　　　■

VIII

Public Library
Directors' Poll

\

THE ADMINISTRATOR'S DIGEST is planning an informal survey of its subscribers, to provide certain information about the work and opinions of our administrators that we believe will be of interest to all our readers. We propose to start with our pubic library administrators, since they constitute over half our total number of subscribers, and would hope to get to our other groups of administrators at a later date. Our thought now is to mail questionnaires to 200 public library directors, within the next four to six weeks. We may, however, decide to substitute a certain number of non-subscribing administrators, to make the sample more representative of all public library directors. Our magazine is designed for the open-minded, creative, energetic administrator and there is much evidence that that is the kind of subscriber that we have. We have the builders and the innovators—and we are afraid that a poll limited to this select group might turn out like the old "Literary Digest" poll. Nevertheless, many of

you will be receiving our questionnaire and we sincerely hope
that you will take the ten minutes or so to fill it out and return
it as soon as possible. We believe we made the first personnel
survey involving public library administrators, back in 1938,
with over 70% of the 270 head librarians returning our questionnaire. We hope to do better this time. We hope everyone
will be completely frank in his or her replies. Certainly nobody will know who you are. The young lady who picks up
our mail will open and throw away all envelopes at the Post
Office, bringing back only the anonymous questionnaires to
be tallied . . . Watch for it! (4/1970)

■   ■   ■   ■   ■

OUR BIG AD POLL: Eight days ago we sent out
questionnaires to the directors of the 200 largest public libraries in the land, and fifty of them have already been filled
out and returned to us. If the percentage of returns proves as
high as we hope, it will simply be due to the fact that (1) Library administrators are an extremely cooperative and professional group, (2) People generally like to answer questions (as I quickly learned years ago when I spent many
evenings asking strangers if I could come into their homes and
ask them a series of questions for the Opinion Research
Corp.; not once was I turned down, as dull as most of these
commercial polls were), and (3) None of these particular
questions require any searching for facts or figures. Most of
them simply ask for one's opinion or feeling about matters
that concern most librarians, and can be answered in a word
or two.

I only hope that those who fill out the questionnaire experience some of the pleasure I had in preparing it. I thought of
everything that I'd ever been curious to know, or that I'd
heard librarians questioning or debating at some time or an-

other, or that seemed to merit some investigation, and later reduced the number to those that would fit into the available space. It came to 210 questions. I have just now multiplied 208 (the average person answers all but two questions) by a hoped-for number of returns and can see that it may take 40,000 tabulations to present the results of this survey. That's enough for a good Ph.D. thesis, and I know too well how long that takes to prepare. Nevertheless, I'm hoping that we can present the first section of the survey report in our September issue.

Perhaps I shouldn't say so much about this Poll, since most of you aren't involved with it . . . but maybe that is the best reason for talking about it here. To get a taste of the thing, let's open up the first questionnaire that we received and look at a few questions and answers:

15. Did you enjoy your year at library school?   NO
55. Could you operate more efficiently and accomplish more without a board?   YES
58. Would you like to see a retirement age for library board members?   YES
83. Do you feel the library is getting its proper share of city funds?   YES
106. Can you generally find good people to fill your professional positions?   NO
112. Do you believe in hiring graduates of NON-accredited library schools?   YES
121. What percentage of your full-time staff would you be happy to replace?   10%
131. Is your staff growing appreciably faster than your circulation?   YES
158. Do you believe public library employees should have the right to strike?   YES
178. Is this the most enjoyable job you have had?   NO
179. Would you like a bigger job?   NO

180. At what age would you like to retire?   55
192. If you had the choice of removing a particular title your board thought highly objectionable, or being fired . . . what would you do?   REMOVE THE BOOK
196. Do you feel that library work is becoming More/Less enjoyable than 10 yrs. ago?   LESS
207. Do you feel that "Intellectual Freedom" should be the main topic of discussion at ALA conventions? NO

Only time will tell whether these opinions represent the minority or the majority of the group. (6/1970)

    ■   ■   ■   ■   ■

THEN AND NOW: It is interesting to compare some of the figures in the above-reported Poll of Public Library Directors with the comparable findings of our study of a similar group of directors 32 years ago. The percentage of men in those cities of over 100,000 pop. was almost exactly the same as it is today, despite all that is said from year to year about the trend in the direction of men taking over more and more of the top positions . . . The percentage of directors coming from the public library field has increased by a third, as has the percentage coming from director's and asst. director's positions, since 1938 . . . A comparison of the two groups of predecessors shows interesting similarities and differences. The percentage separated from their positions by Death has dropped from 34%, in the 1938 study, to 7% . . . while the percentage for Retirement has increased from 14% to 43%. The percentage of predecessors moving to a better job shows only slight change, as does the percentage of those dismissed (14% in the earlier study) . . . All in all, it would seem that the group of chief librarians has not changed as much in general makeup as their institutions. (10/1970)

. . . . .

MORE BRANCHES: It is interesting to note that only 55% of the Library Directors are interested in having MORE branches. The percentage preferring FEWER branches (and larger ones) is doubtless greater than it would have been five years ago . . . We were happy to see that at least three directors recognized the fact that they really didn't need an Assistant Director. It is our belief that no public library in a city of under 100,000 population needs one, and the same applies to many cities above that level. We visited a library yesterday that boasted an Assistant Director—who does all the book selection—and a Head of Adult Services, besides the normal complement of department heads, and left wondering what the Director of this library serving only 80,000 people found to keep himself properly occupied. Many Assistants are doing odds and ends of things that the Director ought either to handle himself/herself or delegate to others down the line . . . It is gratifying to learn that the majority of these Directors have never had any of their recommendations turned down by their board. This may mean in some instances that the Director isn't proposing as many new and challenging ideas as he might, but more than that it reflects the open-minded cooperation that most library boards provide their administrators. These laymen are generally quicker to accept new library ideas than a group of library department heads. (11/1970)

. . . . .

CONTENT WITH LIBRARY BUDGET: I find this section of our Public Library Directors' Poll quite heartening. In view of all the budget complaints that one hears over a period of time it is good to know that most directors are faring quite well, budgetwise. Two thirds of them get at least 90% of the money they request, 83% feel they get sufficient money to enable the library to carry on its essential services, and a good 40% are content with what they get. One in four feel that they could operate on 10% less money, if they really had to, and hold their business to its present level . . . and one in eight have even asked at some time for less money than they felt they could get. Almost half are satisfied that the library is getting its proper share of city funds. And if unlimited funds were available, the median percentage of increase that would be asked for is only 20%. In short, they appear to be more content with their financial support, and with more reason to be so, than some may have thought, and they probably have fewer money problems than most administrators—in either the public or private sectors.

My congratulations to the 29% who said they would prefer a situation where they really had to work to find the money they needed, to one where the library had all the money that might be required. I have experienced both conditions—operating medium-sized public libraries on as little as $1.00 per capita and as much as $12.00 (in today's money)—and would say that operating with a very tight budget was certainly more challenging and exhilarating. An idea that would save $100 was more exciting then than a saving of $1500 in the 1960's. I can remember writing an article entitled "Happy on 50¢" for the Library Journal (1953) and meaning every word of it. It detailed the pleasures of running a library on 50¢ per capita—which might be equivalent to about $2.00 today; we had every kind of service that one could find in a public library at that time—and we appreciated every dollar that came the library's way and knew that we needed it and were using every bit of it to its fullest advantage. That's a good feeling, and one that some of us haven't had in the last few years. (12/1970)

.   .   .   .   .

RE. NON-PROFESSIONALS: Item #2 in this month's report of the Public Library Directors' Poll will probably strike many readers as the most significant, if not the most startling, disclosure of this opinion survey. Here are four of the standard and most representative positions in public library work—ranked in the professional category for years, by librarians and non-professionals alike—and an average of 83 percent of these directors of large public libraries now say that a person who hasn't been to library school can be trained to fill each of these positions. Almost 19 out of 20 directors say an "untrained person" can head a circulation department, while 85% say he or she can be trained to do reference work, 82% say the same thing regarding the running of a branch library, and 70% see no reason why such an individual couldn't become a good children's librarian. Some readers may be surprised that more directors think it possible to run a branch library without library school training than to be a children's librarian without it.

We congratulate these directors on their open-mindedness and honesty. It is our feeling that their answers reflect a certain change in librarians' thinking. We feel sure that we wouldn't have received as many "Yes" answers 10 or 20 years ago. We recall the time we made the mistake of telling a professional audience that we'd appointed some wonderful non-professionals to all four of these positions and that they had worked out beautifully. We had explained that we just couldn't afford to employ library school graduates at that time, but some people still think we are uninterested in professional training. Many other directors have had equally good experience with "untrained" people. Probably most would agree with the person who said "It all depends upon the person . . . but I still believe that anybody would be better for having gone to library school."

All of which calls to mind Michael Ramsden's Presidential

address in '69 before the Assn. of Assistant Librarians, in England. He sparked a real response when he asked "Can we afford, on any sort of cost benefit analysis, to send out expensively trained librarians with our mobile libraries, or to insist on having qualified staff in our small branches?" B. G. Stevenson, from the Leicester City Libraries, agreed with him and said "There is only so much that can be done with a small branch. To staff these places with fully qualified librarians is to pay the librarians for skills which they will very, very rarely need to use. To have a qualified librarian at a small branch is uneconomical for the authority, and frustrating for any librarian worth his or her salt. It debases the profession as a whole." But David Lewis of the Leeds School of Librarianship had an equally thoughtful response. "In Heaven's Name," he asked, "if qualified librarians are not required at grass roots level—working with the community—then where are they required?" (2/1971)

.   .   .   .   .

THE MEN ARE MORE LIBERAL: In making this latest tabulation of the opinions of the directors of our largest public libraries we were struck with the difference between the thinking of the men and the women on certain issues. The men seem to be the more liberal group. For example, of the 10 directors who would like to see a union take over the representation of their employees, 9 are men and possibly the tenth as well; he or she failed to indicate his sex on the questionnaire. The same thing is true of the 20 directors who believe the coming of a union would have a positive effect on library services. All men. None of the women (25% of the total group) want a union or think it would have a positive effect . . . We are at a bit of a loss, however, to understand the three men who "don't care" whether there's a union or not, but believe it would have a "negative effect," or the gentleman who would "strongly dislike" to see a union come in but thinks it would have a "positive effect."

Likewise, on the question of whether the library should buy whatever the public wants, no matter how offensive or poorly written it may be, 10 of the 11 directors who say "yes" to this are men. One person wrote a strong "No—librarians should select materials," and most librarians will be gratified to see that over 80% of the library directors apparently still feel this way. As long as the majority of libraries can afford to buy only a small fraction of the titles published in this country each year, librarians must work hard at selecting those most needed and deserving of a place in their collection. It's a case of selection, not censorship—just as it is when you choose to purchase this automobile or TV set or house instead of others that are being urged on you. A librarian would seem to be on pretty secure ground here in defending himself against any charge of censorship from a patron. From my own memory of twenty years I can't recall any problem we ever had with such a patron, beyond explaining our book selection process. Actually, if a library agrees to automatically buy whatever title is requested by 1, 2, 6, or whatever number of people, it would seem that any small group of citizens with a special interest, whether group sex, the underground press, the Black Panthers, chess, organic food, or what-not, could have their library buy every publication on their favorite topic and reduce the amount of book money left to take care of a thousand other needs. If a librarian is going to buy whatever is requested of his library, he ought to at least keep a record of the people doing the requesting and consider turning down some of the requests from those who have been taken care of too often. There should be some balance and fairness in this business. Sure, we all realize that "they pay our salaries"—as was stated by one director—but let's not forget the thousands of other taxpayers who use the library and want the best possible selection of materials in their particular fields of interest and certainly don't want to be "turned-off" on the library by encountering there too much material falling in the "offensive or poorly written" category. (5/1971)

•   •   •   •   •

ENTHUSIASTIC ABOUT THEIR JOB: Library work comes off very well in this month's report of the opinions of the directors of large-city public libraries, with 70 percent considering it just about the most pleasant way to make a living that they know of. The same percentage think that their present job is the most enjoyable one that they have had. Such people—in their favorite job in their choice of all professions—might be expected to want to continue working as long as they could. Yet we find that the median desired retirement age is only 61—which seems surprisingly early. And 27% would retire right now if they were financially able to do so.

The majority of those with an opinion think that they work harder than most businessmen. My guess is that they may put in about the same number of hours, but generally without the pressures and the anxieties that produce the wear and fatigue. The library administrator has few hard deadlines, nobody breathing down his neck or demanding specific results, no customers or competitors to give him fits, and bears no financial risks or responsibilities. Free of all the fear and uncertainty that plague so many businessmen the librarians can be counted upon to outlive almost any other vocational group. I'm always surprised when I see a list of the past presidents of the American Library Association and count over 25 who are still living. I don't believe there is another national association in the land that can boast more living ex-presidents. The average librarian's long life must be due in part to his relative peace of mind and contentment on the job. Still, we note, with some surprise, that a quarter of these administrators characterize their position as an "ulcer job." That may seem hard to believe to those of us who have never felt that way—but then we are all built differently. It is also interesting to see that two-thirds of these administrators have no desire for a bigger position, and this group includes a good portion of the younger directors, too. It is so easy to assume that the majority of administrators would welcome a still bigger job—but apparently this is not so.

However, I believe the only thing that has really surprised me in the answers to the first 180 questions is that only 27% of these directors have their State and ALA annual dues paid by their library . . . and only 5% have their civic club dues so paid. My surprise is simply due to the fact that all four of the public libraries I've been associated with paid all my professional dues, and two paid my civic club dues as well. In one case, the weekly meals were simply put on my bill and charged to the library. The library board felt that the library was benefiting from my contacts with the Kiwanis Club membership. All of which only goes to show that one should never draw conclusions based on his own experience alone. (6/1971)

■   ■   ■   ■   ■

SATISFIED WITH THEIR PERFORMANCE: Seventy-eight percent of the large-city library directors are frank to say that they have advanced further than they thought they would when starting out in the profession. Asked if they have ever been sorry that they chose this field, less than one in six answered Yes.

Asked if they thought they were:
1) "Doing a good, above-average job?"—92% said Yes.
2) "Using most of your talents?"—83% said Yes.
3) "About as happy as you could be?" 87% said Yes.
4) "Making as much money as you probably could anyhere else?"—59% said Yes.
5) "Overpaid or underpaid?"—2/3rds said "Underpaid," 1/3rd said "Neither."
6) "Enthusiastic?"—93% said they were.
7) "Innovative?"—84% said Yes; 8% "Somewhat."
8) "A good speaker?"—71% said Yes.
9) "Overworked?"—only 37% said they were.
10) "A pretty good politician?"—74% said Yes.

■　　　■　　　■　　　■　　　■

CHAPTER IX

The Staff

HOW THEY RANK: On the Job Prestige scale of one to 100, dentists rank 95. Librarians tie with actors and actresses at 60.

The above note from the San Francisco Examiner's "Grab Bag" may be of interest to librarians who realized they did not rate with dentists on anyone's prestige scale but had no idea they were on the same level with actors and actresses. (6/1982)

■　　　■　　　■　　　■　　　■

LONG LIVE THE LIBRARIANS! I have often remarked that librarians live longer than any other vocational group. This opinion was based on what I have seen over the years and on the fact that the American Library Association generally has over 25 ex-presidents still living, and I have never found any other business or professional association that can match this statistic.

I might add that for years I used to read a publication that listed all the college professors around the country who passed away in the previous month. I would always figure the median age of the many people on these monthly lists and it was always either 70 or 71. This never ceased to amaze me as I knew most librarians, men as well as women, lived appreciably longer than that, and I never considered college teaching to be a high-stress occupation.

In view of all this you can imagine my interest and pleasure to read in a library newsletter that, "According to a study done by Metropolitan Life Insurance Company, librarians are the longest-lived among professionals. Next come curators, political leaders, government officials, community leaders, business executives, scientists, judges, lawyers, architects and designers. Those with the shortest lives are entertainers, physicians, and surgeons."

So now it's official—librarians really do live longer. I hope everyone reading this lives to enjoy his or her 90th birthday party in the best of health. After all, you are librarians, and librarians are expected now to outlive ordinary people. (12/1982)

■   ■   ■   ■   ■

THE WORK BREAK: Somebody in the upper echelon of a California aircraft plant had sufficient sense of humor to post this notice on the bulletin board.

"To all Employees: Due to increased competition and a keen desire to avoid bankruptcy, we find it necessary to institute a new policy. Effective immediately, we are asking that somewhere between starting and quitting time and without infringing too much on the time devoted to lunch period, coffee breaks, rest period, storytelling, ticket selling, golfing, auto racing, vacation planning, and rehashing of yesterday's TV programs that each employee try to find some time that can be set aside and be known as the Work Break.

"To some, this may seem to be a radical innovation, but we honestly believe the idea has possibilities. It may even keep us all in business a few years longer!

THE MANAGEMENT"

(10/1978)

■ ■ ■ ■ ■

MOST WORKERS PUT JOB SATISFACTION ahead of a raise, says a noted industrial psychologist in the Jan. 29th U.S. News & World Report. Professor Witkin asserts that recognition by the boss, the opportunity to participate in management decisions and a feeling that one's work is useful are more important in motivating employees than is salary or job security. Management often doesn't get its money's worth from fringe benefits, he adds, and promotions aren't always welcomed.

Most of us have heard or read such statements many times before but I expect we'll always need to hear them one more time. Emotional needs will always outweigh monetary or material needs, at least for workers already receiving a living wage. As a one-time salary administrator I can recall many times when a man went to see his boss about a raise he felt he deserved and had to have—only to come out with no raise but riding on Cloud Nine—happier and more elated than any raise could have made him—because his boss for the first time really talked with him about his work, letting him know that his superiors were well aware of his good work, appreciated his contribution to the company, felt that he was moving ahead in the department and had a real future in the organization. What person wouldn't rather hear such encouraging remarks from his boss—if he was new and had never heard them before—than receive an increase in salary with no accompanying words of explanation or praise? I remember a few employees who received three raises in one year but seemed to take no satisfaction from them because their bosses didn't care enough or couldn't bring themselves to make a "little ceremony" over the giving of each raise.

I WOULD SIT DOWN WITH EACH department head every three months and learn how all 1400 employees were doing and which ones were deserving of a raise. I was constantly urging the supervisors to call in the favored ones and let them know that they had definitely earned the increase and that the boss was most pleased with their work, and inspire them to continue improving their performance. But most of the department heads simply had their secretary show the people their change-of-rate form, and that was the end of it. Never saw an employee who was truly delighted or inspired with that treatment. Neither did I ever see an employee who was excited about getting an automatic increase or an across-the-board raise. All of which proves again that there are things more important to employes—or anyone else—than more money . . . That's the sad thing about civil service or any other system of salary advancement that treats everyone alike—giving the same amount or percentage of increase at the same time to the hard-working and the lazy alike. It's not only completely unfair but it's equally stupid. (5/1979)

■   ■   ■   ■   ■

TO HELP YOU BECOME AN ASSET to your library, test yourself and see if you do all these things:
   —Do you signal patrons with a greeting?
   —Do you deliver answers promptly and accurately?

—Do you zero in on each person with your individual attention?

—Do you follow through on complaints, seeking to settle differences yourself or with the help of your supervisor?

—Do you accommodate all reasonable requests?

—Do you help keep the place orderly and well-stocked?

These suggestions for service come from a grocery store chain, but they're very applicable to those who work in libraries. So comments a writer in the Oct. 1981 "Prairie Schooner," the newsletter of Rolling Prairie Library System, in Decatur, Illinois. And as Howard Cosell would say, "That's telling it like it is." (12/1981)

■   ■   ■   ■   ■

NO STIMULATION THERE: The January '86 issue of the Solano County Library Newsletter (CA) starts off by quoting from a letter that County Librarian Charles M. Brown had received from a close friend who manages a branch library in another state. He wrote: "Charles, there's just nothing happening to stimulate me here. It's *so* frustrating, the library's administration seems either unwilling or unable to offer the staff any type of motivation or challenge."

What a sad, sad letter that is! One might argue that every worker is entitled to a job with some challenge and motivation. But of course it will never be that way. Fortunately or unfortunately, a great many workers are not looking for a challenge and probably wouldn't recognize one if it were there. But I believe most librarians want a job that really challenges and motivates them. And I feel they are entitled to have such a job and that their supervisors have a definite obligation to make their jobs challenging and exciting for them.

If you have some jobs that just can't be made challenging,

just don't give them to the kind of people who are looking for a challenge. No sensible person wants any unhappy employees, so always give a lot of thought to matching employees and jobs.

Fortunately, there are not many jobs in a library that aren't interesting to begin with, particularly all those that involve contact with the public. There's nothing more interesting than people, even when they are at their worst. For it's then that they offer the greatest challenge.

I'm sure everyone reading this feels a lot of sympathy for the branch librarian who expressed frustration because the library administration didn't offer the staff any challenge or motivation. We can understand how unhappy such a situation must be for an ambitious professional, but at the same time, I would like to ask this librarian if he or she really requires a challenge from the administration to be happy and productive.

So much has been written in the past about the desirability of being strongly self-motivated and the need to set one's own goals and provide one's own challenges. Don't they still hold true? If so, shouldn't we all be responsible for our own state of mind and the maintenance of positive professional attitudes?

We certainly can't find fault with anyone who has felt frustration or depression over an unhappy job situation. I've experienced the same feelings myself on several occasions. I would only suggest that everyone has the capacity to overcome such negative emotions and turn his situation around, regardless of what others do, or fail to do.

LET ME GIVE YOU JUST ONE illustration from my own experience. I believe I mentioned this situation before, some years ago, but don't expect many will remember it. It happened shortly after I left the business world once again to return to the library field.

I became the librarian of a suburban branch of the Oakland Public Library. Most of the time I was there alone, checking books in and out and performing clerical duties that I hadn't had to do for almost thirty years. I was happy to be back in my own field, with a regular paycheck that I could count on, but the work seemed a bit uninspiring after some of the jobs I had had, including three public library directorships.

By the end of the first week I knew I was going to have to change my thinking about that job if I was going to survive in it. I began to think a lot more about the people who came to the library and less about all the books I had to slip and all the cards that had to be stamped and filed. It occurred to me that a lot of the older people were doubtless pretty alone in the world and would be pleased to get a little attention as well as a good book to read on their visits to the library. The more I thought about the opportunity I had to try and give each visitor a lift, the more excited I got about my hitherto routine job.

My first conviction was that anyone coming to this, or any other, library had a right to expect to receive two things at the circulation desk: (1) a smile, and (2) to be spoken to by his or her name. That's certainly not too much to ask, whether in a library or in a business office. And what a difference it would make everywhere if all the customers or patrons were treated in this manner! Not only would the latter behave much better, with far fewer complaints, but so would the staff members who meet the public.

Clearly the first thing I had to do was to learn as many names of patrons as possible. I immediately set myself a quota of so many new names each day. I would glance at each person's library card as I checked out her books and then say something like, "There you are, Mrs. Thompson, I do hope

you like these two books." Anything to use the name and personalize the transaction. Almost always, the person would
look startled, but pleased. And on the way to the door I knew
she was thinking, "How does he know my name already?"
And as the patron walked away I would study everything
about her and try to associate her appearance and her name in
my memory (which has never been very good).

By the end of the first month I knew most of the regulars.
And it was my pleasure to greet them by name as they ap-
proached the desk. Every patron was an individual, with the
same need for attention and appreciation that I had. I like to
think that my efforts to meet this need made their visits to the
library more pleasurable for them. I know for a certainty that
they made the branch library experience more pleasing for
me.

I only hope that this little story reaches someone who feels
bored or frustrated in his or her job, if only to remind them
that their job is what they make it and it is for them to decide
how they will react to it. Frustration can be overcome in a
great many cases. One must always try and avoid letting others determine one's degree of satisfaction in his or her job,
marriage, or whatever else. (4/1986)

.   .   .   .   .

THAT EXTRA SERVICE: We always have an eye
out for that extra little special service that makes one establishment stand out over many others of the same general
type. One can see this "delightful difference" in individual
banks, libraries, stores, and wherever else people work, since
this difference is always created by people . . . people who
truly care about other people and have discovered the great
pleasure of serving them, and going that "extra mile" in doing so.

I encountered my latest place with a difference last summer when I hiked into Sunrise Camp, one of the six high Sierra camps in Yosemite Park. My backpacking partner and I were greeted with a free cup of lemonade. No big deal of course, but most welcome to us who had just climbed 3,000 feet up the mountain from Merced Lake Camp.

None of the other camps had offered us anything like that, so that was the first "difference." The second one appeared at the evening campfire when a member of the staff (all college students) passed around a big bowl full of popcorn. Maybe, again, not a big deal, but none of the other camp staffs were offering anything like this.

The third difference was perhaps the nicest and most surprising one of all. All the camps this year were offering omelets every morning for breakfast instead of scrambled eggs. When we learned the night before that we were again going to have an omelet in the morning I remarked that I was sorry about this as I didn't eat anything with cheese in it. The young lady at the desk heard the conversation and didn't forget it. When breakfast was served the next morning I was presented with a plateful of scrambled eggs—the only one in the dining hall. Naturally, I was most appreciative, and this column is a written expression of my feeling about a group of young people who—like the Avis people—seem to try harder.

All these Yosemite high-country camps are staffed with the finest young people . . . attractive, congenial, helpful, and hardworking. We library employers could learn a lot from Mr. Nick Fiori, the man long in charge of this activity who carefully selects all the camp personnel and does a tremendous job of it. He doesn't hire anybody that comes along, as some librarians do. He wants young people who will work hard and enjoy the work, but perhaps more important, will be a delight to the people who visit and stay in the camps, and to their fellow student-workers. It is most important that the staff like each other and work together well, and all the groups seem to do this. The camps are so isolated, the work so hard, and the nights so cold, that I don't believe many people could enjoy such a summer of work if they didn't have really congenial people to work and socialize with.

PEOPLE WHO WORK WITH PEOPLE they like are generally happy employees who work harder, give the public better service, and are more loyal to the organization than they might be otherwise. When I was in personnel work I felt it was important to assign employees to work with others with whom they might be expected to be congenial. This wasn't always possible, but it seemed to be a factor definitely worth considering. Hence when I got back into library management I tried as much as possible to get people working together who would enjoy each other's company. Actually, it more often took the form of trying to see that individuals were not scheduled to work with people whom they had nothing in common with or didn't seem to like. Working in a small branch or on a bookmobile can be very pleasing if you really like your fellow worker(s); but if you don't particularly care for them because their personalities or interests are so different from yours, it's quite a different scene.

To conclude this whole matter, we might all ask ourselves what is the "extra little special service" that makes our library, or our particular department, stand out in comparison with other libraries, or departments, of the same general size or type? What are the "delightful differences" that we can cite that make us—at least in our opinion—a bit more outstanding than our opinion—a bit more outstanding than the others? It may be something to make our library brighter or more inviting, or something that enables us to give more or better service, or anything else that the public particularly likes about our establishment. If you can think of nothing special or "different" about your library, you are lacking something quite important and denying yourself and your staff—as well as your public—the pleasure of being, or offering, something special and knowing that you are different to such an extent.

Libraries have so many different materials and characteristics and features, and such unlimited opportunities for service, that every library should be different in some way. I'm more amazed to see how alike many libraries are than how different they are, though libraries are far less alike than they were 20 or 30 years ago. With more and more new ideas, and more change each year, our libraries have a much more distinctive and individual look and are in different stages of automation, etc. But it is still hard to find in many libraries any sign of that extra service, that "delightful difference" that we have been talking. (12/1982)

■   ■   ■   ■   ■

WHAT'S THE DIFFERENCE? The Baltimore County Library people were impressed with the service and successful record of Giant Food Stores and decided to do a little research. They discovered that the difference was the "friendly difference." Currently Baltimore staff are putting together a videotape and kit to teach employees how to cultivate this "friendly difference." The Salt Lake County Library people were so impressed that Yvonne Clement sat down at her typewriter and worked up a presentation for Salt Lake County employees.

It would be interesting to hear sometimes whether such presentations, videotapes and kits proved effective in building this "friendly difference." I would guess that the staff of these two libraries are more outgoing than most, to start with, but doubtless they could be reminded to be more friendly with the patrons so that more of them would actually be getting a smile and hearing their name spoken at the front desk, or wherever else they encounter the staff. These are the two things that I've always believed every patron had a right to receive in the library. We can't teach real caring and warmth, but everyone ought to be able to learn to smile and use the patron's name in meeting him or her at the desk.

We recall the bank that posted this sign behind the teller's row: "If you don't get a smile and hear your name from our teller, the bank will pay you a quarter." The bank was required to pay out very little money. I wanted to put a similar sign behind our library loan desk, raising the penalty to $1.00, which I told the Board I would pay out of my own pocket—as I was sure that I would rarely be called upon to pay for such a lapse—but somehow the sign never got up.

I trust all administrators realize that they are the ones who set the tone in the organization, and if the staff sees that they are friendly and outgoing with them as well as with the public, they will have the right example for cultivating this "friendly difference" with the public. I once worked for a short time in a library where the director was never known to have smiled at anyone. Showing a tape on being friendly to the public wouldn't have done much good in that library. I can remember only two really happy-dispositioned people on that staff and they both worked in the office where the public never saw them. The director wasn't able to, or didn't care to, provide the best people to meet the public, but he was smart enough to pick two lovely young ladies to work just outside his office.

SO, DO WHATEVER YOU CAN—starting with yourself—to help build this "friendly difference." The behavior of the people on your staff who actually meet the public is so all important to you and your library that any effort in this direction is worthwhile. Which reminds me of something I read the other day in one of Dr. Robert Schuller's printed sermons. I believe it has meaning for any service operation, so let me quote it to you here:

Just the other day I was talking to a friend of mine who is running a very large retail operation. But business wasn't going too well. "I don't know what's wrong," he said. "Do you know? You come in here quite a bit." I paused for a moment and then I said, "Frank, do you want me to be honest or kind?" "Be honest," he said. "Well, to be honest," I began, "it seems you hire the worst people for the most important jobs."

"What do you mean?" he demanded. "My vice presidents, controller and sales manager are the very best, most qualified people." "I'm sure that's true," I replied. "But they aren't the most important people in your operation. The most important people are the clerks who talk to your customers. Often I get the impression they simply don't care about the business or the customers.

"Let me put it another way," I continued. "You have a very lovely, very expensive car. You have sleek designing, the best leather seats, the most beautiful paint job, an expensive stereo unit, power brakes, power steering and really good mileage. But even with all those assets, if you have a bad spark plug, you'll not be going anywhere. The people in your organization who greet the public are your spark plugs. And yet you hire the most inefficient people for the most important jobs."

AND SINCE I'M QUOTING FROM that particular source, here's a second quotation that might have meaning for librarians worried about their declining budget:

"No church has a money problem, no business has a money problem, no individual has a money problem; it's always an 'idea problem.' If you've got a money problem, you just don't have the ideas that attract money to you. Money flows to ideas that have integrity, human-need filling service and character."

●   ●   ●   ●   ●

I ABHOR WASTE, CORRUPTION, AND bureaucrats who have no interest in saving the taxpayers' money. We like to think that such people are confined to other areas and certainly would never be found operating in a *library*. Well, I'm sorry to say, that just isn't so. For one saddening instance, there is the outrageous case of Frank J. Keliher, a former employee of our own Library of Congress, as reported on p. 211 of James Davidson's important, but most upsetting, new book. *The Squeeze* (Summit Books). Keliher had read the Federal Employee's Code of Ethics, which stated that his duty as a civil servant was to find and employ more efficient ways of doing government's work, and he took his duties to heart.

> "He wrote a memo suggesting that one of the lengthy forms used in the Copyright Office duplicated other forms and could **be** scrapped. On another trip to the suggestion box, he demonstrated the obvious—that money could be saved if employees refrained from destroying rubber bands and paper clips after using them just once. Keliher also designed a more efficient way for the Library of Congress to collect and distribute its mail. For his pains he was banned from the mail room. Undaunted, he composed another memo pointing out an additional means of reducing waste. This time, his superiors ordered him to report to the staff psychiatrist, who soon determined that Keliher had written too many memos and was unfit for service. Keliher, who by this time had become disgusted, concluded that the verdict must be right. He quit his job to find employment someplace where the desire to save money was not considered madness."

We hope everyone reads the Davidson book, despite our strong sense of disgust and shame over this report which sounds like some evil happening from the other side of the Iron Curtain, rather than an action of our respected L of C. But librarians are human beings, too, and most people behave badly when they feel someone is questioning their efficiency or threatening to expose their inefficiency. On my first library job I soon became aware that the average elapsed time between ordering a book and receiving it in our department was two months. I mentioned this to my department head and got her permission to visit the Order Department to check on a list of some 25 new titles. I got a cool reception and gathered that the people there truly didn't like anyone from out front coming back to check on their performance. I didn't know any better at the time, and perhaps my department head didn't either. If she had, I don't believe she would have sent her newest lamb, fresh out of library school, back among those wolves who were bound to resent the intrusion.

YOU HAVE TO SET THE STAGE for such encounters. The person in authority must always let everyone who might be involved know in advance about anything new or unusual that is about to happen. That is one of the most important rules of supervision. Failure to observe this rule causes as much unhappiness and trouble in organizations as anything else I can think of. We all get upset when we hear and read and see things in our work place that we don't know the meaning of. We wonder why this is happening, what it means, and how it will affect us. Change is hard enough for most people to handle, without opening the door also to uncertainty and fear.

If my first boss had come with me to the Order Department and introduced me to the people there with some explanation of what she wished me to do there—or even called the Order Librarian on the phone to see if it would be agreeable and convenient for them to have me visit them, I'm sure that I would have fared much better.

A much better example of what I mean by preparing the way for one's staff members is what I encountered when I went to work years ago for a big company in Cleveland. My first week there, my boss—the head of the Advertising and Public Relations Department—told me he wanted me to make a study of the department's space requirements. But he knew better than to send me out, unannounced, to interview the various members of his group. He knew that any outside surveyor would have a pretty rough time of it, trying to find out from his assorted staff what they did, and how and why, without strong backing from him. There would doubtless have been more opposition and resentment than cooperation, and he would have had to spend a lot of his time in the end straightening everything out. But this dynamic administrator simply called all ten of us into his office, told us that this space study was something that was long needed and that he was particularly interested in, then introduced me and told the group why he had picked me to undertake the study, and, finally, made it unmistakably clear that this project had top priority, that he expected everyone to give me all the time and information that I requested, and that anyone who didn't give me 100 percent cooperation was going to catch hell from him. Actually, he used stronger language than that, and everyone had such great respect for the boss that they wouldn't have even considered giving him less than he asked for—in this or any other matter. They were completely helpful and supportive and made my assignment so much easier and more pleasant that it might otherwise have been (9/1980)

.   .   .   .   .

IT'S NOT WHAT YOU HAVE, but what you do with what you have, that makes the difference. Give two librarians comparable libraries in comparable communities and within two years one library operation will have progressed ahead of the other to an appreciable degree. Put one person in charge of a particular department and everything goes on just like it has been for the past thirty years. Give the same department to another person and marvel at the new life and growth that is imparted to this service. People are so different in the amount of interest and energy and imagination that they put into a given assignment. Which makes it so important to have the right kind of people on your staff to fit the various job responsibilities. Many times administrators have good ideas they would like to implement but must pass them by for lack of someone on their staff who can do them justice.

I'm constantly reminded of this. Today's reminder comes in the form of a letter from Lebby Lamb, the Business Librarian of the Greensboro Public Library (N.C.) which has been using our newsletter for business people. They initially ordered 1000 copies of each issue but have been using 1500 copies the last six years. She writes:

"Business Information has proven to be a valuable public relations tool for us. I have used mailing lists from the Better Business Bureau (membership) and the Chamber of Commerce (membership) to pass along copies; right now I am hoping to use the Merchant Association list to capitalize on a drive to increase use and get more businesses locating downtown . . . Several large firms (Southern Bell and the like) get copies to give new employees and those undergoing any training programs. Libraries in the five colleges here receive copies as do members of the various Business Departments, etc. Keep up the good work!"

IN OTHER WORDS, whenever you add any kind of tool to your library or business you can't just put it on a shelf and let it take care of itself. It must be put to use and promoted constantly if one is to get full value from it. The same thing goes for the programs that are scheduled in library auditoriums. I read about so many interesting programs that are well promoted, which makes me think of some of the lectures and film showings that we didn't give our best shot and that consequently didn't draw a sizable audience. To get back to

Business Information From Your Public Library, I believe most of its users do a good job with it. At least, over 95 percent of them renew their orders for it each year, and seem to feel that a library publication mailed directly to the business and civic leaders of their community presenting a new and vital image of a public service that has something to offer them and wants to be of service to them, can do far more in the way of building the image, the use and the support of the library than spending the same amount of money on a relatively few additional books that will be little noticed among the many hundreds purchased during the year. (9/1981)

■   ■   ■   ■   ■

ROMANCE IN THE LIBRARY: For 19 years we have been looking for and writing about things in a library (ideas, events, services, methods, etc.) that are new and unusual, and I expect we always will. Hence we couldn't fail to spark to the announcement in the Tulsa Public Library's newsletter of six TCCL employees who got married within a week's time.

Now that is really unusual! It is a rare thing for Cupid to strike three library couples on the same staff in a dozen years, and here we see it happening in Tulsa in the course of one week. Dennis Oliphant met Colleen Osborne at the Staff Association's 1983 Wine and Cheese party; Keith Jemison heard Beverly Durant sing at the SA's 1980 Christmas Program; and Dannie Powell and Jim Schultz were brought together three years ago by their interest in motorcycles.

Many times over the years I have heard someone say that library work was the worst possible career for a young woman as she would never have any contact with men. I would always take issue with the speaker, conceding that the librarian might not have any men on the staff to work with but pointing out the number of male library visitors that she would probably meet.

I have worked in business offices where there was one woman and six to ten men. In all three cases the young woman, a secretary, worked with more men than you will find in the great majority of our libraries, but most of the men were married and few outsiders came to these offices. It seemed to me to be better to work in an environment where one might not be working with members of the opposite sex but might possibly encounter a sizable number of them in the course of a year's time, if that was something important to them. And where can young people meet in more agreeable surroundings, particularly for the shy person who doesn't need an introduction or excuse to talk to a desk attendant. I have lost some wonderful young staff members to men who found them in the library. (1/1985)

■　　　■　　　■　　　■　　　■

RESPONSIBILITY: "How do you feel about the amount of responsibility your job entails?" This was one of many questions asked by Elizabeth Bourne, of the Cranston Public Library, in her "Survey of Professional Public Librarians in Rhode Island" (reported on in the R.I.L.A. Bulletin for September). 74 percent of the librarians didn't want any more responsibility. Having been in personnel work in industry, this response didn't really surprise me, but it did interest me as I recall getting the same percentage response when I asked the directors of the 210 largest public libraries in the country if they would like to have a bigger job. I confess I was surprised to learn that three-fourths of them had no interest in moving to a larger library or taking on any more responsibility than they had. A number of them remarked that they had no desire to assume the responsibility that was theirs, but it had been thrust upon them . . .

"Does your job fulfill your needs for status within the library and/or in society at large?" 82 percent of these Rhode Island librarians are content with the degree of status they presently perceive.

Those surveyed felt that the most important job factors are responsibility, recognition of their efforts, their work itself and library policies. They felt the least important factors are job status, opportunities for advancement, and salary. (11/1979)

■   ■   ■   ■   ■

ADMINISTRATIVE OFFICERS: Looking through the latest Annual Report of the Metropolitan Library System in Oklahoma City, my attention was caught by the following list of the Library's Administrative Officers:

Lee B. Brawner, Executive Director

Duane H. Meyers, Associate Director for Management Services

Elsie L. Bell, Chief of Main Library

Nancy L. Fierstien, Public Information Officer

Walter L. Gray, Jr., Program Director of Community Workshop

Jo Ellen Herstand, Materials Coordinator

Joan Jester, Business Manager

Paul Little, Chief of Extension Services

Fred Morris, Supt. of Bldgs. and Grounds

Richard Rea, Personnel Officer

Jimmy C. Welch, Systems Planner/Programmer

What a fine array of library officials I thought, and how I would have enjoyed having the company and support of such a group when I was library director in the '50s of another Southern city of comparable size. Instead of 11 administrative officers, our library had just 1—and that was the library director. He was the head of the main library, and all the branches as well. He neither had an associate or assistant or deputy director, nor any thought or desire to have one. The library had never had one, there was never any money for one, and there really didn't seem to be any need for one.

The director was the library's public information officer, business manager, planning officer, head of the main library and the three branches, chief of extension services (which included the three bookmobiles and the three self-service "booketerias" in supermarkets), the person who selected all the new staff members and promoted and gave salary raises to the older ones as such action seemed desirable, and the library's superintendent of buildings and grounds. There was no Community Workshop and nobody then had ever heard of a "Materials Coordinator" or a "Programmer," or I'm sure the same person would have handled those responsibilities as well.

MUCH THE SAME THING was true of most of the medium-sized public libraries in those days. Clarence Paine was the Chief Librarian in Oklahoma City at that time and if he had the help of any of these other administrative officers we never heard of it. In the four cities I served as Library Director we had a total of just one other "Administrative Officer."

I mention this simply to show how libraries have grown and changed in recent years. Library budgets in these cities are 10–15 times what they were in the 1950s. The library that Lee Brawner heads in Oklahoma City-County in 1982 is a far bigger operation than Clarence Paine had in 1952. He needs a strong administrative group to help manage this larger library and with a budget of over $6.5 million dollars he can afford to create any administrative posts and hire any people he feels he needs.

While I greatly enjoyed the 29 years I was the only administrative officer in the library, and hence could involve myself with every phase of the operation, I am a bit envious of any library director today who has ten or more Administrative Officers to work with. How wonderful just to have all these people to plan with, to talk to, to share one's ideas and enthusiasm with, to delegate work to, to learn from, and—not least of all—to go to lunch with. For most of my administrative career I was the only male librarian on the staff. It can occasionally get a bit lonely, particularly around lunchtime. (12/1983)

■   ■   ■   ■   ■

BELONGING TO UNIONS: Throughout most of my 30 years as a public library director I hardly ever thought of employee unions, except to give thanks for that fact that we didn't have one to bother with. Whether or not they are a net plus factor for the employees, unions have generally been a big "drag" for administrators. They are time-consuming, restrictive, and usually negative in their effect on staff morale and the library spirit that a new director is trying to build.

My only contact with a union was an indirect one, late in my fourth library directorship. I never saw or spoke to any union representative but I was saddened by what happened to my staff when the local city employees union—the old "staff association" that most of the library regulars had joined years earlier—called a strike for more pay and benefits. Half or more of our library employees answered the call to the picket lines and the others stayed on the job, enabling us to keep both buildings open on their regular schedule.

We had a wonderful staff, with everyone seeming to like everyone else, so that the director had no problems as far as the staff was concerned. But then, all of a sudden, half the staff were outside the library, trying to get through another cold, boring day of picketing, while the other half were in the warm, comfortable library keeping the service going and contributing thereby to the prolonging of the unhappy situation. Those who were on strike came to resent those who weren't, and the latter felt this new animosity and felt more and more separated from their erstwhile friends. Each person felt she belonged to one group or the other, and the two groups were separate if not opposed. Some doubted that the two groups would ever be close again when the strike was over. It takes a long time to completely recover from such an experience.

In my time, unions were a phenomenon that was pretty well limited to the large libraries. And, from an administrator's standpoint, I'm happy to note in Carl Sandstedt's 1985 Salary Survey of public libraries in the West-North-Central States, that they are still fairly limited to the libraries with budgets over $1 million. Despite my experience with that citywide strike, I have no objection to labor unions, providing they are voluntary and one doesn't have to pay union dues to get a job. However, I would still prefer to operate a library without them, and my survey of public library directors showed that most of them feel the same way.

But to get back to the Salary Survey, it includes a column about the library's union affiliation. In the 26 libraries with budgets over $1 million, I count 12 with no union, 7 with the AFSCME union (including 1 with the Teamsters as well), 1 with the Service Workers Union, 2 with the Communications Workers union, 2 with local unions, and 2 with "various" unions. Fifty-four percent of these large libraries thus have some kind of union.

The second group of city, county and regional libraries totals 31 having budgets between $340,000 and $1,000,000. I count 27 with no union affiliation, 1 with the Communications Workers Union, and 1 with a local union. That makes only 13 percent of this group of libraries with some type of union for their employees.

The third group of these libraries comprises 51 with budgets of $100,000 to $340,000. Five of them (just under 10 percent of the group) report having the AFSCME union, and the other 46 libraries indicate no union.

In short, the situation regarding union membership in public libraries hasn't changed. Unions are still largely limited to the large cities, which is a good thing as these libraries, and their cities, have the money and the personnel specialists to deal with the problem. (11/1986)

■   ■   ■   ■   ■

MORE MALE LIBRARIANS: A recent study of professional and supervisory employees had an interesting tabulation of the number of men and women employed in two dozen different fields. We were somewhat surprised to read that there are now approximately 100,000 female librarians and 22,000 male librarians. The percentage of men in librarianship has apparently increased 50 percent from the last time I happened to see such a tabulation—from 12 percent to 18 percent. I am glad to see that. For years we heard convention speakers say that we should all try and recruit more men into library work, if only to raise the level of library salaries. But the percentage of men never seemed to rise above 12 percent.

It's always been a particularly good field for men, especially for those interested in administrative work. One can generally become head of a library system at an earlier age than he could become head of a school system or any other public service, to say nothing of the private sector. Librarians in their thirties are found at the head of a sizable number/percentage of libraries serving populations over 50,000. In most other professional fields one would have to wait another ten years to reach the same percentage figure.

Men have always been favored for the top jobs in our

larger cities and counties, though there are more and more exceptions to this old rule. And since populations, and library budgets, continue to grow, the number of library boards looking for a man to fill their vacant directorship is perhaps more likely to increase than decrease. The recent study of the turnover of head librarians in Illinois public libraries seems to support this view. For the most part, females succeeded female head librarians and males followed males, but because only one male was replaced by a female, while four male librarians succeeded female heads, there was a net gain among the 557 libraries of three male librarians between 1981/82 and 1982/83.

Everyone should certainly know by now that there is no relationship between the sex of an administrator and his or her effectiveness on the job. And with so many of the recent female appointees in our larger cities making progress well beyond the limits of their male predecessors, one might have expected to see some movement toward a greater balance in all library administrative appointments. (11/1986)

．　　　．　　　．　　　．　　　．

KNOW ANY GOOD WORDS? Librarians and school people are at a disadvantage in that they can't cite any particular thing that they do in their job that is clearly beyond the understanding of the great majority of college-trained people who are untrained in their field. I first felt this disadvantage years ago when my brother—a Nobel laureate in physics—asked me to tell about some of the advanced training I'd taken for my doctorate in Library Science. I couldn't come up with a single professional concept, operating method, or special idea or technique of any kind that he didn't immediately understand. To my frustration, I couldn't think of a single word or term peculiar to my profession that he lacked a proper meaning for. I never did tell him anything that sounded difficult or complex or mysterious. I came away wondering what it really was that I knew or was capable of doing that suggested that I might make a better library administrator than my brother. At the same time, I was well aware that I couldn't understand the first thing about *his* work. While he could read along with me on any library article, I couldn't comprehend a single sentence of any physics article I've ever seen. Too many thousands of words and ideas that will always be strange to the outsider. (7/1980)

■   ■   ■   ■   ■

CHAPTER X

The Non-professionals

PROFESSIONAL VS. CLERICAL WORK: We once heard a librarian lament the fact that library-school graduates had to do an appreciable amount of clerical work on the job. Of course, this has always been so and doubtless always will be. But this speaker might feel better about the situation if she knew that Booz, Allen & Hamilton recently did a study that showed that professionals spend as much as *one quarter* of their time doing clerical work: running the copying machine, answering the phone, opening mail, and poking in the files. That's unproductive labor that should be left to the non-professional staff as much as possible. When the professional worker reduces his or her "labor input," his output will grow accordingly.

If Booz, Allen & Hamilton were to make a separate study of library professionals I'm sure they would find that most of them spend more than a quarter of their time doing work of a clerical nature. They may spend no more time than other professionals on the kind of labor cited in the BA&H study—copying material, answering the phone, opening mail, and poking in the files—but they doubtless spend more time on duties that a non-professional could easily be trained to do. It's primarily a matter of the nature of the library operation. Doctors, lawyers, engineers & Co. have the great advantage of knowing and doing a great many things that most people realize they could never do without a great deal of the same kind of training. It is generally accepted that a non-professional couldn't quickly be trained to perform a surgical operation or design a safe bridge. Librarians and school people can easily increase the proportion of their time that is spent on professional work, by delegating more and more of their non-professional duties to clerical employees, volunteer workers, and various technicians and aides. (7/1980)

■ ■ ■ ■ ■

IN REGARD TO SUNDAY HOURS: "I cannot help but second Cynthia Dee's opinion that 'how could we ask a clerk to accept supervisorial responsibilities or to make managerial decisions,' writes Frank Hemphill, City Librarian in Portage, Mich. "In this day and age I cannot see how even you could operate an 18,000 square foot library with one nonprofessional on duty. The physical size of a library alone requires more familiarity than a clerical, substitute, or volunteer could master in the time allocated.

"If the problems encountered in this library during a 65-hour library week correlate in any manner with use, then how many more problems will arise on a Sunday when per-hour use will be higher than any other time during the week. Staff needs to know how to turn off the fire alarm, activate the security system, handle the verbally abusive phone call from the patron who owes 5 cents, and all the other possibilities for problems which can arise. At a minimum, Sunday service requires an employee who is familiar with the procedures and policies of the library and can safely operate the building. The liability aspects of operating on Sunday with less than experienced employees frightens the dickens out of me. Besides the above, the institution pays for that very elusive quality, good judgment, a factor upon which the individual ultimately responsible (the administrator) must rely on choosing staff.

"I do agree that a library should have Sunday hours if at all possible. If I could have one full-time staff member (prof.) on duty and fill out the other service areas with good subs—prof. and clerical—this library would be open, given two books per capita."

The above paragraphs are well stated and require no editorial comment. However, I'm tempted to say a few words about the feeling that so many librarians have, in common with the great majority of teachers and other professionals, that the difference between professionals and their nonprofessional colleagues is vast and all encompassing. The professional employee is credited with good judgment, common sense, interest in his or her job, devotion to the library, professional integrity, hard work, intelligence, and much more besides. Many people seem to think they can handle anything in a library because they are librarians, while a "clerical" can't be counted upon to handle anything unusual or difficult because they are not professionals.

There's a lot of talk these days about people being racists, or sexists . . . perhaps we should add a word to represent the majority of us who discriminate in our thinking against classes of workers who fall below us in the scale of employment because they haven't had the training we have had. What's a good word . . . "professionalist?" That's not to say such thinkers are to be criticized . . . but only that we should always be careful to give other classes of workers the full credit due them.

I have great respect for professional training. I wouldn't

have suffered through three or four years of it if I didn't set a pretty high value on it. But I try to be realistic and not give it more credit than it rightfully deserves. I don't think it changed my basic qualities and aptitudes, nor do I think it added in any way to whatever amount of creativity, common sense, and administrative capacity that I had before. Likewise, when I was a library school instructor I never had the feeling that I was changing the personalities or the potential of my students. By the end of the first week I knew which ones were blessed with curiosity, imagination, animation, good sense, and a willingness to work—in short, the people I'd like to hire myself—and that's the way they rated at the end of the course, in the great majority of cases.

Frank Hemphill's letter seems at first reading to suggest that only a professional librarian could operate the library alone, but closer attention convinces me that he is thinking more of experience than professional training.

For instance, he starts by saying, "The physical size of a library alone requires more familiarity than a clerical, substitute, or volunteer could master in the time allocated." The last four words suggest an experience requirement, though rightfully one that should be looked for from professionals as well.

In the next paragraph he wants staff that know how to turn off the fire alarm, activate the security system, handle the abusive phone calls and other problems . . . but it doesn't take professional training to equip one for such tasks. Just that amount of experience and good judgment that he seems to imply. He does call for a "professional," but that, in our smaller libraries, doesn't always signify library school training.

But that's enough treading on thin ice for me today. I know I should stay away from this topic entirely, but I recall too many wonderful library staff members—both professional and clerical employees—who had more than their share of imagination, enthusiasm, common sense, dedication, and the other positive virtues . . . everything, in fact, but a year of library school training. There are thousands of such individuals working in our libraries. We mustn't ever let their lack of professional training—which grows less and less important with every additional year of experience they have in the library—blind us to all they have to offer and are capable of doing if we are smart enough to give them the opportunity.

Every library employee deserves to be considered as an individual human being, not just a member of a group or class who must not be thought of in connection with any assignment above that level. Take another look at each one separately and try to discover what he or she is capable of and would like to do. Never forget that staff development is one of the greatest responsibilities of any administrator. It is generally the one most neglected. Let's hope not in *your* library! (4/1984)

■　　　■　　　■　　　■　　　■

CLERICAL-PROFESSIONAL DEBATE: "Bravo! for your short exposition concerning the clerical-professional debate that gnaws at the innards of so many library directors and other professionals," writes Phil Hearne, director of the East Shore Area branch of the Dauphin County Library System (Harrisburg, Pa.).

"I have yet to find an enthusiastic, dedicated, experienced, non-degreed staff member who could not, with the proper guidance, perform most professional tasks.

"After only seven years in this line of work I believe that the MLS is only a ticket to on the job training which prepares most librarians to move into management and administration positions.

"At East Shore I must use clerical staff to perform some

professional duties because the branch runs on a 62 hour week, circulates 250,000 books a year, has 14,000 square feet of public space, and only eight (count them, eight) FTEs, pros included.

"There is no choice, but it is also good management to involve the staff in professional affairs. We need their input and ideas that come from a different frame of reference. I know what some readers of these statements will say: that it takes too much time to manage in this style, that you won't be able to keep them down on the circ desk after they have seen life in the fast lane, that the cost is too high. Only one response to these arguments is necessary: as a manager you will be ignoring and losing valuable resources and potential from each staff member whom you inhibit.

"The knowledge that I allow one of my volunteers to weed the collection will probably elicit gasps, cries of horror, and guffaws, but she is competent, experienced, and from checks of the materials she has pulled, is probably a more ruthless weeder than I am. Of course, I review the materials behind her, but return only 5 to 10 percent of them to the shelf. She has saved me at least 80 percent of the time it takes to weed! The investment was well worth the effort.

"Clerks vs. pros—bah! Every one of us pseudo-pros started off learning the ropes like any clerk. Don't underestimate the intelligence and expertise sitting at your circ-desk dismally filing 3×5 book cards.

". . . and please, Mr. Alvarez, keep treading on that thin ice so that the library profession continues to re-evaluate itself and change for the better."

MOST WOULD AGREE: Mr. Hearne may hear from a few people in his area who disagree with him on this matter but I daresay that most library administrators would agree with him in his thinking about the MLS degree and the capability of experienced clerical people to master most professional tasks. I am sure that he would be both pleased and surprised to know the percentage of our administrators who are in agreement with him on these two points. (9/1984)

•   •   •   •   •

GIVE THEM MORE CREATIVE DUTIES: Our attention was caught by the following letter to the editor of "Main Entry"—the newsletter of the Salt Lake County Library System in Utah. It was written by Marsha Leclair-Marzolf, the Children's Coordinator, and makes a lot of sense. Most of us have been guilty at some time of assigning pretty boring jobs to young people who are obliged to contribute a certain number of hours of work to the library. Ms. Leclair-Marzolf writes:

"When I read the suggested tasks for boy scout volunteers in last month's *Main Entry* I had some misgivings with the suggested tasks, which included checking reserves, shelving popular paperback books, straightening bulletin board announcements, shelving JE and JP books, straightening shelves, stamping reminders and cleaning books. These are all routine and fairly boring jobs for active young people. True, they are necessary and important tasks that pages and clerks perform on a daily basis. However, pages and clerks also have other more interesting and challenging duties to intersperse with the routine ones.

"I am worried that a boy scout who only stamps reminders or shelves JE books will leave thinking library work is dull and unrewarding. Couldn't these routine projects be interspersed with more creative activities? I submit the following suggestions:

1. Reading books on a one-to-one basis to whatever children are in the library at the time.

2. Helping a librarian or a resource person with a program—passing out materials, helping smaller children cut out patterns, etc.

3. Putting on a puppet show. Scripts and puppets can be borrowed from my office. Scripts are also available in many library books. Children love puppets and any kind of homemade production will go over well.

4. Learning a craft from any of our multitudes of craft books and teaching it to younger children.

5. Helping to select records from Billboard.

6. Using a tape recorder and camera to interview patrons about the library or their favorite book and then putting it together as a simple slide-tape show.

7. Putting quotes from patrons about their favorite books on the bulletin board along with book jackets.

8. Creating their own bulletin board or display.

9. Laminating and preparing simple story hour material.

10. Distributing posters and other publicity to stores, malls, churches, community centers and schools.

11. Delivering books to the elderly or shut-ins.

12. Reading stories at the hospital.

All these ideas take minimal time or preparation on the part of the librarian—certainly no more time than explaining JE shelving patterns. If you describe the project choices, let the child choose the project. Then you can give an outline of the steps involved and turn the details over to the scout. The scout can use initiative and creativity to implement the project. If they don't carry through, you're no worse off than if they hadn't tried. I think that in most cases you'll be surprised at what they can accomplish. And, besides, they will have more fun than if they clean books for three hours and the scouts will have a better feeling about the library." (6/1982)

.   .   .   .   .

LIBRARY PAGES HONORED: A one-time award for pages, "the unsung heroes of the library," was presented this year at the Enoch Pratt Free Library in Baltimore as the result of a generous gift from Joseph Rice, former Superintendent of the Stacks and Shelving Department. A committee of main library supervisors narrowed the choice of possible recipients to four worthy members of the Stacks and Shelving staff—each of whom was awarded a savings bond.

This is the first we have heard of any special recognition of library pages—those essential and hard-working members of the staff who sometimes do get taken for granted. We hope to hear of similar awards already made or perhaps inspired by this report. Our library, which always has an outstanding group of pages, normally has a farewell party for each departing member . . . and honors each with a "Day" when all staff members wear a ribbon saying "Mary Thompson Day," or whatever the name is. Which, of course, calls for many explanations to curious patrons.

The only thing I have ever done for the pages myself, besides offering a lot of praise and appreciation, was to take eight of them to lunch at the country club a few years ago. I enjoyed it tremendously, until the moment when three of the young people driving the golf carts I had borrowed to give the group a tour of the course, had to stop suddenly, forgot what I told them about how to stop the carts, and so made abrupt turns to avoid hitting the cart ahead. I looked back to see bodies flying right and left. It was one of the worst moments in my life, but the young people acted as if it was one of the best in theirs. (1/1980)

■   ■   ■   ■   ■

CHAPTER XI

Volunteer Workers

LIBRARY VOLUNTEERS: The Volunteer Program has been one of the fastest growing and most important developments in public libraries in the past ten years. The idea of enlisting unpaid "volunteers" for service in the library was almost unheard of before 1975, but now almost all public libraries have one or more volunteers. Some have the help of over 100 such workers and a few others have branches that are entirely staffed with volunteers. It is indeed heartening to know that there are people out there that are both willing and able to help a library out when it can't afford to hire sufficient staff to do all its essential work or is trying to improve the quality of its service. (1/1985)

■   ■   ■   ■   ■

RECRUITING VOLUNTEERS: As we have said before, a library should do more than just ask for volunteers.

People need to know what the library has in mind for them, how much time would be involved, and whether they have the training or other qualifications that would be needed. The average individual isn't likely to think seriously about volunteering for any job until he or she has the answers to these questions.

You don't enlist volunteers at your church by simply putting out a call for volunteers. People have to be told what, when, and for how long. Thus, with your library, the best way to recruit volunteers is to cite the various jobs you need help with, and tell exactly what each job consists of and requires.

No library does a better job of going after the volunteer personnel it needs than the Passadene (CA) Public Library.

Every issue of the PPL newsletter describes about eight jobs for which the library needs volunteers. Here are two examples from the January 1985 issue:

"CENTRAL CHILDREN'S ROOM GAMES ASSISTANT: A volunteer having knowledge or ability to plan children's board games and familiarity with libraries is needed to sign out games for use in the library, instruct children in playing games and put games in order after use. This volunteer must be comfortable and enjoy working with children, and is needed for one or both sessions: Monday 3-5, Thursday 3-5.

"CLERICAL ASSISTANT/REFERENCE SECTION. The Reference Section needs someone to assist clerical staff with general duties: filing, processing new materials, etc. The volunteer should have a high school education and ability to alphabetize accurately, neat handwriting, reliability and ability to work independently on routine tasks. Typing is helpful but not essential and a commitment of 4 hours per week is required."

Most people reading those paragraphs would be apt to say, "That sounds like something that I ought to be able to do. I think I would enjoy that." You have given them a picture of the job and allowed them to see themselves performing in it. With no reason left to be uncertain or negative about this interesting opportunity, they may well volunteer their services. However, it is generally not enough to simply convince someone that he or she can and would enjoy becoming a library volunteer. Most of us are lazy and inclined to procrastinate, and it can be a long way between saying yes to an appeal in a library newsletter and actually visiting a library office to register for a volunteer's job.

Therefore, don't leave everything up to the unknown public who may read your library newsletter or see your appeal in the newspaper or on a library poster. Have these volunteer jobs in the back of your mind every time you talk with a library patron and when you see the kind of person you are looking for, bring up the matter and show them these job descriptions and see if you can't sell them on the idea of enlisting with you. (3/1985)

■　　　■　　　■　　　■　　　■

JOBS FOR VOLUNTEERS: The majority of libraries are using volunteer workers these days, and making good use of them. The Contra Costa County Library (CA) has employed 80 volunteers in the past year, and I believe it would be both interesting and helpful to many of our readers to see the following list of some of the jobs that their volunteers have assisted with:

Delivering and returning books for convalescent hospitals and shut-ins
Updating community resource files
Developing a local history file
Preparing analytics for plays, short stories, etc. for index files
Arranging floral displays

    Coordinating exhibits and displays
    Washing the bookmobile
    Developing and processing picture files
    Calling patrons who have overdue books
    Processing books for electronic security system
    Processing paperback books for circulation
    Cleaning book jackets
    Hosting open house and library tours
    Delivering flyers and publicity to community organizations
and schools
    Running projector for film programs
    Making name-tags for children attending story hours
    Watering plants
    Stuffing envelopes for mailings

That's an impressive list and should suggest some new assignments to other library administrators. Good volunteers can be found, but how much good they do for your library depends on how good you are in finding interesting and meaningful work for them to do. (12/1982)

      ■   ■   ■   ■   ■

VOLUNTEERS: The Iowa City Public Library has issued a nice 8-page publication, "Volunteers 1985," which mentions all the people who have contributed to the operation of the ICPL. We haven't seen anything quite like it, and it is something that would never have been possible anywhere half a dozen years ago.

It starts by listing the names of the 241 service volunteers who gave a total of 5,837 hours of work to the library last year. This represents the equivalent of 2.9 full-time employees. Over half of the total hours was spent helping to check in books to further a top priority of the Library—speeding up the re-shelving process.

A volunteer who accumulates 80 hours becomes eligible to buy books at the staff discount. At 100 hours, the volunteer is given a certificate of appreciation and a purchase coupon enabling the person to select an item for the Library's collection. When a volunteer achieves 500 hours of service, his or her name will be engraved on an Honor Roll in the Library Lobby.

Youth Services Department sponsors a volunteer program for young persons in sixth grade or under. In 1985 thirteen volunteers contributed 173 hours of service to the Children's Room. Their names are listed here.

The next section is about the Friends of the Library and their contribution to the Library. Listed are the 11 Board members and the 53 persons who contributed time or materials to Friends' projects in '85.

Then come information about, and names of the members of: The Library Board of Trustees, the Art Advisory Committee, the Iowa City Public Library Foundation, and, lastly, the members of the Centennial Endowment Committee, and the members of the Centennial Kickoff Committee, and subcommittees.

■   ■   ■   ■   ■

OVER 600 VOLUNTEERS: "Your thoughts regarding the importance of volunteers are *very* appropriate," writes William Schell, the director of the Martin Memorial Library in York, Pa. "In Pennsylvania . . . public libraries (like fire companies) are usually private associations and not public service (government) agencies.

"To double our circulation of items since 1981, the 14 libraries of our York County Library System have recruited over 600 volunteers who worked more than 43,000 hours in 1985.

"Thus we hope to have created enough 'positive feelings'

about public library service in York County to pass a special library tax referendum in May for operating support."

York County, Pa., may well be the No. 1 county in the U.S. for library volunteers. 600 volunteers is a tremendous number of enlisted helpers for any library system. And these people have got to be the hardest working group of volunteers that we have yet heard about. I might add that 43,000 hours is equivalent to the work of almost 21 full-time employees.

We feel very optimistic about the passage of that special library tax referendum in May. With 600 library volunteers, and all their families and friends, added to those of all the library staff and board members, along with the hundreds of devoted library users who are well known to the librarians in York County, the supporters of the referendum start off in great shape. They need only concentrate on seeing that everyone who would be inclined to vote for its passage actually goes and votes. With the hard work and support of all those wonderful Friends of the Library groups, how can the library cause fail?

Before leaving York County I would like to say that the Martin Memorial Library has the most effective bookmark for attracting volunteers that we have seen. It answers the question "WHAT WILL YOU DO?" by listing the following jobs:

> Help people find books and records
> Check books in and out
> Work on a computer
> Make phone calls
> Help to publicize the library
> Mend books
> Repair art prints
> Build a better card catalog
> Borrow books from other libraries
> Write book reviews

Arrange library displays
Put our books in order
Maintain the library scrapbook and there's so much more.
(5/1986)

■   ■   ■   ■   ■

VOLUNTEERS—THE TEENAGE VARIETY: The Anoka County Library (MN) uses teenage volunteers all summer long to help with the summer reading program. They are used primarily to help in recording the names of the books the children who are in the reading program read. Using volunteers, who sign up at the beginning of the summer for daily shifts, saves the children's librarians a great deal of time. Volunteers also frequently man the projectors at summer movie programs, alphabetize, do artwork and help in controlling and supervising large crowds. As a "thank you," the library puts on a picnic for the volunteers at summer's end. (12/1978)

■   ■   ■   ■   ■

JUNIOR LIBRARY VOLUNTEERS: "We've been so overwhelmed with the success of our Youth Services' Junior Library Volunteers summer program that I wanted you to know about it," writes Marilyn Shuman, the Public Information Officer of the Arlington Heights, Ill., Memorial Library.

"You can imagine the flurry of activity when 74 kids signed up, over a couple of days, and the coordinators of the program realized how many jobs they had to come up with. (They did very well . . . but these kids were not here to just sit around!)

"The postscript is that a JLV program is being offered in our fall program brochure—with a limited number of applicants accepted. They have all been great kids and helpful in many departments."

The youngsters, all of junior high school age, registered to volunteer two hours or more a week at the Library. The job of assigning work to all the young helpers, who work in teams of two or more, is immense. But the Library staff, as well as patrons, were quickly impressed with the value of having all the new helping hands around, and with the seriousness with which they performed their duties.

Some of the jobs they have done are: Helping with the Youth Services reading program for younger children, helping maintain audio-visual supplies, including scrubbing records and putting away filmstrips, dry-mounting and laminating, sorting book slips, stapling, labeling and helping mail the Library's monthly newsletter, and monitoring the Apple II computer while youngsters use it to play video games.

This is the kind of program that most public libraries can and should offer—at least for the summer months, and throughout the year if possible. It's really surprising that only a very few libraries have ever even thought of doing anything like this. We hope that this report from Chicago area will inspire others to attempt such a useful program. (11/1982)

.   .   .   .   .

CHAPTER **XII**

Shared Administrators

DIRECTING MORE THAN ONE LIBRARY: A number of city librarians are also directors of their country or regional library—which should make their job doubly interesting. Six or eight librarians have the pleasure of directing two completely separate library operations. An example would be Herbert Johnson who heads both the Oberlin College Library and the public library in Oberlin, Ohio. But the busiest person in this select group has been William R. (Bill) Gordon who, since 1966, has been the director of the Arrowhead Library System which includes seven northern Minnesota counties with a population of approx. 315,000. In 1974, when the directors of the Duluth and Virginia, Minnesota, municipal libraries retired, he was appointed city librarian for both jurisdictions in addition to administering the Arrowhead System, a position which required that he maintain two residences and work with numerous library boards and government officials. In the Arrowhead System, a staff of 185

provides service through 28 member libraries, six bookmobiles, and mail-a-book service to rural areas; in Duluth, 52
staff members provide service through four branches and one
bookmobile; and in Virginia, 13 staff members serve the community. Bill gave up all this to assume the position of director
of the big Prince George's County Memorial Library System
(Greenbelt, Md.) on April 18. He now has almost twice as
many staff members but only half as many residences, which
sounds like a good trade.

WE HAVE ALWAYS WANTED TO DIRECT more
than one library system at one time—if only to be completely
busy and to add to the interest and sense of accomplishment
afforded in one's work. After all, so many of the things that
an administrator does—book selection, professional reading,
conferences, etc.—can serve a number of libraries at the
same time, and if the second library is fairly small and not far
away, assuming responsibility for it would be not much more
difficult than adding another branch library. And it could
save the two jurisdictions some money . . . Such were my
thoughts when, some time ago, the adjoining city was looking
for a new city librarian. I lunched with its city manager and
asked him if he would be at all interested in having a highly
trained and experienced library administrator for half what
he was offering to pay. This person would provide all the
needed ideas, supervision and control . . . the only catch was
that he would not be on the premises all the time. He would
be in and out three times a week and the rest of the time
would be only a quick call and a 7-minute drive away. Many
librarians who have their offices outside the main library
aren't seen there that often. As to costs, I suggested he could
pay me three or four thousand dollars for my extra work, and
a like amount to my city fathers to compensate them for this
partial sharing of one of their department heads, and save the

rest of the Librarian's salary (perhaps $20,000). Seemed like an interesting idea to profit all parties, but it never got far enough for presentation to my city manager or city council. Would have been interesting to have their reaction to this unusual proposal. (10/1977)

■   ■   ■   ■   ■

SHARED ADMINISTRATOR: Shirley Apley is the shared administrative librarian for the Oklahoma cities of Bristow and Prague. As such, Apley will assist the local libraries in the administrative aspects of library service to their communities.

This innovative concept will allow each community library to maintain its local autonomy while benefiting from the support of a half-time administrator.

I have always considered this a great idea. In fact, as I mentioned once before, I once tried to arrange with the adjoining city of San Bruno to operate both their public library and the one I then directed in South San Francisco, only 3 miles away. The arrangement would have meant more work for me in the areas of planning, budgeting, personnel management, public relations, and working with a second city administration, but I am certain that there would have been time for all these extra duties. The work that took most of my time—e.g., book selection, professional reading, and meetings—could have been done for both libraries at the same time.

The library director in San Bruno could have taken over the So. S.F. Library just as well, when I left there. Perhaps if money for libraries ever gets real tight we will see some "shared administrators" in places a good bit larger than these two cities in Oklahoma. (12/1984)

■   ■   ■   ■   ■

ANOTHER SHARED ADMINISTRATOR: You may recall my telling you last month about two small Oklahoma libraries that are sharing the services of a single administrative librarian, and expressing my approval of the idea and predicting that some day we would see "shared administrators" in places a good bit larger than these cities in Oklahoma.

I had hardly gotten that editorial column off to the printers before I read—in the newsletter of the River Bend Library System (Ill.)—about the exact same type of shared administratorship in larger libraries that I had pictured in the December issue and had tried without success to effect for myself in San Mateo County.

The Boards of the Bloomfield Township (pop. served 46,861) and Baldwin (pop. served 35,410) Public Libraries have chosen a joint director, Stephen A. Kershner, who has been director of the Geauga County (Ohio) Public Library. The two libraries, although under separate boards and separate governmental jurisdictions (City of Birmingham and Bloomfield Township, Michigan), have traditionally worked together since the days when Baldwin library served the whole region. The libraries have a joint automation system and cooperate in many ways. (They are even listed next to each other in the Amer. Library Directory, which shows budgets of $767,844 and $916,322 for the two libraries).

We would like to congratulate Mr. Kershner and express the hope that his first year in his new two-library job is as pleasing and exciting as we would expect it to be. We are most envious. It is interesting to think of all the places where time and money can be saved by having one director instead of two to manage the two systems. That's half as many hours of administrators' time spent representing the two libraries at all kinds of meetings and workshops, half as many hours spent in book selection and professional reading at the top level, half as many hours deducted for trips to library conventions, vacations, etc.

And just as important, having a joint administrator should open the door for a number of other joint positions that would help both libraries. Perhaps neither library could justify or afford a separate personnel officer or public relations assistant; but when the work and the funds of the two libraries are combined there may be sufficient need to warrant the employment of such specialists and enough money to pay for them.

Let us hope that Mr. Kershner will let us know a year from now how everything worked out and what it meant for both him and the two libraries. What was the reaction of the two staffs, what did it mean for collection development, and for community relations, and what savings were realized, and so on. (1/1985)

. . . . .

DIRECTING FOUR LIBRARIES: "I am always amazed at the number of things that pop up in print as 'innovative' and 'creative' that we've been doing routinely here in Southern Maryland," writes Kitty Hurrey, the director of the Southern Maryland Regional Library Association. "For instance, in the December issue of LAD you talk about the 'Shared Administrator' in Oklahoma. The Southern Maryland Counties of Clavert, Charles and St. Mary's have shared a Director since 1959.

"The organization was formed for very practical reasons. At that time, each county library system in Maryland was required to hire a Professional Librarian to be eligible for State aid. These three counties were very rural and quite poor so with the help of the Division of Library Extension, they formed a cooperative association and hired 1 professional librarian to act as Director of all 3 county library systems. Twenty-five years later, despite huge growth, (the 3 systems now circulate over 1,000,000 items per year), the 3 Boards of Library Trustees have never found a reason to change the modus operandi—it works!"

It was nice to hear from Mrs. Hurrey. I believe I remarked some yeas ago on the fact that she headed four separate libraries listed in the *American Library Directory*—the So. Md. Reg. Lib. Assn. and the Charles Co., Calvert Co., and St. Mary's County libraries—and that I was most envious, being the director of only one library system. A number of librarians head two library organizations headquartered in the same building. A typical example would be John Jones who is the director of both the Kinston-Lenoir County Public Library, in Kinston, N.C., and the Neuse Regional Library. Another instance would be that of Art Goetz, the director of the Wicomico County Free Library, in Salisbury, Md., who also runs the East Shore Regional Library out of the same facility, serving 8 Shore counties. But Kitty Hurrey really stands out as a "Shared Administrator"; she is the head of distinct library organizations in three different locations.) (3/1985)

. . . . .

JOINT MANAGEMENT: We've run across 2 or 3 libraries in the American Library Directory that show two people as the Librarian. For example, the Librarian of the Marylhurst College Library in Marylhurst, Oregon, is "Paula Hamilton & Barbara O'Neill." Don't see why that wouldn't work out all right in some smaller libraries, but it certainly wouldn't be my preference.

There are probably 10 instances of a person serving as the

director of two separate and independent libraries. In some cases, the libraries are located in different communities, miles apart. More often, they are in the same city, as in the case of Patricia Ann Sacks who is the director of both the Cressman Library at Cedar Crest College and the John A. W. Haas Library at Muhlenberg College—with a combined staff of 26 people—in Allentown, Pa. I like this arrangement better than the one mentioned above. It offers possibilities for saving a good amount of money and for providing better management of the second library in each hookup.

Needless to say, there are many cases of one person serving as the director of both a municipal library and a county or regional library system, both generally headquartered in the same building. Both have separate staffs, budgets, etc. (12/1979)

■　　　■　　　■　　　■　　　■

HUSBAND & WIFE DIRECTORSHIPS: It is interesting to note the increase in the number of cases where two libraries in the same community are headed by husband & wife combinations. For example, one of the subscribers to the AD is the Gilson family of Lincoln, Illinois, where Preston is Librarian of the Lincoln College Library and Christine is director of the Lincoln Public Library.

To mention a few other cases, Lee Cage is director of the Nacagodoches Public Library and Alvin C. Cage is the director of the Stephen F. Austin State University Library, also in Nacogdoches, Texas. In Abilene, Texas, Joe W. Specht is the head librarian at McMurry College and Alice W. Specht runs the Bay County Library System. In all such cases I can't help wondering whether the couple married after they were in these positions or whether they were married before and

looked all around for a community that offered two top positions open at the same time. Either way, they are indeed fortunate to live and work in this situation. (12/1979)

■   ■   ■   ■   ■

CHAPTER XIII

Retirement

ETHEL CROCKET, California's very capable State Librarian, has announced her plans to retire next August. She has performed beautifully in what may be the most demanding library job in the land, and will indeed be hard to replace. This is a job that very few of us would want and even fewer would be able to fill satisfactorily.

It's refreshing, to me, to see someone make such a commitment ten months in advance. That's decision-making and goal-setting of the most difficult kind. It reinforces my own intention to resign from the directorship of the public library system that I have been with for over 13 years now. I am sure that I would enjoy "retirement" but I have put it off because I enjoy greatly every day at work and know I would miss the people I work with and everything and everyone associated with my library position. I know I'm luckier than most employees—to live within walking distance of my "work" (though that doesn't seem the right word to cover my pleasurable occupation), to be able to have my office windows open every day in the year, to lunch with fellow members and then spend an hour on the beautiful golf course next to the library three days a week throughout the year (which breaks up the day beautifully), to be able to select and see all the fascinating new adult books . . . But next July 1st I believe I will try experiencing this retirement life that so many people recommend so highly. (11/1979)

■   ■   ■   ■   ■

THE JOYS OF RETIREMENT: Lynda Lee writes from Lake Charles, La.: "As I struggle with preparation of next year's budget I'll think of you enjoying leisurely mornings and unstructured days for exploring any new interest that catches your fancy. These should be the rewards for years of service."

That's a good picture of this "retired" person except for the fact that I haven't had time yet to explore any new interest. I find I'm working about as many hours a day as before—but at a more leisurely pace and in more attractive surroundings. So far, I'm enjoying retirement (self-employment would be a better word) immensely, but I'm not sure I would be as crazy about it if I didn't have the *AD* to help fill my time so enjoyably. I do most of my writing in the backyard, with one or two golf-breaks in the park across the street—which the dog and I have all to ourselves during the day. I'm sure he thinks my retirement is the greatest thing ever.

I DON'T MISS THE LIBRARY as much as I thought I would. If I didn't pass it three or four times a week while visiting the country club next door, I might not even think about it. It is necessary for me to visit it once a week to scan some of the new periodicals, but I may stop by more infrequently after my successor comes aboard. (This was written a year ago, two months after my retirement). My predecessors in three other cities rarely came to the library after they retired and I don't want the new director to feel that I'm looking over his or her shoulder / or trying to maintain contact with some of the staff.

The hardest thing in visiting the library is keeping my hands to myself. I have to constantly remind myself that I am just a patron now, like everyone else, and have no right to go behind the desks, or pop into the offices, or take material home without its being properly charged out. I just got the first library card I've had in forty years.

The most difficult thing for me is to pass by the 12-foot long serpentine shelving that has always displayed our new books, fiction on one side and non-fiction on the other. There's room for 100 books on each side, displayed frontally, as all popular new books deserve to be, and as I started doing back in 1946. I've always taken on the care and constant replenishment of the new-book shelf as my one job outside the director's office, and it was always the library's No. 1 attraction. Now, with no director and an overworked staff, this special section is not getting the proper attention and most of the books are just shelved (spines out), rather than displayed, and many volumes have outstayed their proper time on these shelves. Many times I've wanted to take ten minutes to straighten the place up, but have refrained. Another thing, books are being left on the reading room tables long after their users have departed, so that it is difficult for the evening crowd to find a cleared off table to work on. I always took a few minutes before leaving the building at 6:15 to clear off any tables that the pages hadn't gotten around to. I don't believe a messy building of any kind is very inviting, but I've seen a number of libraries that don't appear to have anyone on the staff with the responsibility of maintaining a neat, attractive appearance. I've always felt that this was an important matter, and one essential to the building of the right library image, but I've just let things alone the past two months. I just mention these things to indicate what it is like to be newly retired.

INCIDENTALLY, Ms. Lee writes that, "Although we did not actually meet when you were in Lake Charles for L.L.A., I can say with complete honesty that I remember more of your speech than any of the countless others I have heard at such meetings. Never will I forget your admonition concerning the much greater difficulty getting rid of a staff member than a spouse. How true time has proven that."

Isn't it amazing what an individual will remember from a particular speech? I'm sure every speaker would like to know some time later what, if anything, his hearers recalled from his or her talk. Ninety-five percent probably couldn't recall a single thing said, and the remaining 5% would remember only one thing. This would most likely be an idea they felt they could use in their own work, or something the speaker said that expressed and reinforced their own feelings. The sad thing about public speaking is that most everything said is due to be quickly forgotten and the speaker rarely has any feedback to know what, if anything, registered with a portion of his or her audience and what ideas were ever implemented. The speaker generally can only hope that someone was helped in some way by the talk, or that someone at least found something interesting in it.

I CERTAINLY DO REMEMBER SAYING that it is easier getting rid of a staff member that you can't abide than a husband or wife that you can't live with—hence one should take extreme care in employing new people, whether full-time or part-time, professional or clerical. As a former personnel man I have always been amazed at the way most people will hire just about anybody who meets the written specifications for the job to be filled. It's as if they believed that one person was just as good as any other person and there was no reason to consider their interests, attitudes, disposition or other personal factors. Back in the days when librarians were in short supply, some library employers would write to a library school and say, "Send me a cataloger," or reference librarian, or whatever else they might be needing. Just anybody to fill a position and do a job.

I would never hire anyone sight unseen, and I would never take anyone that I wasn't enthusiastic about no matter how badly I needed to fill a position. I've often been urged to make an appointment by a department head who admitted that the person being interviewed wasn't just what they wanted but "we need somebody right away." It's my belief that any organization can get along without a particular replacement for any reasonable length of time, and that it is far better to hold off and wait for the right person than be stampeded into hiring someone that lacks the capacity to be a real contributing member of the staff. Such a person is likely to be a problem, and a source of regret for you for a very long time. For years you will be waiting for this person to leave, but of course it's the ones you want to see leave who outlast you on the job. When I asked the directors of the 200 largest public libraries in the land what percentage of their staff they would like to get rid of if they could, the average response was 10 percent.

ANY EMPLOYER WHO WOULD LIKE to be rid of 10% of his staff—but knows he is stuck with them (as they are stuck with him, or her)—is bearing a real unhappiness load. If they are pleasant enough but just not able to perform above a minimum level, the employer will be able to live with them fairly well. But if they are disloyal or unpleasant and troublesome, the boss will probably have to learn to suffer their presence and not let the situation rob him or her of all the pleasure that the job should provide.

People are the most important element in any job situation. They are the most interesting, the most productive, the most responsive and pleasant, and have the greatest capacity for change and improvement. When considering a move to a new directorship, the wise individual looks first and longest at the staff he will be inheriting. One can always do something to improve the building or the book collection but if you take over a negative-minded, poor-dispositioned staff that has 10 or 15 years to go to retirement, you will likely get resistance and little support for every improvement you try to make. If you have good ideas and the support of a happy, positive-thinking staff, there is no limit to what you can accomplish and the joy that you will experience.

IN SHORT, WE WOULD ENCOURAGE every employer to be a lot more careful in his or her selection of personnel, since one's happiness is determined more by the people one works with and for than by anything else. I have talked over the years with many library directors who had some kind of library problem at the time that was cutting into their happiness. I believe that in almost every case it was "people trouble." One may not be satisfied with buildings, equipment, or library materials but I never knew anyone to become really unhappy or troubled over such matters. But every profession has a good percentage of people who have truly suffered at one time or another through something that another member of the organization said or did to them. Since supportive, contented, capable people are your best key to satisfaction and achievement in your job, employ only top people for every job—and you can generally find the kind you want, at the established rate of pay, if you try hard enough and wait long enough. When we needed a staff to work in the new South San Francisco Library I interviewed 225 people in one week, grading each one as I talked to her. I then hired all 20 of the A and A− people, and they all started to work the same day. All of them were attractive, pleasant, animated human beings, far better educated than their job specifications required, and they immediately liked each other. In fourteen years I never heard of the slightest unpleasantness from or about any of this group and they helped to make my job the "Easiest and most pleasant job" I ever had.

THAT WAS THE WAY the stories about my retirement were headed in the county newspapers. I regret the use of the word "Easiest" in the headline, as I don't want to undercut any of my colleagues who are still working, but that's calling it the way it was for me. For the first time, I had taken over a library with a brand new building and no particular problems. The job wasn't as challenging, and didn't afford the same opportunities for accomplishment with the joy etc.—but if you wanted pleasant relationships and peace of mind, you couldn't find a better location. I might add that in looking back over my various positions and those held by many of my colleagues I have come to the opinion that most library administrators—and probably school superintendents, too—should serve for four or five years and then move on. In all my positions I was able to make all the changes and improvements that seemed desirable, in the first years on the job. These were always extremely busy and interesting years, but by the third year there was less to do, and by the fifth year I seemed to be doing little more than keeping the operation running smoothly. Then it seemed a good time for somebody else to take over, bringing his or her own new ideas and point of view. When a job becomes somewhat routine and one feels that he or she has accomplished about all that can be done with it, then it is time for a change.

NOW—A YEAR AFTER WRITING THE ABOVE paragraphs—I'm still delighted with my change to being completely self-employed. Though I'm averaging 40 hours a week working on my three newsletters *(AD, Superintendent's Digest,* and *Business Information From Your Public Library),* the freedom to come and go and work only when I want to, is really great. I particularly enjoy being able to spend more hours of the day out-doors. And my golf game is better than it ever has been—though that isn't saying a whole lot. Last month I played 63 holes of golf on one gorgeous day . . . walking and carrying my golf bag all the way, which was about 18 miles. Thanks to the natural air-conditioning from the nearby ocean, I quit after $3^{1/2}$ complete rounds not because I was tired but because I was bored and hungry. The other members were startled to hear of this as I don't believe any of us had ever before thought to play more than 18 holes at one time.

Meanwhile, I find that I don't miss my old job at all. And this is the job I stayed with so long because I enjoyed it so much and felt sure I would miss it so greatly. When I visit the library now, except for the greetings from staff members it's almost as if I never worked there. I'm detached from it, except for those moments when I see half a dozen renewal notices that have fallen from periodicals onto the reading room carpet. The staff member who picked up such litter for 14 years is no longer there. (11/1981)

.   .   .   .   .

FEW INDEED ARE THE LIBRARY DIRECTORS who leave the profession for new careers in the business world. Walter Curley is a prominent example of some years ago, leaving the directorship of the great Cleveland Public Library to become president of Gaylord's, the library supply firm. A 1981 instance is that of J. Randall Peyser, Director of Lincoln Library in Springfield, Ill., who has accepted the position of Vice-President in charge of Electronic Financial Services at the Springfield Marine Bank. Which reminds us that we twice left the profession for a new career in business . . . but were later delighted—in both cases—to get back into library management. (11/1981)

■ ■ ■ ■ ■

RETIREMENT IS WONDERFUL, BUT . . . It's 2½ years since I retired as a public library director but I still get asked how I like retirement (self-employment, actually). I still like it, and probably will continue feeling that way as long as I have this writing job to help fill my time and thoughts.

But I've just come in from 18 holes of golf in the rain and, for the first time, feel envious of all you people doing interesting work in dry libraries. Our foursome plays golf every Tuesday and Friday, rain or shine, and it's rained our last six outings. That's winter in the Bay Area for you.

I thought, for instance, of Dan Bradbury who has just moved from the directorship of the Janesville Public Library (Wis.) to that of the Kansas City, Mo., Library. What a wonderful time he must be having in his new position . . . serving 6 times the population and with almost 5 times as much money to work with. His opportunities in KC are limitless. The Kansas City Public Library has always been one of those large libraries that either never did anything interesting or was exceedingly modest about letting anyone know about it.

A note from him this week says: "Your advice to do the same things here that we did there was well taken. We've started to move in some of the same directions, but it all takes time. (Four weeks on the job already and no *major* accomplishment!) The biggest trick will be how to keep the staff from tiring of hearing 'well the way we did it in Janesville was . . .' "

As some of you know, the KCPL's board is the elected school board. They are one of the few remaining libraries with this type of structure in the U.S. As a matter of fact, I believe they are the largest library in this group. Perhaps some of our readers have seen a picture of the big downtown library in Kansas City. The first seven floors are library, and the top six floors are school administration offices. It was a picture of this building that gave me the idea for building a main public library at no cost to the public . . . by building it with floors of offices or apartments overhead and letting the rent from these floors pay the cost of the entire building. I presented this idea in my first editorial column, back in December 1965. (2/1984)

·   ·   ·   ·   ·

WHAT HAPPENED TO THEM? We receive newsletters from many libraries and we read many news items telling of the appointment of new library directors. But the thing that we greatly miss is some indication of what happened to the new appointee's predecessor. We rarely can find any word of what happened to this noble individual. Did he or she die, or move to a better job, or retire and move to the Sun Belt, or simply depart—with or without the board's urging? We know so many library directors, at least by name, that we are always interested to know what happened to the person who is no longer there. Do the editors of library system newsletters really believe that all their readers know what befell their departed colleagues, or do they feel that all the Ms. Smiths and Mr. Browns who have headed libraries for many years are no longer of any interest to anyone once they are out of the library?

Let me give you an example from the excellent newsletter of the DuPage Library System (Geneva, Ill.). After introducing the new librarian, the reporter tells us that, "The Board and staff at Bensenville Public Library chose a special way to recognize the services of former Library Director, Bill Schell. A blue spruce was planted and dedicated to Bill in honor of his six years of service to the library and the community." That's a grand idea and I'm happy to hear of it. But I'd still be interested in knowing whether the departed librarian moved to a larger library, left library work to take over his father's business, married a wealthy woman and retired, accepted a job on the faculty of a library school, went into politics, decided to devote all his time to writing, or did any of a great many other things that departing librarians have been known to do. (12/1981)

■   ■   ■   ■   ■

CHAPTER XIV

Visiting the L.A. Convention

I HOPE TO SEE YOU THERE: I'm scheduled to give a talk to the Small and Medium-Sized Libraries Section of PLA at the Los Angeles convention, on Saturday, June 25th, and hope that those of you who are there will come up afterwards and say hello. I know the names of most of "our libraries" and it's always a thrill to me to meet "one of the family."

The topic given me is "First Aid for the First Time Library Director"—which sounds like a "dream assignment" for any speaker. Sounds to me like the talk one would want to give to a library school graduating class, or to any group of active librarians, if he/she could only give one talk.

Any person who has been around libraries for 30 years or more is bound to have acquired some unusual opinions. I expect most of you will agree with some of mine, but just as certainly will disagree with some others. For instance, I've asked many librarians where they think they waste the most money—if they will admit to wasting any—and what they think their library's greatest need is. Their answers to these two questions are quite different from what mine would be. In other words, we librarians don't think alike on many matters, which is a good thing, and we should listen to each other with an open mind to try and decide what approach is the right one.

While the topic is addressed to library directors you can be sure that the talk—as yet unprepared—will be aimed at all grades and types of librarians. I don't believe any of us would bother to prepare and deliver a speech if we didn't believe it could be helpful to the entire audience. One thing you can be sure about this program: you won't hear anything about computers or library automation or networking or anything that is strictly informational. I'm one of those who believe that plain information is better provided in written form, is too quickly forgotten anyway, and doesn't affect the listener in any significant manner—as a good speech should.

No one enjoys public speaking more than I do, but I often think that many of us get away with murder. I believe that anyone who gives a speech and fails to say anything significant that the audience didn't already know should pay a penalty to the association. Anyone who does no more than provide some information that one could read just as well in the quiet of his office should pay a smaller, but still sizable fine. Every speaker would know of these penalties before agreeing to speak. No one should speak, fine-free, who didn't challenge his or her audience to think, who didn't suggest a new approach or direction, or stimulate his listeners to do something new, or in a different manner, or simply motivate them to go back to their libraries and start doing some of the things they know ought to be done.

So I expect to have a wonderful time doing just what most of you would do in the same position: pointing out a number of things that I see librarians doing that I believe they would be better off not doing, and also a number of things that they generally fail to do that, in my opinion, are most important to do. I'm thinking primarily of librarian's attitudes, and the way they think about and approach the various aspects of their job. I'm thinking about the factors that make some libraries great and prevent others from being more than "just average." (6/1983)

■   ■   ■   ■   ■

EVALUATING THE SPEAKERS: While I didn't attend any of the meetings at the ALA convention in Los Angeles, other than the one where I had the pleasure of speaking for an hour and a half on the topic, "First Aid for the First Time Director," I was there for three days and came away with the feeling that these conventions have improved in recent years and that the chances of someone's departing with some helpful information have definitely improved.

One thing that really impressed me was the way in which program speakers were evaluated by the Public Library Association's Small and Medium-Sized Libraries Section. Perhaps ALL the convention speakers were evaluated in the same way, I just don't know. This is something that has long been done in other business and professional associations, and that I had recommended years ago for library speakers, but this was my first encounter with it.

Everyone attending this June 25th program was handed a Program Evaluation Sheet and invited to fill it out during and after the session. 86 Evaluations were returned. John Moorman, the program chairman, has just sent me a copy of the four-page evaluation report. I may have been evaluated before at various state library conventions but, if so, I was never informed. Hence I am most appreciative of the PLA's policy of letting its speakers see how they were rated. This is understandably most interesting and helpful to them.

For the benefit of other library groups interested in doing the same sort of thing, let me say that the program was rated on a six-point scale where 0 is poor and 5 is excellent, for each of the following six factors: (A) Interest and timeliness of topic, (B) Accuracy and quality of information, (C) Appropriateness of program format, (D) Value of program to your professional growth, (E) Quantity of new or innovative concepts presented, and (F) Overall evaluation of the program.

A SEXIST SPEAKER? I am puzzled by the comment, "Please avoid sexist speakers in future programs." I don't know whether these three listeners felt that I favored men as administrators or whether I leaned toward the women. Since I have no such preferences, and don't recall mentioning either men or women in my talk, and have written this newsletter for 18 years without anyone suggesting that I might be a sexist, I am curious.

As I review the talk—and I had no written speech—I recall only one time when I indicated someone's sex, and that was when I was saying again how much I am impressed with the tremendous difference that one person can make in a given situation. In both the public and private sectors one can think of so many cases where a new chief executive came in and made some long-needed decisions and quickly turned around an organization that for some time had been going nowhere. The buildings, the budget, the staff, the organization's materials and services and purposes were the same as before. But now there was some real leadership, which introduced new attitudes and a new "can do" spirit that was quickly felt by both the staff and the people served. As the staff took on new life, they became more productive on the job and more helpful to the "customers." As the service improved, so did the image of the organization. Business picked up, which brought an increased demand for service. Everything was now on the increase—growing, improving, giving more and better service to more people.

AND ALL OF THIS WAS BROUGHT ABOUT by one person—the new administrator. He or she had to have the help of many people—don't forget, a supervisor gets results through his or her staff—but all these people were on the scene before. Whether board members or department heads, they hadn't been able to "move the ball." It took a new administrator—just one person—with ideas and initiative and enthusiasm to breathe new life into the organization and start it moving forward. And there—in that one sentence—you have the best argument I know of for being an administrator. As an administrator you can make a difference . . . a very great difference. This difference will affect not only the amount of satisfaction, pleasure and pride that your staff will derive from their work, but—more than that—the amount of help that the public will get from your organization for a long time to come.

Most of us wouldn't want a job where we couldn't make a difference. Hopefully, we appreciate how fortunate we are to have a position so full of opportunities and satisfactions. Ninety-nine percent of the world's population is not nearly as fortunate.

I cited the case of the new superintendent of schools in Boston, and that of the new superintendent in Council Bluffs, Iowa. Both took over a school system that was said to be a public disgrace and in a matter of months turned it into an operation that won the confidence and support of the public. Many library administrators have accomplished the same kind of turn-around and known the same joy and sense of accomplishment.

AS A "BEST ILLUSTRATION," I offered the case of
the new vicar of our local Episcopal church. She came aboard
a year ago, the first woman vicar any of us had known. In the
previous 14 years the mission church had had a succession of
six or seven male vicars, none of whom was able to "make a
difference." Sunday attendance averaged from 18 to 24 people all these years.

Then came the Rev. Lynn Bowdish—with more love and
enthusiasm and energy than anyone has a right to have—and
in three or four months the average Sunday attendance was
up to 50, and the number of people actively working in the
church was as many as the total membership four months before.

Almost immediately the new vicar enlisted a full-time volunteer secretary, along with your editor as the new church
Treasurer, and many church members to paint the building
inside and out, to combine two basement rooms to make a
needed meeting and dining hall, and to help her plant flowers
all around the church building so that plain old St. Elizabeth's
now has probably the most colorful and attractive grounds of
any church in the area. Church services have been increased
from just one on Sunday to four a week, an organist and choir
has been added, along with a Sunday school and active youth
organization. Art shows, rummage sales and other fund-
raising programs have become quite common this past year.

ANYONE CAN TAKE THIS PICTURE of change
and growth and put it up against his or her library scene and
perhaps be inspired to go and perform a similar miracle. At
least no one reading this can any longer say that such transfor-
mations are not possible. They always are, have been, and
will be, possible. If they have yet to happen in your library,
it's up to you to decide whether you want them enough to
make the effort. If you do, make your plans, set your goals,

and get moving! Remind yourself: "If it's to be, it's up to me!"

And don't be discouraged if you feel you can't make as big a difference as the vicar, at least not in such a short period of time. Pick out certain areas where you see needs that *can* be met. When these are taken care of, other needs will show up.

A number of things can be learned from this brief report of Rev. Bowdish's activities. The first lesson is that one can't do all the work him/herself. It is most important to enlist all the possible helpers one can find. To be sure, a church has members many of whom can be persuaded to carry part of the load of operating the institution. But the library administrator probably has just as many people in the community who can be called upon for advice and assistance in particular situations, to say nothing of all the volunteer workers who are contributing their time to libraries these days on a regular basis. Most public administrators make relatively little use of the outside help that could be available to them.

A second lesson to be learned from seeing this church is how much more attractive and inviting a building can be when one provides some simple landscaping and surrounds it with beautiful flowers and some nice lawn and rock paths. I've seen many public libraries that greatly need the treatment that the new vicar gave our church. I'm thinking particularly of a library in Arizona that I firmly believe would experience a 10 percent increase in use if its drab exterior were transformed as the church's was. Such a dramatic "facelift" would at least make the library the talk of the town.

A GREAT CHURCH: Churches and libraries have much in common. They come in all sizes. And some are dull and drab while others are full of activity and a spirit of helpfulness. Some are growing while others seem to be going nowhere. And in all of them the quality of the leadership is the predominant factor. We have seen above what this can mean in a small church. Sunday morning several of us went out to Garden Grove in Orange County to see what an exceptional minister has been able to accomplish in 25 years.

We wanted to see the beautiful Crystal Cathedral—the home of the Hour of Power television program that many of you have probably seen on some Sunday morning. You may remember our telling in an earlier issue how Dr. Robert Schuller raised the money to build his dream church. After receiving a few gifts of a million dollars he invited people to "buy" a window for $500. This was an intriguing idea and it didn't take long to "sell" all 10,000 windows, bringing in a total of $5,000,000. The name of each donor is on a plaque on his or her window and one can go to the office and quickly find the location of this particular window among the total 10,000.

Schuller next offered the 10,000 stars hanging from the ceiling of the 13-stories-high structure for the same amount, raising another needed $5,000,000. There are almost 3,000 seats in the Cathedral and these brought $1500 per seat. So that's how a person with real imagination secures the funds for a new building when there are no Federal grants and no money from the city or any other outside agency to pay for it.

The bus service in Los Angeles on a Sunday morning leaves much to be desired, and we were 50 minutes late getting to church. After the service the substitute minister invited everyone who was a first-time visitor and would like to have a tour of the church and its 22-acre property, to come forward. About 300 of us did so and were divided into five tour groups, each led by a lay minister who wore a distinctive "uniform" for easy identification and carried a mike and sound amplifying equipment.

I might add that the seats were the most comfortable I ever encountered in a church, the acoustics were excellent, and I particularly delighted in the fountains of water down the center of the cathedral, the trees and plants along the front, and the chirping of birds (in cages) that could be heard during the sermon. The pools and fountains and trees outside the building contributed even more to the beauty of the place.

Our guide told us that the church (belonging to the same group as Dr. Peale's great church in New York City) had 10,000 members, 13 ministers, 2,000 active volunteer workers, and 70 different ministries. For example, there was a Singles group with 3,000 members, and a Prisons Ministry that distributed 60,000 baskets there last Christmas. The Church has now started four churches in other areas; it will support a new church for a full year and then let it swim by itself.

One thing that particularly interested me was the amount of training they give their volunteer workers. This is something that most libraries don't do and probably should do more of. Our guide told us that every Wednesday evening there will be 3,000 people on the "campus" taking some kind of course. He himself has taken 2700 hours of instruction to prepare for work as a counselor and lay minister.

There were many other good-sized buildings on the campus. The one that most interested me was the large, attractive bookstore. There must have been 150 people buying books and gift items while we were there. I saw so many interesting volumes that ought to be in most public libraries but aren't for the reason that they haven't been reviewed or even listed in most book announcement columns. If I were still an active librarian I would have ordered about fifty of these books.

GIVE YOUR STAFF MORE INFORMATION: Most people who work for an organization don't know enough about it. They know enough to do their assigned job and that's about all. They should be given more information and more training so they could fill in for some fellow workers when they are absent for some reason, and so they might be able to answer some of the questions that come to them from outsiders.

It is irritating to most people to be told, "I'm sorry; I don't work in that department," when they ask a clerk a question that anyone in the organization ought to be able to answer offhand. Employees—and this includes library personnel—ought to know more about their place of business. They ought to know who's who and what's where. If they don't know, they should not just admit it and stop there. They should add, "but I'll find out for you right away," and then do it. They are much better fixed to obtain the desired information than any outsider. They can easily find out who and where to call.

Our guide at the Cathedral—an unpaid volunteer—was able to answer every kind of question asked about the church and its history. I tried asking some questions of a loan desk attendant in a library outside the Bay Area last month and quickly gave up when it was clear that she knew nothing beyond her circulation department duties. I then visited the children's department and after commenting on the attractiveness of the room I asked the professional at the desk what their approximate circulation was. She had no idea. It's been my experience over the years that the great majority of professional librarians can't tell you the circulation of their library or its annual budget. In fact, they won't even hazard a guess as to these figures.

What brought this to mind was our experience trying to get a bus back to downtown Los Angeles from the Crystal Cathedral. It took us almost four hours—due largely to the ignorance of the insufficiently trained bus drivers. We started off by asking the driver of each bus that came down the avenue, "Where can we catch a bus to take us back to downtown Los Angeles." Most of them admitted they didn't know, but one driver felt sure that No. 35 would get us there. "Where do you find a No. 35?" The driver directed us around the corner to the bus stop and said No. 35 should be along shortly.

Well we waited there an hour and a quarter and no bus of any kind came by. We didn't particularly mind because it was good to sit in the warm sun and chat. But when a bus finally came—of the wrong number—we got aboard anyway and asked the driver to let us off anywhere that we might catch a bus going to L.A. She said she'd let us know, but she forgot about it until we'd gone five miles past the exchange point. It was a mixup all the way . . . Why don't they give each driver some sort of directory that would provide immediate correct answers to every kind of question that the public might ask? And let every library director make sure that every library employee is prepared to handle any and all questions that come his or her way. A little training along this line might prove time well spent in some libraries.

SOME DIFFERENCE OF OPINION: I started off my talk at the convention by remarking that librarians are a most happy and fortunate group of people. "You work in the nicest surroundings, doing what you like, enjoying a high degree of job security and experiencing a relatively low amount of job stress, with the satisfaction of helping others, and ultimately living longer than most people.

"And those of you who are administrators have it the best of all. You are somebody in the community, you have been given a business already well established and a pretty free hand to run it. You call most of the shots; it's your baby to nurture and develop; if you get an idea for it you can go with it. You can't lose any money in this business of yours, and you aren't even likely to lose your job unless you rock the boat a bit too much. It's hard to find anything to match a library director's job. The opportunities are unlimited. And you'll never suffer from boredom, or the lack of something to do. Almost everything about the job is a plus."

Perhaps I should have left out the remark about little stress on library jobs. I still believe it but it was immediately apparent that a good portion of my audience didn't agree with this judgment. I could have predicted that they wouldn't, but I often say things in talking to my fellow professionals that I know many will disagree with and possibly be irritated with me for expressing such an opinion. I believe it is helpful to one to be obliged to consider "strange" opinions, particularly when they might well be valid after all.

When I asked the directors of our 200 largest public libraries whether they felt their position was an "ulcer job," 40 percent of them said yes. However, that's still a minority, and the average librarian certainly experiences less job pressure than the average library director.

I expect I feel differently about this matter than most librarians because I have had experience in business and industry and have built seven businesses of my own. I can recall single days in the private sector when I felt more stress than I can recall experiencing in my thirty years as a library director.

I remember the first day I tried selling a new product to individual housewives who had no knowledge of or interest in it. After the first 25 rebuffs I felt completely rejected and it took all the courage I could muster to continue ringing the doorbells. In another job I was selling a new service to executives of large companies who never heard of my company or the service before. It was nothing but pressure for me as I was constantly aware that if I didn't make a certain number of sales each month I would be out of a job. Any job in a library seemed like heaven to me at that time.

But my worst time was shortly after I borrowed a large sum of money to take over a dormant country club that had failed three times before, and found that new members weren't joining as fast as I had expected. When the bills are three times your income and you are losing a five-figure amount every month, that's pressure! And that's real stress! At least the librarian who feels pressure on the job isn't losing a lot of money at the same time.

Everything is relative and one judges things on the basis of his or her experience. I shouldn't have said that the librarian's job involves relatively little stress—even though that was my individual experience—and hope that I will remember not to ever say it again. As my mother used to say, "some things are better left unsaid." (9/1983)

■　　　　■　　　　■　　　　■　　　　■

CHAPTER XV

Having the Right Attitudes

WHAT WONDERFUL PLACES LIBRARIES
ARE: Madelyn Helling, our Nevada County Librarian
writes:

"A note to comment on your Dec. issue . . . with thanks for
writing about new ideas and on what wonderful places libraries are for work."

"I'm sure my staff gets tired of hearing me discourse (they
probably call it harp!) on these two things—and since I route
your publication around—they will see it well-stated by you.

"Pulling new ideas out of employees is not easy even when
they are given every encouragement—but one keeps trying!

"I know few people who work outside of libraries who are
happy in their work. I see many happy librarians, tho, and
those of us who worked in the jungle of the business world before becoming librarians know first-hand how wonderful and
worthwhile the field is."

I BELIEVE, AND CERTAINLY HOPE, that she is
expressing the sentiments of most of you reading this. I have

met few librarians who seemed not to like their work, and very few who wanted to get out of the profession. The great majority seemed to be happy enough, if not enthusiastic about their chosen career. To be sure, I've heard a good bit of grumbling and complaining about this and that from librarians over the years, but less than I encountered in the business world. Generally, the matters fussed about seemed of the trivial and "can't-be-helped" type, and one tended to wonder why human beings would make themselves unhappy over such matters. After all, do they really believe that everything should always work out to their complete satisfaction, and that there should never be any emergencies, or snafus, or unfairness, or unreasonable demands or "foolish" decisions by their bosses. Most people expect a certain amount of "bitter with the better," try and understand its causes and not get emotionally involved in it, and recognize that it's not a big deal anyway and that there are still far more things right and happy about the situation than there are things wrong. Such people appreciate how fortunate they are to be working in such a congenial field, and don't let other people or events detract from their job happiness. I'm sure many of us have wished that this or that employee had worked in the business world or somewhere else where the work situation wasn't as pleasant as in the library. Such experience might help them approach more closely that "attitude of gratitude" which makes for true happiness.

A LIBRARY DIRECTOR WITH THIS ATTITUDE was Lawrence Eaton of the Pawtucket Public Library in Rhode Island. In his "Greetings from the Director," which constitutes the 11th page of the beautiful holiday greeting card which Lee Eaton and Pat Desilets produced for the PPL, he wrote:

"My message this year is a simple, but profound, 'thank

you' for letting me serve as Pawtucket's Library Director. The pleasure is all mine! It's a happy experience to work in Pawtucket. Mayor Dennis M. Lynch, our Board of Trustees, our Staff, and people all over New England—all are loyal friends of the Pawtucket Public Library. As I travel throughout New England, people tell me our Library is tops and many assure me the word is out that we have the best public library in Rhode Island.

"I often hear other library directors warn their patrons that these are unhappy times for libraries and that services are being threatened by our inflationary economy. Yes, inflation presents a serious problem. But with the community support we enjoy in Pawtucket, we'll overcome any and all future problems . . ."

THAT'S REAL POSITIVE THINKING! That's the way one should feel about his job, whatever kind it is. It is my constant hope that more people will come to feel that way. Millions more. It clearly makes for greater happiness and greater accomplishment. I can recall some minor jobs in years past when I didn't feel particularly elated about the work I was doing, but in my thirty years' work as a library director there were very few days that I didn't say to myself how lucky I was to have that particular position, with its unlimited opportunities and satisfactions. In the whole country there were only a hundred or so such positions with an equally desirable combination of size and location, and so considering the thousands of trained librarians the library board could have picked from, anyone so favored—and the others fortunate enough to be appointed to the comparable posts—certainly ought to feel well blessed. As someone has remarked, "Just think. Being able to do the kind of work you most enjoy doing . . . and getting paid for it at the same time!"

I LIKE TO HEAR ADMINISTRATORS SAY they have the best library—or school system, or parks department, or paper manufacturing plant, or bank, or whatever—in the area. I've heard people say all these things, and they have generally been telling it like it is. If they weren't actually the best, they were approaching that position. They were doing some outstanding things that gave them the decided feeling that they were really outstanding and a jump or two ahead of the competition. People don't normally think they have the best organization unless they have certain things in mind that would support such an opinion. The person who believes his operation is superior is thinking in terms of excellence and accomplishment and progress. He wants to be the first with new ideas, and the one to have the biggest increase in circulation, the most programs, etc. He or she is a real competitor and wants and means to be the best. Any library—or other organization—fortunate enough to have such a person at the helm, is bound to go forward at an unusual pace. As we have said before, it is really amazing what a difference such a person can make in an organization, in a relatively short time. Sometime, somebody is going to make a study of this phenomenon—and I hope I'll still be around to read it. (2/1981)

＊　　　＊　　　＊　　　＊　　　＊

EXPECT THE BEST—AND GET IT! I have been talking for forty years about the tremendous difference that one person can make in any organization. We all know of many cases where a new director took over a library that was going downhill and turned it around completely in a relatively short time, or a new school superintendent breathed new life into an unhappy school situation, or a new company president changed annual losses of millions of dollars into equally large yearly profits. The sports fans remember how Vince Lombardi turned things around for the Green Bay Packers, and how Bill Walsh did the same thing years later for the San Francisco 49ers. Clearly, a good leader with imagination and enterprise can make all the difference in the world.

■   ■   ■   ■   ■

BEING A PROFESSIONAL: I heard John Ralston, the former coach of the Denver Broncos football team, give a talk recently on attitudinal motivation. He told of Floyd Little, the great running back, who, when asked how he gained 128 yards against Minnesota, explained: "Every time my number is called I tell myself, 'This is the last time I'll ever carry the ball.' " Motivation is inner thought in action, and most of us could certainly use that kind of thinking.

But some of the players don't act like professionals. There are three ingredients to being a professional, he said:

1) Are you really and truly having a love affair with your job? You have the freedom to choose what you want to do.

2) Are you continuing to learn and trying to do better? You've got to run to stand still today. You can't learn by experience, the tuition is too high. We must all learn from others as much as we can.

3) Do you try to set personal standards that are well above most?

"The professional doesn't worry about what happens around him, what others are doing . . . only about himself and his doing the best job possible. He's just trying to satisfy himself and trying to meet his standards.

"Want to get better!—it's the price you pay for the air you breathe."

That's a good thought for today and I pass it along because everything Ralston said applies just as well to the library or any other field as to football. Are all of us getting

better every day? The great ones, said the coach, grit their
teeth and say, "I've got to be better."

         ▪   ▪   ▪   ▪   ▪

   INTERPERSONAL RELATIONS: We are indebted
to Don Reynolds, the Asst. Administrator of the Central
Kansas Library System, for sending along a copy of the pref-
ace to Anne Mathews new A.L.A. publication, *Communicate! A Librarian's Guide to Interpersonal Relations,* which
Reynolds developed for use in the CKLS. They make good
sense so we're happy to pass them along to you:

   1. Each of us has control of our lives. Who we are is who we
   want to be. What we do is what we truly mean. Being reactive
   instead of active keeps our minds in neutral rather than drive.
   We acquiesce by our silence to what others do if we don't
   speak up for our ideas and our feelings. Silence is indeed as-
   sent.
   2. To find answers and get information, ask questions. If
   we ask not, we will never find out why. If we don't know why
   something is happening, it is better to ask than to sit around
   grumbling about "nobody ever tells me anything." By saying
   that, we indicate our disinterest in searching for ourselves.
   3. Clear up gripes as soon as possible. If we have a gripe or
   complaint about what is being done or the way things are going, we should share our feelings with whoever is in charge of
   that area to see if a change can be made to eliminate the irrita-
   tion. If not, and we still feel irritated, we should examine what
   in us is causing it, possibly changing our attitude. A continuing
   gripe signals our unwillingness to take a positive self action.
   4. Monday quarterbacking is unhealthy for the soul. It's
   very easy to point out the errors of other's ways and what
   could or should have been done after it's all over and the deci-
   sion(s) made. If we don't care for the result, we should keep it
   to ourselves unless continuing evaluation and development
   are called for and allow for future change.

5. Reliving the past is toxic. The past is over and we can't do anything more about it. So forget it.

6. Say what you mean and really listen to others. We must learn to transmit our thoughts clearly and to listen to our colleagues so as to grasp the real meaning of what they're telling us. We must listen to nuances and be aware of hidden meanings in our own messages . . .

7. There is no mysterious "they." We are all in this together. We are they.

8. Don't be disturbed. Nobody or nothing can upset us or cause us stress. It is only what we feel about people and events that may bring disturbance to our heads. If we look for and expect the best, we will find it—almost all the time. We are what we think.

9. Be of good cheer. A giggle a day keeps the gloomies away. A glad heart makes a cheerful countenance; a cheerful heart is a good medicine; a downcast spirit dries up the bones. We are as happy or unhappy, content or miserable as we suppose ourselves to be." (1/1984)

■　　■　　■　　■　　■

ARE YOU ENGAGED IN WORK? Someone asked me recently, "How many years have you been working in the library business?" I gave him a number that seemed like a good rough guess. But after hearing "Dear Abby" Van Buren talk about her career on television this morning, I am afraid I gave the man the wrong answer. Abby made this statement: "It's only work if you would rather be doing something else." That immediately registered with me because I've often felt the same way about what I do—that it's too pleasing to be considered as "work." Particularly since there was nothing else I'd rather be doing. I've had a few positions outside the library field that were really work, since I would have been much happier back running a library again, and I remember a few lower-rung library jobs that were also work because I would have preferred to be working out of one of the upstairs offices, but I can't recall a single one of my 31 years as a public library director where I thought of my daily occupation as "work." And the busier I was, the less likely I was to entertain such a thought.

My Dad worked 14 hours a day, 7 days a week, for almost 70 years, as a busy physician and medical writer, and I never heard of him speak of it as work. He seemed to enjoy every bit of it, and certainly there was never anything else he would rather have been doing. Every Saturday and Sunday, as every evening, he could be found on his bed in the big upstairs front bedroom, either reading or writing. Since he didn't spend any time fishing, hunting, playing cards, golfing, or just wasting time, as so many men do, he was able to get so much more work done—though, by Abby's definition, it wasn't work at all.

USING THE SAME DEFINITION, I know many of you have never done any work either. Which reminds me of what I said long ago to several library school classes, on my first session with them. I made the remark that, "Library work is the easiest, most pleasant way to make a living that I know of." I remember the incidents because of the look of shock and disbelief on the students' faces as I said this to them. I had the feeling that they felt that this was just something that shouldn't be said . . . perhaps not even thought. But that was the way I honestly felt, and I proceeded to explain why. First, I told them something of what I had seen and experienced in other occupations—which were clearly less attractive than what these students were contemplating. Some had undesirable working conditions, and others involved far more pressure from one's supervisors, and hassles with one's customers. Librarians generally worked in pleasant surroundings and with interesting materials (books are far more interesting to handle than shoes, furniture, plumbing equipment, or whatever), and since they lent their material and gave their service for free they avoided most of the uptightness and unpleasantness that is apt to enter into dealings where money is involved.

I went on to say that librarians don't work under the pressure of quotas or deadlines, nor do they run out of work and face the problem of boredom and trying to look busy when there's nothing to do. All of which, I added, is why librarians seem to like what they are doing more than any other professional group ("I know of only 2 or 3 people who left the profession voluntarily"—but that was back in the 1950s), and why they live longer. And if librarians do live appreciably longer than people in other occupations, isn't the pleasant nature of their work, and their enjoyment of it, deserving of some of the credit?" (12/1980)

■   ■   ■   ■   ■

BE ENTHUSIASTIC: Marvin Thomas, the director of the Howard County Library (Md.), writes to say that, "Our circulation is increasing each month by over 10 percent more than the preceding month. Also our information services in March were more than our information services for all of last year. As a result, our Central Library parking lot is overflowing all the time."

We congratulate the Howard County librarians and, at the same time, we envy them their new and people-filled library. It has got to be a tremendous pleasure for them, and particularly for Mr. Thomas, to see the continually increasing number of people using the library. My happiest moments as a librarian were seeing the library parking lot with every spot occupied and the reading rooms with every seat filled. The busier the library was the better I liked it. The morning hours might have been the best time to get work done, but it was the after-school hours when the building filled with people that provided the most gratification and excitement. A library is a wonderful place whether anybody else is in the building or not, but any real public-service librarian has got to be thrilled by seeing his or her library swarming with people. It's the same with any service or establishment that one operates; there's nothing more pleasing than seeing a lot of people in one's place of business, showing interest in what one has to offer.

One of the saddest things to see in a library, or any other institution, is an employee—and there are many of them—who seems in no way to respond to an increase in the public's interest in or call for his or her services. Such library employees don't seem to know or care whether the circulation or the number of information requests go up or down, or whether anybody comes in the library or not. Increased traffic may be resented more than welcomed. Some people are happier the less busy they are, even though the time passes much faster when one is really busy. It is most important in hiring new staff members to be sure that you don't take on someone like that. Such an employee you will probably be stuck with for many years, and you will always be sorry you made such a poor selection. It's always possible to find happy people, enthusiastic people, people who can get excited about library developments, so don't be in a hurry to give one of your limited number of staff positions to someone who doesn't have this important capacity. (6/1981)

■   ■   ■   ■   ■

BE KIND: Ann Landers gave some good advice to the members of the San Francisco Rotary Club.

"If I could give just one bit of advice to everybody in the world," she said, "it would be, 'Be Kind.' You can't imagine how much a pleasant smile, a little handshake, a warm word, can mean to someone fighting depression, carrying burdens you never expect.

"Sometimes the most cheerful people are the ones with the most problems. Some people deserve an Academy Award for just getting out of bed in the morning."

That's all so true, and we hope library administrators will always be mindful of this when selecting or assigning staff to stations where they will be meeting the public. We have often said in these columns that library patrons are entitled to a smile and to hear their name spoken at the circulation desk . . . and to receive an equally warm reception at every other point of public contact. I can't think of anything more important than this, yet it often seems that people are employed to work at the main desk—the most important spot in the library—with no thought at all of their capacity to be kind and warm and friendly to the many lonely and burdened people who come there.

Library desk attendants are a fine group of people. But in my experience, and probably yours also, some libraries have a more pleasant, more "kind," staff out front than others. They tend to give patrons a "lift," rather than sending them away as lonely as they came in. I always feel that these libraries are more alive, more attractive, and somewhat superior to the others, and that all this didn't just happen by accident.

I've known too many library administrators who have had no interest and have played no part in the selection of their library staff. They have been content to leave the choice of new personnel to others who have often failed to understand the qualities that are most important in library employees working with the public. It's always a delight to me to visit a library and meet staff members that suggest to me that the administrator has a special appreciation for people of that quality and doubtless makes an unusual effort to recruit them. If, like Ann Landers, I could express "one bit of advice" or one wish—for all library administrators—it would be that they give more thought and effort to selecting new personnel who are warm and "kind."

BE RESPONSIBLE: That's another bit of good advice that might well be given to the human race. How wonderful it would be if everyone did what he promised to do or what others had a right to expect him to do. When one sees the poor service, the neglect and discourtesy that is so common in both the public and private sectors, one tends to wonder how so many of these businesses and other institutions continue to operate.

This column rarely ever says anything critical about a particular library or individual. But two things came to mind today that make me feel critical of a certain type of behavior, which might be characterized as the failure to *Be Responsible*:

(1) Last summer I dropped my prized Lincoln letter off at a shop in Berkeley to be treated some way to prevent further deterioration in the 125-year-old paper and print. Months have passed since then, and every time I call the shop the person in charge is very sorry, he's been under the weather, but he will surely complete the job and return the letter to me in the next two weeks. I'm still waiting. Frankly, I can't understand this type of behavior. If you promise to have a job done at a particular time, you ought to do it even if you have to stay up half the last night to finish it. One thing I can say for sure is that no city manager ever failed to get the information or report he requested from my office when he wanted it.

(2) Approximately a year ago I sent a manuscript to the library journal I consider the best of them all. I still haven't even had an acknowledgment that the article was received. After six or seven months I wrote the editor to inquire what was happening with it. No reply. Three months later I wrote

again, begging to hear whether they had any intention of publishing it or might return it to me. Still no reply. After waiting another month or so, I called the editor long-distance. He was at the Midwinter meeting, but the person on the phone took my name and address and assured me that an assistant editor would return my call the next day. No such luck, or perhaps I should say, no such courtesy. A week later I sent a registered letter to the editor and am now waiting for some response.

Needless to say, such behavior is indefensible—as I stated in my last letter to the editor. How much time does it take to ask your secretary to return a manuscript to someone, or even drop him a card yourself? It's ridiculous when you consider that's a journal's business: publishing articles, along with other news, etc. Half a dozen years ago when I sent the same person another article for possible publication I didn't hear a thing until after five months I was obliged to write to see if it had been received.

I don't have any feelings about the editor himself. But I do deplore such behavior. (3/1983)

■　　■　　■　　■　　■

NEXT TO CLOSE-MINDEDNESS and the reluctance to even consider a new idea, perhaps nothing blocks progress in all areas more than this idea of perfectionism—that whatever one does should be as complete and perfect as possible, and if one can't have it that way, it's better to do nothing at all. That kind of thinking will certainly cut into the amount of joy and satisfaction one will derive from his or her work to say nothing of all the service benefits that will be denied to the people using one's institution.

We recall the library that put off for years starting a record collection because it never had the extra $5,000 that it

thought essential to adding such material ($100 would have
made a nice start), the reference librarian who never let a new
professional in her department answer the phone until she'd
worked there for six months, the couple who put off buying a
house for so long—since they always found something wrong
with the place they had about made up their mind to
buy—that they finally had to pay twice as much to get one, the
people who would like to play tennis, or the piano, but feel
they would never be good enough, the catalogers who won't
accept the work of other catalogers elsewhere without
double-checking everything and who waste hundreds of
hours making their cards more complete—despite the fact
that the public uses the catalog as a simple book-finding tool
and not as a source of bibliographical information. Check the
author and title, jot down the call number, and go . . . (I'm
proud of the way catalogers have simplified their work in
non-academic libraries, so that the average non-fiction main
entry card is now only three lines but I'm always puzzled as to
why the cataloging process seems to take as long as it did 20 or
30 years ago. The people who cataloged no more than two or
three books an hour in 1948 are still turning books out at the
same rate in '78.)

LIBRARIANS ARE STILL putting off taking inventory as often as they should—because they don't have the
staff time to do the whole job in a short period of time; doing
much less weeding than they should—because they think the
entire job should be done by professionals and they don't believe they can afford the time; closing library branches entirely when hit by budget cuts—because they overlook the
fact that most branches *can* be operated, on reduced schedules, by a fraction of the regular staff, and if one's total branch
staff is cut in half, or by two-thirds, it is doubtless better for
the public to have four buildings open with one staff member

apiece than to operate only two buildings with two staff in each, or to have one person in each of three branches rather than three people in only one open building; spending as much as a full week's time on their state library's annual statistical questionnaire, making it 100 percent complete and accurate—overlooking the fact that most of the statistics are of little use or interest to outsiders and that the really significant figures—most of which should be in the Librarian's head—shouldn't require more than an hour or two to supply; etc., etc.

YOUNG PEOPLE, PARTICULARLY, should try out all the new ideas they have an opportunity to, accept all the responsibility that is offered them, and try to be as open and alive and eager as possible—even though they may have doubts as to their ability to handle the new challenges and responsibilities. A good try, if it's one's best effort, is a lot better than no attempt at all. A small collection, or an understaffed service, is better than none at all; a vacation trip on a shoestring is better than going nowhere; an incomplete index is better than no index at all; writing a book that one has to publish himself is a lot better than just dreaming about writing one; and so it goes. Each of us has only one professional life to live—so we better get with it. The more we attempt, the happier we are. (2/1979)

▪   ▪   ▪   ▪   ▪

ONE AT A TIME: Whatever you are trying to build—a publication, a library service, or any other business—you build it one unit at a time. If your operation is to succeed, you must value each individual subscriber, library user, or customer. You must think of them, go after them, and care about them individually and not as just part of a

large mass. My first four to six months as director of the Nashville Public Library (TN), I wrote individually typed letters of
welcome to every new library borrower, letting them know
that the new library director was aware that they had just
"joined the library," and that this was a matter of some importance and pleasure to him. It also gave me an opportunity
to tell the newcomers something more about the library and
its services, and to invite them to contact me at any time
should they have any suggestions, questions or complaints
about the library.

Have you ever called on people in their homes, trying to
get them started as library users? Do you particularly care if
book circulation in some of your units shows a decrease for
the year, and do you try to do anything about it? If some of
your best patrons suddenly stop coming to the library, are you
aware of it, do you particularly care, and do you take any
steps to ascertain why they have stopped coming to the library
and whether you can still be of service to them?

I have visited libraries where I have had the feeling that the
staff treats people as separate individuals—each with his or
her own problems and needs—and tries to really help them
and send them away satisfied. We all know particular hotels
or markets or cruise ships, or whatever, that look on their customers the same way.

But I'm sorry to say that I have visited other libraries,
along with other stores and service agencies, where people
seem to be viewed as just part of a troublesome stream of humanity that must be taken care of one way or another. The
fewer of them there are, the better, and the quicker they can
be dispatched, the better. Who they are, what they really
need, and whether they ever return, are seemingly no particular concern of the employees.

IT'S MORE FUN THAT WAY: Whatever kind of
work one does, it is a lot of fun when you look on the people

you serve as separate personalities. Every time I cross the Bay bridge I am interested to see the reaction of the money collectors as the various lines of automobiles approach their booths. Many of them accept the coins we hold out to them with no interest or animation. A vending machine would work about as well and experience no less enjoyment. But there are one or two young people along the row that truly seem to enjoy their routine job. They always greet one with a real smile and say "Thank You" as if they really meant it. They look right at each driver and seem to understand that most of them have problems and unhappiness and that a warm and cheery greeting might make a difference. I am sure it often does, and am certain that it transforms a dull job into something fairly interesting and pleasant for these toll collectors.

Almost any type of service job can be made of some interest if one thinks about the people being served and tries to give each one some sort of a lift, whether through an encouraging smile, a few kind words, an extra helping hand, or all three. As I quickly learned when I was in charge of job evaluation and employee rating for a large company, people tend to make their own jobs what they are, and the attitudes of individual employees are of prime importance. (10/1984)

■　　　■　　　■　　　■　　　■

START WITH ATTITUDE-CHANGING. I have always delighted in reading about people who took on difficult and unattractive assignments and found ways to turn them into highly successful ventures. And when I stumble on such an account I want to share it with others. Hence the following article (from *Guideposts* magazine) about the changes wrought in the school system in Council Bluffs (Ia.) by an enterprising new superintendent. I particularly like it because of its emphasis on the importance of attitudes. Situations don't change until people change, and people don't change unless and until their attitudes change.

Dr. Chopra's article is not only the longest to appear in this publication, but it gets my vote for the one with the greatest potential for helping all of us. If his "power principles" were applied in the lives of all who read this fine article they would do more to change libraries and improve the morale of librarians than anything else one might imagine.

When Dr. Raj Chopra was offered the post of school superintendent in Council Bluffs, Iowa, he went there to learn more about the community and the school situation. He remembered the CBS *60 Minutes* television report on Council Bluffs' school system two years before. In that report CBS' Mike Wallace had pointed out that Council Bluffs' student test scores were the lowest in Iowa; he went on to describe a run-down school system presided over by an embittered school board.

When he got to Council Bluffs for his 3-day exploratory visit, he heard much of irate parents, school board meetings exploding into shouting matches, and demoralized teachers fleeing to other jobs.

"But it wasn't just the school system that seemed to be in trouble. I sensed something wrong about the general community attitude . . . Maybe they're still smarting from that television report," I told Sue, "but everyone seems to be suffering from a poor self-image. Hardly anyone had anything good to say about the schools, and some even advised me not to take the job. 'You'll only hurt yourself,' they said."

But Dr. Chopra took the job. And three years later when Council Bluffs' civic and business leaders were polled on their opinions about the city's strengths and weaknesses, they ranked the school system as a community *strength*.

What had changed?

Nothing, really, in a material way. The students, schools, teachers and townspeople were the same.

Yet student test scores had soared to a new high, teacher morale was up, and parents were proud—so proud that they'd begun sponsoring an annual "Council Bluffs Pride Week" with a big parade down Main Street honoring their schools and community.

What made the difference?

"Simple principles of positive thinking, or 'power principles' as I like to call them," says Dr. Chopra. "Here they are:

1. Be enthusiastic.
2. See the good.
3. Expect the best.
4. Learn that 'I can make the difference.'
5. Believe!

But these power principles won't do you any good unless you put them to work. Here's what I mean:

BE ENTHUSIASTIC

Too often we refuse to look at the bright side of things. We dwell on what's wrong or discouraging. My first priority in Council Bluffs was getting out into the schools and visiting with students and teachers. One morning as I walked through a school hall, a teacher came toward me. I greeted her. "Good Morning, Mrs. Jones."

"What's good about it?" she grumped.

"It's good because I have the opportunity to look at your beautiful face."

She looked a bit startled, but I continued. "Mrs. Jones, it's good because both of us are looking forward to working with twenty-five young people today. It's exciting to know that we are going to make this day better for them."

Enthusiasm is contagious; it's transmitted from one to another. But you can't generate it in others unless you have it yourself.

SEE THE GOOD

To make progress in any difficult situation, you have to start with what's right about it and build on that. When a hue and cry is raised that 20 percent of the students cannot read, I've found that first I have to tell parents that 80 percent of the students *can* read. After that we start thinking about what to do with the other 20 percent. With any tough situation, the best hope is to start working on it from the positive side.

Let's take the problem we faced with the media in Council

Bluffs. Often local newspapers, TV and radio stations can break a school system by reporting only the defects they see. Because of that, some school board members and superintendents get hypersensitive and assume that the media are out to do a hatchet job.

I looked at the media from the plus side. We had to accept the fact that reporters were not working as our own public-relations agents. But they *did* want to do the best possible job of informing the public of community affairs. So we set out to be completely open with them. We also realized it was our job to give them *good* news. Each day of the week we tried to give them at least one good story about the school. And that was an easy thing to do. A school can have as many human-interest stories as it has students. But you have to look for them.

We learned to work with—not against—reporters, looking upon them as basically decent people, which they are. People, I have found, usually respond to your expectations. If you believe that they are good, one way or another, consciously or subconsciously, they are going to respond with goodness. You have to learn to:

EXPECT THE BEST

When I visited my first classroom in Council Bluffs, I was impressed by the inquisitive young faces I saw there. Were these the same children who had ranked so low on test scores? They didn't look any different from students I'd seen in other cities. In fact, they looked very intelligent to me. And I decided to tell them so.

"I want you all to know that I think you are among the brightest children I have met," I said. "I'm proud to be associated with you." As I told them how certain I felt that they would do exceedingly well in the coming year, I saw a look of expectancy brighten their faces.

When the teacher walked out into the hall with me, I said, "I noticed your rapport with the children and how well they respond to you." Shaking her hand, I added, "I know you're going to do great things with them."

I'm not talking about a Pollyanna outlook. In telling our teachers that we appreciated their skills, we also let them know we *expected* the best.

"We will help you to grow," we said, "but if you cannot grow, we'll help you find satisfaction in some other job."

We found that 90 percent of the teachers were doing a good job. Most of the rest were surprised when we told them they weren't doing well. "No one has told me that for ten years," said one. "What am I doing wrong? I'll try to correct it." These we were able to help.

As for the few who were not designed to be teachers in the first place, we helped them see this and then helped them find vocations elsewhere in which they could be productive and happy.

By the same token we let our principals know that we wanted supervisors who would spend some time in the classrooms to find out what was happening to the young people, who would work with teachers in helping them grow, who were willing to give them encouragement. And we always tried to impress upon our principals, supervisors and teachers the power that lies within each and every one of us to make a difference in other people's lives.

LEARN THAT "I CAN MAKE THE DIFFERENCE."

We can be the difference between hope and despair, love and hate, understanding and anger, success and failure. Often a simple comment will do it: "I like that dress" or "You sang so well in church last Sunday." A phone call, a note—in a thousand little ways we can give others a lift by letting them know we've seen or heard something good about them. You can always find a way to show you care—and caring gives encouragement.

Simple principles of positive thinking, yes. But none of them will make a difference in your life unless you

BELIEVE

The Bible proverb says: *As a man thinketh, so is he.* As we believe, so shall we be.

Just look at what happened in Council Bluffs once the people believed their school system could be great. The same power principles can be applied in your own life, in everything you do. They can be summed up in seven powerful, positive words: Expect the best, and you'll get it. (6/1983)

.   .   .   .   .

IMPROVE ATTITUDES: This is the key to the turn-around, according to Charles "Red" Scott, who has been reviving near-dead companies for a decade. And the process begins with you. The manager must have absolute faith in his own ability and the company's ability to carry out the plan. As soon as the leader loses faith, the plan is functionally dead.

"The manager who has faith is enthusiastic, determined, and committed," says Scott (in the Feb. *Inc.*). "These emotions and attitudes are contagious and soon spread to other workers. Improved attitudes result in an improved bottom line.

"The real secret to making a profit is to increase human productivity. The key to increasing productivity is to improve employee attitudes. Therefore, the job of management is to continually improve attitudes.

"The single most important ingredient in achieving a turn-around is the building of an enthusiastic, cohesive team. The key to that is communication."

Unless you know the company intimately, it's virtually impossible for the smartest analyst to look at the surface and see what's really happening.

"Instead," Scott recommends, "I'd look at the people. Check out the person at the helm. If he or she is a winner, is honest, and has a deep personal commitment to the company, you've got a good bet on a turnaround. If any of those three elements is missing, don't touch it." (10/1986)

■　　■　　■　　■　　■

TRY ANOTHER WAY: We have often said in this column that "Everything is Possible." If you come up against a closed door, or lose a bond-issue election, or suffer any other seeming misfortune, don't give up. You are never defeated until you admit defeat. Look for a different approach, or alternative sources of financing. The challenge and the opportunity is still there, and so are you and all the library forces you can muster. So regroup, get better organized and prepared, and take another crack at it. If it's a new building that you need, really believe and know that you are going to get it. It then becomes just a question of when, and on what attempt. Looking at it that way will take away most of the pain and depression of an early loss or defeat. You won't feel that you have lost the new library; you have simply suffered a delay. The construction has been postponed, not lost or abandoned. You have other options and other ways to get to your goal. Don't wait more than six months to try another way.

One library that sought another way is the Cumberland County Public Library (Fayetteville, NC). Less than a year after the defeat of a county-wide referendum on a $4.5 million bond issue to finance construction of a new central library, the CCPL has received the go-ahead from the County Commissioners to proceed with the project. This is great news and we do want to congratulate Jerry Thrasher and his fine staff and library friends. We hope that their use of 3,000 copies of each of the last three issues of BUSINESS INFORMATION FROM YOUR PUBLIC LIBRARY had some part to play in this development.

Approval came after an energetic group of community leaders and Friends of the Library pulled together commitments of $497,000 in federal jobs bill funds, $250,000 from the Cumberland Community Foundation, $350,000 from the City of Fayetteville and over $1.1 million from a local fund-raising effort. The Commissioners are adding $3 million to complete the funding for the 65,000 square foot $4.8 million facility that will consolidate main library services, now divided among three buildings in downtown Fayetteville. (12/1983)

■   ■   ■   ■   ■

A STORY TO REMEMBER: I heard recently about another library administrator who lost his job. My immediate reaction was, "What a shame. What tough luck, losing a fine job like that, when new ones are so hard to find." And then I happened to recall a favorite story of Dr. Robert Schuller's which has become a favorite of mine, too. The story is centered around a Chinese man. He had all the material things he needed. He had a beloved son, and a prized horse. But one day his horse broke out of the corral and ran to the mountains. Since all of his assets were tied up in this horse, he lost in one brief moment all of his life's savings.

All his neighbors, hearing that the horse was gone to the hills forever, came to offer their sympathy. They all said to him, "Your horse is gone. Oh, what bad luck." Then they cried and they tried to console and comfort him.

But he said, "How do you know it's bad luck?"

Sure enough, a few days later, the horse being well-domesticated, came back to where he could be sure there would be water and food. In the process he brought back twelve wild stallions with him. They were all captured and ushered into the corral.

Now when all of the town heard the news, they came and they applauded and said, "Oh, thirteen horses, what good luck."

And the wise, old Chinese man said, "How do you know it's good luck?"

The townspeople remembered his words the next day when his son, his *only* child, tried to break one of the wild stallions. In the process, he was thrown off, he broke his leg and was left with a limp forever.

When the neighbors heard about that, they came to him again and said, "Your son, forever a cripple. What bad luck."

But the wise, old man said, "How do you know that's bad luck?"

Sure enough, about a year later, a Chinese warlord came through town, conscripted every able-bodied young man, and took them off to battle. They lost the battle. In fact, every young warrior was killed. The only young man left in the village was the maimed son of the wise Chinese man, for he had never been conscripted, thanks to his limp.

The moral of the story is this: How do you know when something is bad luck? And how do you know when it's good luck?

Only God knows what's good and what isn't, says Schuller. And even when something bad happens He has a way of turning it into something fantastic.

I found this out for myself in the 1960s when I lost an attractive job. My neighbors all said, "Oh, lost your job, what bad luck." Unlike the wise Chinese man, I didn't think to reply, "How do you know that's bad luck."

I've long since come to realize that that was truly good luck. If things hadn't happened that way I would never have come to start this newsletter, or my other two, either. I would never have had the pleasure of these monthly visits with you people . . . Let's hope that things turn out equally well for all the librarians who lose their jobs in 1985.

(Since writing the above, I was reading an article in TIME magazine about Irwin Jacobs, one of the big business raiders like Boone Pickens. My attention was caught by this sentence, "As it turned out, failing at brewing was one of the best things that ever happened to him." He sold his beer brands and auctioned off machinery, thus making a $5 million profit that he immediately put to good use. And when a firm he acquired in 1978 went bankrupt, he salvaged some of the pieces to form a new company called Minstar which made a profit of $23 million for 1984. Which proves again that failures can be transformed into successes.) (6/1985)

■　　　■　　　■　　　■　　　■

HOW THE LIBRARY HELPED THEM SUC-
CEED: Phillip K. Barton, the director of the Rowan Public
Library in Salisbury, N.C., writes "to share with you and your
readers an idea we developed here for a new brochure explaining library resources and services. (I won't say the idea is
original with us, for I've seen some similar ideas used for brochures.)

"Earlier this year we decided to do something different for
National Library Week. What we did was to get our Friends of
the RPL to sponsor a contest entitled 'Has the library helped
you succeed . . .?' Entries consisted of narratives in 250
words or less which described how the library had helped the
individual succeed in some endeavor. I must admit the response was not overwhelming, but what we received was
great! (Enclosed is a copy of the entry form.)

"Six winners were selected from the entries. Each winner
was recognized at the annual meeting of the Friends during
National Library Week and given a cash award of $25. Also
the winners were to be featured in a new library services' brochure. When the awards were presented at the Friends' meeting each winner's story was told. It was so wonderful to sit
there and hear how great the library was and not be the one
who was saying it. I don't believe any of us on the inside could
say it any better than these folks did . . .

"It is my hope that we can make the contest an annual
event. I feel this is a very reciprocal venture in that some of our
public can get recognition because they are library users and at
the same time the library gets some good public relations (and
praise) without being the one blowing the horn."

The entry form is fine and the enclosed brochure listing all
the materials and services the library has "To Help You Succeed," is excellent. It includes pictures of the six contest winners with each one's statement as to how the library helped
him/her succeed.

I like everything about this "contest." I particularly like
expression of the thought that libraries are in the business of

helping people succeed . . . that personal success is the name of their game . . . that they are interested in helping people succeed in life, and have the means of accomplishing this. Libraries are almost never mentioned in connection with the idea of individual success. I believe this is the first library advertising I've ever seen that used the word "success," or "succeed." People are urged to use the library for information and recreation, but librarians have always stopped there. Apparently, we never went far enough in our thinking and caring to be concerned with what happened to our patrons after they got the information or other service that they requested from us. They got help from the library but what did they do with it and what did it do for them?

It's possible for two people to receive the same service from the library but make entirely different use of it. In one case, the information or service may be put to no real use; in the other, it may help one start a small business or prepare an important publication.

Should librarians devote any thought to the final use made of the help they provided? You give good service to a patron; is there any point in being concerned about what use is made of this service and whether it helps the person succeed in some significant way? I believe it is healthy to occasionally remind ourselves and our public that helping people—which should mean helping them succeed in life—is truly a primary and highly important part of our job, as well as a major reason for our professional existence.

This Rowan Public Library contest lets everyone know that the Library is thinking about their success and is not just interested in giving service to give service. Who wants a doctor who provides medical assistance simply because that's his job and those are the logical steps for him to take? Don't we all want a physician who truly cares what happens to us after he has done his thing with us, and who is out to make us well, rather than just perform his assigned part of the treatment process? Of course we do. But, unfortunately, not all medical doctors are like TV's popular Dr. Welby. And maybe all librarians are not equally concerned with the success or well-being of their patrons. (6/1983)

■   ■   ■   ■   ■

"LIBRARY SPOTLIGHT," a relatively new feature of the Baker & Taylor Company's monthly *Forecast* (new books) is doing a splendid job of highlighting the interesting services of some of our more progressive public libraries. The Columbus report is particularly interesting as it covers a large-city library that was relatively unheard of outside its state and had no reputation as an innovative institution until just a few years ago. Donald Sager stepped up from the Mobile, Ala., library directorship to head the larger library, conducting a successful campaign for a large increase in funds. His fine work, and the money obtained thereby, brought additional staff and library materials that really transformed the big library in Columbus and Franklin County. Which all goes to show again what one person can accomplish in any institution. The public, the buildings, the staff, the resources may stay the same, but a new leader with ideas and energy and enthusiasm can make all the difference in the world. Applicable new ideas are always essential, and exciting, and they attract new "customers," build support, and create a better image for the institution. They are generally helpful and desirable, but too often are viewed as such by everyone except some of the institution's department heads whose old work habits are affected, or threatened, in some way, by the changes. If none of these people are upset or complaining, then the proposed idea probably doesn't amount to very much and isn't going to change anything to an appreciable degree. Of course, one shouldn't generalize, but the above is true more times than not.

THEY ARE DOING A LOT OF INTERESTING things in Columbus. Many of the things you read about in this B&T article you won't find in most libraries this size—or any other size. And the thing which I'm sure you all noticed is that almost all these resources and services that seemed unusual to you have been added to the library in the past half dozen years. Which tells us that any enterprise—school system, library, business—can be transformed and given new life in far less time than most people think. I know two libraries that were modernized and given new life in less than a year . . . and the two city populations recognized the transformation in their library and gave it unstinting praise. So if you are the head of just an average institution and have felt that it couldn't be greatly improved because of its lack-luster past, forget it! It will change just as fast as you change your thinking about it. It's all up to you—and you only have one life to change it in. If you don't get the place moving, your successor will. Why leave all the fun to this unknown person? And that's what we are really talking about—*fun!* One of the greatest joys in life is to take a department, a library, a little business, a school system, whatever . . . and build it, improve it, try out new ideas in it and see them succeed, and watch it grow in every good way. Millions of people never have the opportunity to experience the great pleasure that comes with this sense of accomplishment—and that is truly a sad thing. But everyone who reads this publication is in a position to gain this type of reward. And I do so hope that he or she will make it happen—many times. (1/1981)

■   ■   ■   ■   ■

I HEARD A WELL-KNOWN TV PREACHER say, "Inch by inch, anything's a cinch." I mention this because I have always preached "Think small, and get started," rather than "Think big"—which generally means, "Try and get a grant, and hold off until you have all the money, or until victory is assured." The poeple who get things done are the ones who, when they get an idea, take some action on it in a reasonably short time. They make a start, and a commitment, so there will be something underway, no matter how small. And they add something to it, whenever they can, until—inch by inch—they have put together something worthwhile. Such people generally have half-a-dozen inch-by-inch projects on the burner at the same time. Your "Think Big" individual is likely to be so overawed by the immensity of his All-Complete project that he never gets to first-base with it. If there is something in your work that you have long wanted to do, or see done, see if you can't break it down into a number of small parts, and then list these parts in the order in which they should be accomplished, and get moving on the first one this week. Have someone make you a sign saying, "Inch by Inch, Anything's a Cinch," and keep it on your desk until your retirement party.

■　　　■　　　■　　　■　　　■

INVINCIBLE! What a great word that is. Dr. Norman Vincent Peale explained its meaning in one of his sermons years ago. "It means simply that nothing can destroy you, that nothing can defeat you, that you have an unconquerable self that never needs to give up . . .

"There are people everywhere ready to give up. There are others who will never give up; these latter are the invincible ones.

"It is *always* too soon to quit . . .

"We have had some very great men in the history of our

country, the kind of men who had invincibility built into them . . . Let me read you some of the life history of one of them. He failed in business in '31. He was defeated for the Legislature in '32. He failed once again in business in '34. His sweetheart, his fiancée, died in '35. He had a nervous breakdown in '36. He went into politics and was defeated in the election of '38. He decided to run for Congress and was defeated in '43. He was defeated for Congress in '46. He was defeated for Congress in '48. He was defeated for the Senate in '55. He was defeated for Vice President in '56. He was defeated for the Senate in '58. After that he was through, wasn't he? He was, as they say, 'washed up,' wasn't he? He had had it, had he not? No, he hadn't at all. He was elected President in 1860! The man, of course, is Abraham Lincoln. Invincible!"

I always thought that was a wonderful story and decided to share it with you today as I know some of you have faced situations—may even be facing one now—where you must decide whether to continue to push forward toward your particular goal, or give up.

How invincible are you?

■   ■   ■   ■   ■

"LIFE IS A MATTER OF PERSPECTIVE," began a recent message delivered by Dr. Robert Schuller from the Crystal Cathedral in Garden Grove, California. "Consider, for instance, the story of the two shoe salesmen who were sent to Africa to check into the potential international market there. Like the two spies who returned to Joshua in the Old Testament after reviewing the promised land, the salesmen returned to their shoe company with their reports. One salesman had a negative report. 'There is no market there,' he said, 'nobody wears shoes in Africa.' The positive salesman reported, 'On the contrary, it's a fantastic opportunity, no one has bought shoes yet!' "

That's really tremendous! Two people look at the same scene and come away with totally different conclusions. It *is* all a matter of perspective and one's perspective is a self-fulfilling prophecy. If you perceive that business is going to be bad, it will be bad. If you perceive the possibility of a good, successful year you will set off intangible forces that will likely make the possibility a reality. (2/1983)

■   ■   ■   ■   ■

XVI

Welcoming New Ideas

NEW IDEAS: We do a lot of talking about new ideas. They come in all sizes, and one doesn't have to be tremendous or earth-shaking to be exciting and pleasing to the persons affected. Any new thought that offers an easier or more economical way to do something, even though it has meaning for only one person and affects only the simplest of tasks, can provide great delight to the person who conceives the idea.

A good example is the idea—small, perhaps, but exciting —that public services librarian Jean Amelang picked up at a library promotion workshop in Kinston (N.C.). As reported in the popular newsletter *Down East,* "Jean is in seventh heaven because she learned a way to prevent one of her pet peeves: bibliographies and hand-outs overhanging brochure racks whose support bars are too low. (Mount a sample copy on cardboard or posterboard of identical size, laminate it, and utilize its stiffness as the first copy in the rack to hold up the giveaway copies behind it, to avoid droopiness.) Simple!"

I don't know Ms. Amelang but she sounds like the best kind of librarian: Somebody who is smart enough to recognize a new idea when she reads or hears about it, and who cares enough about her work to be interested in any idea that might speed or improve any aspect of it. The greatest need of libraries or any other type of organization is for more employees who have a real enthusiasm for their work and who can get excited about new ideas that can affect its performance.

Many employees in every field are inclined to think that an idea of the magnitude described above is not worth noting or remembering or doing anything about. We've seen many libraries where everyone seems to feel that new ideas are the province of the administrator alone. The staff leaves all the planning and thinking, and all the making of improvements and other changes, to the boss. They seem to feel that that is his or her responsibility.

We all know libraries that have made great progress on the ideas of a single person—the library director—but who doubts that they could have gone even further if all the staff had contributed their share of good ideas, as well as making the changes needed in their individual departments.

Many times a library staff leaves the thinking and innovating to a boss who is no more creative than they are. After all, there is nothing in the title or job of an administrator that provides the incumbent with imagination or any other powers that he or she didn't have before. And since most library directors started out as low-level staff members it would seem highly desirable for all professional library employees to be given a definite responsibility for innovation and work improvement in their service area. They should be taught where to look for new ideas, how to recognize those that have merit, and how to go about implementing good, usable ideas.

We certainly weren't taught anything like this in library school, but I believe we should have been. I believe that it could provide the most interesting and useful course that could be found anywhere. When I taught a course on supervision to engineers, we had a saying, "A Supervisor Gets Results Through People." Maybe now we should add another saying to that: "A Supervisor Gets New Ideas Through People" (or should).

■　　　■　　　■　　　■　　　■

BE AN IDEA COPIER: Our September issue carried an enthusiastic item about the Harford County (Md.) Library's "Reading a Family of Four," one of the best annual reports that we have seen. We passed our copy along to Patti Bergsing, the director of the Burlingame Public Library, who was looking for a good new idea for her forthcoming annual report. She was equally delighted with the Harford report and proceeded to turn out a Burlingame copy that is like the original in every way except that the book titles and figures are different. It is a compliment to Jim Gosier and his Harford staff, and also to Mrs. Bergsing who had the good sense to recognize a good idea and then make use of it. Most people wouldn't see the applicability of such a report in their own institution and, if they did, they probably wouldn't do anything about it.

The Burlingame Library has already received some compliments on its interesting report. I'm sure its patrons feel this is a unique presentation, which is quite all right. Anything's new, if it's new to you. And equally true is this statement: "It's new, if it's new to them." Let me give you another example of this. Twenty-seven years ago, as I may have mentioned some time before, I read in a library journal about the self-service book collection that a Nebraska librarian had set up in a grocery store. Housewives could pick books off the shelves, along with their bread, and milk, and soup, and charge them out to themselves . . . entirely on the honor system. No attendants and no checking at the exits. I thought it a wonderful idea and quickly arranged with a local supermarket chain to establish such "booketerias" in three big suburban stores. It was a bigger deal than the one in Nebraska so I wrote it up in the same journal. It obviously was not a new idea, as I credited the Nebraska librarian, Stewart Smith, with the idea, but Newsweek magazine ran a story on the Nashville booketerias, and Business Week ran a full-page photograph. The idea was new to them and their readers.

SO LET'S DO MORE IDEA BORROWING. After all, what's the point in someone's writing an article in a business or professional journal about something interesting his organization has done, if people are just going to read it and forget it. And that is what usually happens because the reader isn't looking for possible adaptations and uses in his own operation. In the case of the "booketeria," our library was apparently the only one to act on the Nebraskan's article, and only 2 or 3 librarians around the country acted on mine. And it was really a tremendous idea; we circulated books like hotcakes, and at the nation's lowest cost per circulation.

SOMEONE HAS MADE A STUDY OF NEW IDEAS and has stated that the average person doesn't act on anything he reads until he has heard or read about the idea three different times. It takes three encounters to register on one's mind. So, if you can get moving on the first or second encounter, you are going to be well ahead of the pack. Actually, if you move on the idea at all, you are going to be ahead of most people. For the great majority of people have NO interest in new ideas. They don't have any of their own, and they don't want to hear about any, or be asked to consider any, and they fervently wish nobody else had any either. Most people have an abhorrence for change, and this reluctance to even consider a new idea is the greatest barrier to progress in every field. And the life of an innovator is apt to be a rough one. A recent study shows that most of them are fired, or run off by their fellow professionals who can't accept their "ridiculous" ideas.

BUT WE ALL CONTINUALLY NEED new ideas in our business. I hope you are getting some from your employees. I remember a librarian who worked for us in Nashville. She was head of the reference department—and a good one—but was troubled by the thought that she had never had a new idea in her work. I encouraged her to read the professional journals and let me know whenever she found something that could be applied to her department. Several months later she came into my office with an article she wanted me to read. It was about a seemingly good idea from a northern library. I said, "Wow, that's great. That ought to be worth a raise." And I gave her one on the spot. I wanted her to see the connection between creativity and more money . . . and she got the idea. Five months later she was back with an even better idea—also taken from another library—and we gave her another raise on the spot. We could do that in those days, at least in Nashville, which had a corporation-type public library.

"HAVE YOU HAD A NEW IDEA LATELY?": That was the title of my talk yesterday to the Menlo Park Rotary Club. I believe they wanted me to talk about books and libraries, but I thought the above title would attract a bigger audience. I talked more about the basic content of libraries—ideas—but pointed up the library as the city's Arsenal of Ideas. I began with an account of how a young man came into my office years ago and surprised me with this ques-

tion: "How do you get a new idea? You seem to have so many, but I've never had one, and I've got to come up with some at the radio station or I'll be out of a job."

All I could think of was to tell him to open his eyes and mind as wide as possible and try relating everything he saw, and read, and heard, to his job situation. Once one gets into this habit, he or she will see interesting possibilities for his business on all sides. I never could go into a department store without seeing some color, or material, or arrangement, or new idea that I could use in the library. The two leading journals on banking were another good source of ideas—on displays and public relations programs—that one could use in libraries.

Most people just don't relate things. For example, there was the director of a large library that operated a cafeteria that went about $40,000 into the red each year. Taking a train trip one summer, he went into the dining car for lunch— which turned out to be just a car filled with vending machines. The passengers seemed infatuated with this new food service, and he was too, but it never occurred to him that here might be the answer to his money-losing food operation. Replace the cafeteria with vending machines and make a little money instead of losing a lot.

AN EQUALLY GOOD SOURCE OF NEW IDEAS—and I won't burden you with any more of my talk to the Rotarians—is the practice of constantly questioning everything you do and see. Why do we do this? Isn't there a better way of doing that? Do we really need to keep this material? Can't we eliminate that job? Etc., etc. I am convinced that many, if not most, people go through their working lifetime without ever asking a single one of these questions, even to themselves. They were never trained to question anything about their job, and feel no need or obligation to improve any aspect of it.

Questioning things OTHER people do, can be difficult, as I found out shortly after assuming my first library directorship in Massachusetts. Becoming aware that it was taking six weeks on the average to get new books out of the catalog department, I suggested to the cataloger that we play a game.

"Let's go over everything you people do," I said, "and in every instance where you can't give me a good reason for doing it, let's try doing without it for a few months and see what happens." We went over every notation that was printed on a catalog card, every kind of card they made, every file they kept, etc.

In the majority of cases, the only explanation she could give was: "That's the way it has been done for 20 years," or "That's the way I was taught to do." So we eliminated all these steps, with the result that the Catalog Department was quickly reduced from 3 people, in full-time equivalent, to 1¹/₂—and no new book ever again took more than four days to get out to the public. The public loved it . . . but the cataloger never forgave me. I should have waited longer before making any changes, although things would probably have come out the same if I'd waited 10 years. (12/1980)

■   ■   ■   ■   ■

THERE ARE MANY PROFESSIONALS in all fields who don't seem to think they can learn anything that would be useful to them from a report about activity in a different field. Many of us read articles about the public schools, or museums, or about banks, department stores, supermarkets, or other service operations, in a rather inattentive sort of way. The material is interesting to read but we certainly aren't expecting to learn anything from such a "foreign" field and aren't looking for any ideas that we might use in our own work, which is indeed most unfortunate. All these fields are important sources of new ideas for libraries. The percentage of innovative people in banking, merchandising, and in the other fields, is as high as in the library profession, and any library manager who can't recall half a dozen helpful ideas that he borrowed from these outside fields is missing some fine opportunities.

For a number of years we never missed an issue of *Banking or Sales Management* or *Administrative Management*, to say nothing of *Chain Store Age, Motel-Motor Inn Journal, Office, Personnel Journal, Nation's Schools, Progressive Grocer,* and a dozen other lesser journals that we skimmed for ideas.

Too many librarians look only to library publications for ideas, if they do any looking at all. And a high percentage of us have become so specialized in our thinking that no nuggets of ideas are likely to register on our minds unless they come from our own special field of librarianship. Our average public librarian isn't likely to pay very much attention to a new development that is proving helpful to some university librarians, and the average college librarian isn't apt to stop and try to figure out how he can adapt to his own use something new that seems limited to the public library field. (4/1983)

·   ·   ·   ·   ·

PROFESSOR'S ADVICE: Professor Neusner quoted his mentor at Harvard, the late, great scholar of Judaica, Harry Wolfson. "If you want to be accepted and even liked," Wolfson told Neusner when he was an undergraduate, "then do not say anything that has not already been said, nor do anything that has not already been done. Do not disagree with anyone. Do not say anything new. Best of all, do nothing at all. Then you will be a great scholar in the eyes of the world . . ."

Wolfson's advice is obviously pertinent to other fields as well, which certainly includes public administration. I've said much the same thing many times before in these columns, and have quoted other writers making the same observation. This is just a fact of life that doubtless everyone knows anyway. The sad thing is that most professionals have no need for such advice as they are not likely to ever say anything or do anything that has not been said or done before, anyway. The number of people who are going to say something new or do something different is always going to constitute a small minority.

Most of the innovators will suffer some difficulties and unhappiness because of their "strange" ideas and actions, but the appreciative response of the public and their own personal satisfaction and sense of accomplishment will more than make up for this. Even if, and when, the jealousy and intolerance of some of their colleagues causes them to lose a prized position to someone who is thought to be a more desirable applicant because he or she has no record of ever having irritated or antagonized anyone. The explanation for this of course is that the preferred candidate never expressed an original or unorthodox idea in his professional life, but the average library board is not going to consider that. (10/1986)

．　　　．　　　．　　　．　　　．

10 RULES FOR POSSIBILITY THINKERS: In one of Dr. Robert Schuller's printed sermons, we ran across the following rules which tell how to handle an idea and live by it:

    I. "Never reject a good idea because it is impossible— When God's ideas come they are always impossible. That's

His way of making sure that you are operating on a level of faith and not depending on your own strength!

II. "Never reject a positive idea because it may fill your own personal desires and ego.—It's shocking how many Christians throw away a great idea because they feel it would be ego fulfillment. Your work must fulfill your ego needs!

III. "Never oppose an idea because it will lead to a problem.—Every great possibility is going to create problems and the bigger the possibility the bigger the problem.

IV. "Never reject an idea because there is something wrong with it.—No idea is perfect. They come from God but they pass through faulty human minds.

V. "Never make your decisions on your ability but on your adaptability.—When God calls you He always calls you beyond your human resources.

VI. "Never wait to launch the idea until you have solved all the problems.—Impossibilities never turn into possibilities until God begins to perform a miracle. And God will not perform a miracle until you have made the plunge. Miracles happen! Decide to go ahead with a beautiful idea even though you do not know how you are going to solve the problem.

VII. Never use an immovable, unsolvable problem as an excuse for quitting.—Problems are intended by God to be guidelines, not stop signs.

VIII. "Never back away from a great idea because the price is too high.

IX. "Never reject an idea because of conflict with your present thinking or the past position that you may have taken.—God's ideas are intended for you to grow. You know where the growing edge of your life is and mine. It's where there must be changes in our attitude or thinking. Almost every God-given inspired possibility will demand that you change your attitude. Change your mind. Say to someone, 'I was wrong. You were right. I'm sorry. Forgive me, I was locked in my thinking. I wasn't thinking straight.' God can do great things for the person who can change his mind.

ANYBODY WHO LIVES BY THESE COMMAND-MENTS is a real possibility thinker, and that's the kind of administrator every library should have.

To put it another way, it is highly important for you and your community that your library be operated by positive-thinking people rather than by the negative-thinking variety—which, of course, are far more numerous. The former see opportunities where the latter only see problems, which is why one finds very few if any successful operations headed by negative-thinkers. All of which explains why I write and talk so much about attitudes and positive thinking and the importance of keeping an open mind and trying out new ideas and staying "cool" and not getting upset over the thoughts or deeds of colleagues, etc. From what I've seen in many fields, the need of all of us for right attitudes and perceptions is far greater than that for straight information, and a thought that can change a person's way of thinking about or reacting to a particular situation is likely to accomplish more than the imparting of a lot of information. And its effect will be more lasting. (2/1979)

■   ■   ■   ■   ■

CHAPTER XVII

Quality of Service

PRODUCTIVITY: White-collar workers are unproductive at least 4 of the normal 8 hours on the job. So concludes a research report by Theodore Barry & Associates, a management-consulting firm. Another finding of this study, as reported in a recent issue of U.S. News & World Report, is that the typical office worker is almost 10 percent less productive than the typical blue-collar worker, who pulls the oars about 55 percent of the time.

While we can believe the second finding, it is harder to accept the thought that white-collar workers are unproductive half of the time. We have known some, both in and out of the library profession, who were in this category but never would have categorized this whole working class in such a manner.

It would seem to be a matter of what one means by the words "productive" and "unproductive." Does the latter mean doing nothing or just wasting a lot of time, or does it encompass a normal amount of work that is simply judged to be meaningless or "unproductive" because it doesn't advance the organization or produce any of the goods or services which it was established to do.

We have observed enough business and professional organizations at work to believe that the average white-collar worker is "out of service" perhaps 10 percent of his or her scheduled time. This is the time lost in coming late to work, in leaving early at the end of the day, in taking longer breaks, and a longer lunch hour than one should, plus the time spent on personal phone calls and at the water fountain and coffee bar. Some who stay in the restroom or go elsewhere to smoke, run this stolen-time percentage to 15 percent or more, as do others who write letters and attend to personal business on company time.

Then there is the multitude of workers who can easily spend an hour or more a day sitting, standing or moving around just chatting about nothing important. A great many others just like to observe the scene around them, as if waiting for something interesting to happen. Governmental offices seem to have a much higher percentage of these time-wasters than offices in the private sector, particularly those where the owner is on the premises. When a manager is paying all the expenses out of his own pocket, his tolerance for every kind of waste is much lower.

NON-PRODUCTIVITY, OR TIME-WASTING, is much harder to recognize in libraries than in any other work environment that I can think of. The main reason of course is that there is so much reading material everywhere that staff members can legitimately read, that no one is ever without something interesting to read or busy herself with, and any observer finding a half dozen employees so engaged would never be able to tell who was really working and who was just pleasantly passing the time. To be sure, the majority of library employees are busily working at any given moment, but I know from my own experience how easy it is to spend more time looking at some of the new books, or new magazines, or the morning paper, than is truly necessary.

I've worked in business establishments where most people were clearly seen to be either working or not-working. There was nothing to read or half-work with. If you were there and not working you felt uncomfortable and hoped the boss wouldn't see you and consider you expendable. Actually, more people left that company voluntarily because they didn't have enough work to do, than for any other reason. A number of them remarked to me, in the personnel office, that "trying to look busy" when they didn't have the work to do was killing them.

I don't recall ever hearing this complaint in the library field. Even when I surveyed some large libraries where it certainly seemed that some of the departments had more people than they needed, I didn't see any evidence of employees suffering for lack of something to be busy with, and have yet to hear of someone wanting to quit because there was nothing to do.

On the other hand, I know libraries that have three or four extra positions at the top that others don't have, or a variety of coordinators, supervisors, administrators or consultants that the majority of comparable institutions are obliged to get along without. Those that feel no need for these extra positions, or can't afford them, seem to get along all right without them. Yet, I have encountered very few people in these categories who didn't seem busy, and capable, and engaged in productive work a good part of the time.

STILL, WE HAVE ALL SEEN a great deal of waste motion in libraries. Too much keeping of statistics that serve no real purpose, too much filing of paper that should be thrown out, too many card files that should be abandoned, too many surveys that aren't productive of anything, too much time spent on book selection and on checking orders, etc., too much time spent cataloging an average book, too much time spent interviewing job applicants when no jobs are open, too much time spent going to meetings, etc. Librarians should make a bigger effort to streamline their department(s) and eliminate *everything* that isn't essential . . . and that means staff as well as materials and methods. Don't do anything, or keep anything, unless you know *why* it is necessary to do so. Never stop questioning everything you do, and your people do. If the only reason to do it is that it's always been done that way, stop it immediately!

Some people might like to designate January as "Streamlining Month" or "Throw-It-Away Month." This would be a time for examining everything in your library offices and departments. Skip the book collection for now as weeding should be a continuous process and if one started on the bookshelves there would not be time for anything else. January should be a time for looking primarily at the material on your office shelves and in your various files, and for questioning also every routine or work practice that is used there.

This could be a really enjoyable time for the entire staff. Or maybe I'm unusual in that I find considerable pleasure in cleaning out cabinets and throwing things away that are no longer needed. To me, weeding a book collection is every bit as satisfying as adding new books to it. One can improve a collection faster through proper weeding than in any other way. I was just talking to a housewife who retired last month; she said she has been doing nothing but cleaning out closets and has been having a wonderful time and making great improvements in her home.

Several large companies report that they place a large bin

in the middle of each of their plants, at the same time each year, and have a competition to see which one can come forth with the most waste material. The plant that cleans out the most tons of paper gets a prize, and all employees take part in the week-long throwaway. I know some libraries that would be hard to beat in this department if they ever let go and started cleaning out. I know a reference desk that has been completely covered with stacks of material for 15 years—since the library opened. I know administrators who have never weeded a single drawer in their office, and librarians who have never thrown anything away once someone has decided—perhaps years ago—to keep it. My idea of the choicest job in the library world would be that of a "Chief Streamliner" who would be employed by individual libraries to eliminate all unnecessary paper in whatever form, as well as all unnecessary motion on the part of the staff. I would like to be paid on the basis of the weight of the material weeded and the amount of staff time saved in the future operation of the library. If one could work and be appropriately paid on that basis, it would easily be the top-paying job in the profession, and one would have the satisfaction of knowing that he or she did more to benefit libraries than anyone else.

QUALITY OF SERVICE: I was pleased to read about a workshop that a large library recently scheduled for its staff to help improve their service to the public. This is something relatively new in the library field, and it is in line with the intense new interest in quality of service that we see in the business field. We now live in Service America, where organizations must perform rather than produce, and where service is, and will be, the competitive advantage.

Restaurants, hotels, hospitals, banks, public utilities, airlines, colleges and universities—all have the problem of gain-ing and retaining the patronage of their customers, and people are getting more and more critical of the quality of service they experience in their daily lives.

The times call for a new focus on service, and a helpful new book that shows how service management can turn an organization in any kind of service field into a customer-driven and service-oriented business is *Service America!* by Karl Albrecht and Ron Zemke (Dow Jones-Irwin, 1985). Their *service management concept* will help managers think about their businesses in a new and effective way. Library administrators should derive equal benefit from the authors' ideas.

They believe that "high-quality service at the front line has to start with a concept of service that exists in the minds of top management. This service concept must find its way into the structure and operation of the organization. There must be a customer-oriented culture in the organization, and it is the leaders of the enterprise who must build and maintain this culture.

"We also believe in the value and importance of measuring service. An intimate and objective knowledge of how you are doing—in the customer's eyes—is critical. Market research, the service audit, and a process for measuring service quality and feeding back this information to the frontline people are crucial ingredients in moving an organization to a high level of service orientation . . .

"Managers need to see their roles in the context of helping service people do their jobs better. The role of management in a service-driven organization is to enhance the culture, set expectations of quality, provide a motivating climate, furnish the necessary resources, help solve problems, remove obstacles, and make sure high-quality job performance pays off."

EVERYBODY IS SERVING SOMEBODY: Everyone in a service organization has a service role, even those who never see the customers. They are all there to support the people who serve the customer. But I expect we have all known library employees who were oblivious of this responsibility. It's easy to become so involved that one becomes completely introverted in his or her point of view. "It's somebody else's job to take care of the customer. My job is to make sure these reports get in on time."

"When inside people lose the sense of being connected to the customer, regardless of how distant the connection may be, they become bureaucrats," say Albrecht and Zemke . . . The simple message to all of the people in a service organization is:

"IF YOU'RE NOT SERVING THE CUSTOMER,
YOU'D BETTER BE SERVING SOMEONE WHO IS."

To have a high standard of service, say the authors, it is necessary to create and maintain a *motivating environment* in which service people can find personal reasons for committing their energies to the benefit of the customer. There are four indications of such an environment, all measurable through employee surveys.

The first is the overall *quality of work life*. This includes factors like job satisfaction, job security, pay and benefits, opportunities for advancement, competent supervision, harmonious surroundings, and justice and fair play.

The second important indication is the overall *morale*. The third is a prevailing *energy level,* measured largely in terms of a sense of individual wellness and psychological well-being. The fourth is a general sense of *optimism*—a belief that there are new possibilities, new ways to do things, new levels to achieve.

WE ALMOST NEVER RECOMMEND BOOKS to our readers but one volume all administrators would find interesting and helpful reading is *Working Smarter,* by The Editors of *Fortune* (pub. by Viking Press). It is a series of articles that analyze management style, the quality of worklife, production management, and worker participation, and shows how organizations can lift productivity, improve quality, and regain the competitive edge by working not harder but smarter. There are concrete examples from many of the best-run companies in this country.

I could find something to quote to you on most pages of this book but let me just draw from pages 173–74 because they cover several of the points I was trying to make in my recent talk in Los Angeles. There I urged the new administrators to clean up their libraries and keep them that way. A messy library, I said, will turn off people. I hope that you believe in neatness, and will pick up litter in the parking lot and inside the library, because your staff probably won't. In the libraries I visit I generally see three or more of those magazine renewal notices on the floor. The librarian doesn't check on the appearance of her library and the public sees the junky look and thinks nobody at the library cares. Incidentally, why don't the periodical clerks shake out those pesky slips before they put the new issues on the magazine shelves?

We had a Dairy Queen near the library that made the best hamburgers I've ever tasted. But I finally stopped going there because I was always turned off by the messy appearance of the place. Nobody ever seemed to pick up anything during business hours and the amount of unappetizing litter on the floor didn't help one's appetite. The result was inevitable: they went out of business.

I've probably picked up more paper on public library floors than anyone else. And before going home at 6 o'clock I'd walk through the reading rooms and take a few minutes to clear off tables that the pages missed so the evening crowd could find a place to work. Every hour or so during the day I'd come out of my office, pick out a pile of newly returned books that qualified for our beautiful section of new books and refill the empty spots on the shelves with them, displaying each book front cover out. This was my one special work assignment and I valued it because it gave me an opportunity to check on the popularity of individual titles and a chance to visit with some of the library patrons.

I see so many racks of "new books" in libraries that have nothing in them but government documents and unattractive material that nobody would want to read. The staff doesn't renew the shelves often enough—sort of like some of those buffet dinners where the first people down the line take the best food and leave the table a mess, and the kitchen staff doesn't replenish the food sufficiently.

WORKING SMARTER emphasizes that, "For all the improvements made possible by technology, the quality of service still often depends on the individual who delivers it. All too often he is underpaid, untrained, unmotivated, and half-educated. Even the mighty oil industry may be represented before the public by a grubby, indolent teenager who seems more interested in picking his nose than coming over to the pump to help.

"A few of the biggest service companies manage to be pleasantly efficient, even when they have thousands of employees dealing with millions of customers. Visitors to Walt Disney World come home impressed with its cleanliness and the courtesy and competence of the staff. Disney World management work hard to make sure the 14,200 employees are 'people who fulfill an expectation of wholesomeness, always smiling, always warm, forever positive in their approach.'

"Even for dishwashers, employment at Disney World begins with three days of training and indoctrination in an on-site center known as Disney University. Disney doesn't 'hire' people for a 'job' but 'casts' them in a 'role' to look after the 'guests' (never 'customers').

"They learn that everyone pitches in to make Disney World work. When the crowds get too big to handle even the top managers and their secretaries leave their offices to work behind counters or in ticket booths. New employees begin to pick up the pride that goes with working for a first-class organization . . . Periodically, employees return to the classroom for more training and indoctrination—a process some of them call 'fairy dusting.'

"The secret of keeping Disney World so clean is never to let it get dirty. Disney himself set an example by picking up rubbish when he walked around. Employees on 'potty patrol' have walkie-talkies so they can radio for help to keep the toilets clean on busy days. Every night the Magic Kingdom is scrubbed squeaky clean. Crews steam-clean the streets, polish every window, shine all the brass. The results, as Mary Poppins would say, are supercalifragilisticexpialidocious."

The authors go on to tell how at McDonald's the quality of service is the envy of the industry. They all go by the same book. "Cooks must turn, never flip, hamburgers one, never two, at a time. If they haven't been purchased, Big Macs must be discarded ten minutes after being cooked and French fries in seven minutes. Cashiers must make eye contact with and smile at every customer. Exact specifications alone aren't enough, however. The help, mostly eager youngsters, must also be motivated to perform a monotonous, low-paying job with sustained enthusiasm . . ." One manager sometimes livens up the lunchtime rush hour by offering $5 bonuses to the cashiers who take in the most dollars and handle the most customers. She gives a plaque to the crew member of the month. Another manager gives every employee a daily rating on a scale of one to five. Both managers sometimes put the store on "sixty-second service": any customer not served within sixty seconds of placing an order gets free French fries. "You've got to create excitement and instant recognition," says one of them.

.　　　.　　　.　　　.　　　.

TELEPHONE DIPLOMACY: Most of the things that library employees do, they do better than other people would do them. If there is one thing that they do less well, it would be answering the telephone. I've often felt that the average library would get a lower rating on its telephone answering than on anything else it did. Most of its services would receive an enthusiastic plus value from library patrons; they are making a positive contribution to the library's image. But how many people are given a lift, or an improved image of the library, through a telephone call to the library that involved no real service? In 30 years of running a public library I have had very few complaints from the public about anything, but the majority of those I did hear were about the quality of our telephone answering. Half of these were concerned with waiting on the line, and the other half were simply comments on the voice quality—the "lifelessness"—of the library employees answering the phone, whether at the circulation desk, in the Reference Department, or wherever.

I KNEW WHAT BOTHERED THEM, because it bothered me, too. I thought of the excellent reference librarian who always answered the phone as if it were 3 a.m. and she had just been awakened from a sound sleep, the branch librarian who was abrupt to everyone on the phone, and the loan desk attendants who could never get any animation into their telephone voice. I've called enough other libraries in every part of the country to know that this is a problem that all of us need to work on. We're turning many people off, and reinforcing the feelings of others that the library is a dull place, before they have a chance to find out that their library is really quite an active and pleasant establishment.

WHAT CAN ONE DO ABOUT THE SITUATION?

Not too much . . . and not nearly as much as one would like. You have to live with all your staff as they are, just as they have to live with you as you are. You can't change them very much by talking to them, or having a Telephone Company representative give them some instruction, or have them read some of the best training manuals. And you can't confine your telephone answering to the one or two people who handle this assignment the best. All the people in your public departments will be involved in the telephone service. Most of them will need no help; their natural interest and pleasantness will be immediately apparent to all callers. They will be as friendly and helpful on the phone as they always are to everyone off it. It's just the minority who think of callers as problems rather than people, or who aren't really concerned whether the caller gets all of the information he needs, or—more likely—have no animation or spirit, that you will have to work with. In some cases, you may get some good results. When there's a real desire to improve, and such improvement is recognized and rewarded, much is possible. But to be a real asset on the telephone, one must have a real interest in people, a happy disposition, and a desire to make friends for the library. Your warm, outgoing personalities will always do well on the telephone, but you may have one or two people on your staff who are always going to sound cold and uncaring, or lifeless. Nothing is going to change them, so don't fret about them. I've occasionally contemplated making a tape recording of such a person on the telephone and using it with her to help her improve her performance, but never could see how to do this successfully.

■   ■   ■   ■   ■

THE WRONG INFORMATION: Friday morning I called the library at San Francisco State University to ask what hours they were open on Saturdays as I was thinking of doing some work there the next day. They told me 8 a.m. to 4:45 p.m. So I got up early Saturday morning and drove a dozen miles to the University only to find a CLOSED sign on the front doors of the library. The information person had given me the normal Saturday hours and left out the words, "Except from August 2 through August 23 when the library will be closed entirely on Saturdays." The same thing happened to me several years ago, at another university library, when I was told the hours that the place would be open throughout the following week. On one of the days, I drove well out of my way only to find that the library was closed because of some school vacation period. I remember thinking at the time that this was a mighty poor way to run a railroad. And since these PR disasters doubtless happen frequently on our campuses—due to all the semester breaks, etc.—our academic library friends may want to remind their people to take care in giving out with their hours.

A FUNNY/SAD NOTE ABOUT THIS is that I returned to my own public library at 9:15 Saturday morning, after a visit to a second university campus found nobody home there for the day either. While I sat in my office, the phone rang three times. The library was closed and I should have let the thing ring. But I never could stand to hear a phone ring and ring while I thought of the person on the other end of the line needing some sort of service. All three persons wanted to know when the Reference Department would be open. I told them, "10 o'clock this morning," forgetting that the building doesn't open on Saturdays until 11 a.m. Several said they would come right in at 10 o'clock. I didn't realize my mistake until 10:30 when there were staff members working in a still-closed building. For the next half hour I was trying to intercept cars coming out of the library parking lot . . . trying to catch and make things right for the people who I'd led to visit the library when it was still closed. I let a number of people slip into the building early, and hope that my three callers came later rather than earlier. All of which proves again that library representatives don't always give the correct information, and one can't expect to maintain perfect public relations with everyone.

EVEN REFERENCE LIBRARIANS MAKE MISTAKES, and when it happens it generally isn't possible to locate the person to whom you gave the wrong information, so that you can make a correction. It is easy for the conscientious librarian to imagine the trouble that her mistake could have caused, and to be quite upset by the thought. I still remember the time—though I haven't thought about it in many years—when I was working in the Reference Department of the Rochester, N.Y., Public Library (my first job) and a man called to ask "What is the 7th Wedding Anniversary?" I checked the almanac and it listed all the anniversaries in one paragraph—number, material, number, material, etc. I read him the name next to the number 7 but discovered—after he had hung up—that I had given him the wrong answer; I should have gone to the other side of the number.

Well, I worried about that for some time after, imagining what his wife said to him when she caught "our" mistake, and then imagining all the people he later told about "those bumblers at the library." I was always very conscious of the fact that I represented the Library to everyone who visited it—on the phone or in person—and that their opinion of the institution was going to be based on how nice and how helpful I was to them. So it was difficult for me to consider that I had goofed and let the library down.

SINCE THEN, I HAVE LEARNED to live a day at a time, in "day-tight compartments." No regretting of mistakes made in the past, or things said by one's self or others that would have been better not said, etc., and no worrying about the future, trying to cross a thousand bridges that one will probably never get to. That certainly makes life much easier, and that goes for running a library, too. Anybody can make it through *one* day. And tomorrow is always a brand new ballgame . . . and one that never happened before in all history. You start fresh, with unlimited opportunities, and you still only have to make it through a period of 24 hours.

■   ■   ■   ■   ■

LIBRARY WORK is like a game of tennis; the player who serves well seldom loses.

■   ■   ■   ■   ■

INVITATION

If, after reading this book, you think you'd like a subscription to *Library Administrator's Digest*—and don't already have one—just write to Box 993, So. San Francisco, CA 94080 and say you would like to continue on from *Library Boss,* and a one-year trial subscription will be yours for only $16.95

No publication has a finer and more creative and enthusiastic group of subscribers. The following is a sample of the unsolicited comments that we have received from some of them in the past year. As you can see, these are dedicated, caring librarians who are continually seeking ways to improve the quality of their service. If you have the same interest, do come and join the *LAD* family.

"LAD is my first priority in professional reading. Thanks."
    Hilma Cooper, Dir., Cheltenham Twp. Libs., Glenside, PA

"Thanks for the many hours of creative thought your *Library Administrator's Digest* has inspired in me."
    Marilyn Hinshaw, Dir., Eastern Okla. Dist. Library System

"I think *LAD* is a super publication."
    Donald Fought, Dir., Public Library, Port Clinton, Ohio

"The *LAD* is still my favorite reading of the month."
    Alan Woodland, Chief Ln., New Westminster, Br. Columbia

"I thoroughly enjoy *LAD*. it is an informative, eye-opening publication, which always provides some good ideas."
    George Needham, Dir., Fairfield Co. Dist. Library, Ohio

"I enjoy your newsletter, and while I don't always agree with what you say, it does make me think."
    Michael Golrick, Director, Wilton Library Assn., CT

"Your publication does more to renew my library spirits than any one other thing I can find. Thanks for sharing with us your enthusiasm for the good ideas you hear about."
    Mrs. Lou Hewlett, Assoc. Dir., Jackson-George Reg. Lib., MS.

"I've been getting your Digest for several years and never fail to find some good idea that we can use. It's one of my most valuable resources."
    LaVonne Leitner, Dir., Rampart Regional Lib. Dist., CO

"I love *LAD*. It is one of only two library journals which actually has practical ideas. I can count at least 5 in the last year that were a real help, and lots of others that were interesting and provocative. I wouldn't miss it."
    Carol Hole, Outreach Supervisor, Alachua Co. Library Dist., FL

"All of the staff enjoy this publication."
    Agnes Fansler, Librarian, Sun City Public Library, Arizona